Comments from the Health Profession

The LIFE Parent Education Seminars were evaluated in 1993 by Dr. Marcia Hills of the University of Victoria, under the auspices of the British Columbia Health Care Research Foundation. Dr. Hills wrote:

"Both the qualitative and quantitative data support an overall positive effect (of the LIFE Seminars) on parental knowledge, attitude and parent-child interactive behaviour. (...) Overall the interview results support the quantitative data results of a shift from autocratic to democratic parenting styles, and increase in confidence of their parenting abilities... (The data) indicate major changes in parents' perceptions of their interactions with their children and these changes seem to be substantiated by their children.

(...) In the words of one parent, 'The most useful thing in this course was the acknowledgement of different temperaments and individual differences. (...) I'm more accepting of who my children are -- they don't annoy me as much.' (...) Another parent wrote: 'We're learning to let our child be responsible for himself. By encouraging independence it frees everybody.' Older children noted better communication and understanding, a feeling of being listened to, a sense of fairness, being offered more choices, and given more responsibility.

(...) All parents reported experiencing a change in their relationship with their child as a result of the program. When asked in the final interview about the overall impact of the course, four of the 26 parents cried. They could not have better expressed the impact the course had on their lives. As one parent said quietly through tears, "I think my son might be dead if I hadn't taken this course." This response speaks clearly to the need to continue to offer parents the opportunity to take this course. Both the format and the context areas of the program are unique when compared to other available parenting programs in the province."

"In summary, the LIFE program is very effective in assisting parents to learn to cope more effectively with their children." -- Dr. Marcia Hills

Sidestepping the Power Struggle

SideStepping the Power Struggle

Power Struggle

A Manual for Effective Parenting

By

Alison Miller, Ph.D.

and

Allison Rees, Ph.D.

Publisher:
Living in Families Effectively (LIFE) Seminars
Victoria, BC, Canada

Living in Families Effectively (LIFE) Seminars
#217 - 2186 Oak Bay Avenue
Victoria, BC, Canada V8R 1G3
Telephone: 250-595-2649
Website: www.lifeseminars.com

Living in Families Effectively Seminars is a registered name owned by Alison Miller.

Library and Archives Canada Cataloguing in Publication

Miller, Alison
Sidestepping the power struggle; a manual for parents / by Alison Miller and Allison Rees
Miller and Allison Rees.

Includes bibliographical references and index.
ISBN 0-9696774-8-0

1. Parent and child. 2. Child rearing. 3. Child psychology.
I. Rees, Allison II. Title

HQ769.M5318 2006   649.1   C2006-901946-0

Production and Editorial Management: Mary P. Brooke, Brookeline Publishing House Inc., Victoria, BC
Front Cover Photography: iStock International Inc.
Back Cover Photography (author portraits): Tammy Murdock, Embellish Studios, Victoria, BC
Cover Artwork: Robert Kabwe - ProtopopDesign.com, Westmount, QC

Printed in Canada. First and second runs printed in Victoria, British Columbia.

This book is dedicated to all of our children.

Quick-Reference Summary

[See full Table of Contents starting on page *x*.]

CHAPTER 1: I Gotta Be Me!
Understanding Your Child's Inborn Temperament

Social scientists now generally agree that children are born with at least nine temperament traits. These traits influence behavior and it is easier to parent your children once you are aware of their inherited temperament (and your own inherited temperament, for that matter). This chapter includes comments on the pros and cons of each trait, parenting pointers and some things to think about.

CHAPTER 2: Tell Me It's a Stage
Development of the Child's Self

Perhaps the main goal of any child is to become independent. The road to independence is marked by transition stages (e.g. from preschooler to school-age child) which are usually characterized by challenging behavior (defiance, stubbornness, etc.) This chapter looks at the stages in developing independence, as well as children's learning to handle emotions, learning to recognize others' needs, and sexual development.

CHAPTER 3: Act Your Age
Development of the Child's Understanding

Children are both immature and inexperienced in the world. This chapter explores many of the ways they behave because of this immaturity and inexperience: their worries, their insecurities, their difficulty adapting to adult notions of time, their embarrassing candor, their need to explore, their endless questions, their tendency to make messes and their poor memory. If we know what to expect from children, we will be more likely to relax and enjoy them for what they are.

CHAPTER 4: Taming the Triggers
Managing Antecedents of Behavior

Behavior (both our children's and our own) is not only influenced by individual temperament and stage of development. It is also affected by what happens to us in life, both the big upsetting events and the little everyday things. These "triggers" cause problematic behavior and emotional outbursts. If we as parents can detect triggers before they begin to create problems we can prevent many difficulties.

CHAPTER 5: The Freedom of Responsibility
Helping Children Develop Responsibility

If your child takes on responsibility he can learn from the natural consequences of his choices, pleasurable or sometimes painful. It is important to know which responsibilities to hand over and when to hand them over. The process is made much easier if you distinguish between "kid issues" and "family issues". Letting your child be in charge of certain things minimizes conflict in the family and helps your child mature and become responsible.

CHAPTER 6: Developing Caring People
Helping Children Develop Values and Empathy

We want our children to grow up into caring, honest adults. This chapter describes the stages of moral development and shows us how to help our children mature beyond either selfishness or blind obedience. Specific problems discussed include counteracting the negative effects of the media, lying, and stealing.

CHAPTER 7: Love, Limits and Consequences
How to Set Limits and Use Consequences

Parents need to set limits on children's behavior, at least regarding family issues, and impose consequences if necessary. But the use of consequences for negative behavior often creates more problems than it solves. Certainly it doesn't foster a relationship of harmony and mutual respect. We discuss alternatives to the use of consequences, as well as the pros and cons of various commonly used consequences: time-outs, grounding, removal of privileges, etc. This chapter explores how and when to use consequences, and how to negotiate them with your child.

Acknowledgements

We owe a great deal to those people who've read our material and given us feedback: Pat and Peter Kirchner, Wendy Lum, Randine Mariona, Carol McDougal, Tracy McMicking, Trevor Murdock, Jeremy Schwartzentruber, Tamara Schwartzentruber, Allen Specht, Jenny Spring, Kristina Stewart, Marion Stokes, and Erin Wilcox. We would like to give special thanks to those people who reviewed all of our material in the editing process: Janet Bauer, Mary P. Brooke, Ben Schwartzentruber, Robert Stuart Thomson, and Anne Tolson. Their work gave this book clarity and made it an easy read. We would like to thank Tracy Yarr for her great ideas and humor for the cartoons and Joan Badke for drawing them. Thanks to Tammy Murdock for her photography assistance, including our headshot photos on the back cover. We also appreciate Mary Brooke's superb job of editorial management and page design.

These books would never have come about if it weren't for the thousands of parents who've taken our LIFE Seminars over the past 25 years. You have inspired us by working with the material and making positive changes in your lives. We have learned from you what works and what doesn't work and refined our ideas bit by bit. Our volunteer facilitators have helped stimulate our thinking and have been the team we relied on to keep our vision going in spite of obstacles. Those who've stayed with us for a long time include Keith Hiscock, Doug McCallum, Paul Nicholson, Alan Poole, Randy Rochefort, Connie Thomas, and Brenda Zimmer as well as several of those who helped edit the books. There are so many others in our community who have volunteered their time or supported our courses and we simply can't name them all, but we do express our appreciation.

I (Allison Rees) would like to thank Alison Miller for her friendship, her mentorship and her incredible gift for writing and courageous ability to see the truth. My husband Bruce who gave me the support which allowed me to pursue my passion. My mom, Anne, who has always been a steady voice of reason. My sister Anne for being there for me. Finally, my two wonderful children, you both amaze me, inspire me and teach me beyond words.

I (Alison Miller) would like to thank my valued friend and colleague Allison Rees for her steadfastness, her vision of our professional future, her courage to try new things, and her ability to translate my abstract ideas into practical living skills. My good friend Adrienne Carter for her encouragement in the early days when we wrote together. My father, Ron Miller, for his example of independent thinking. And of course my three children, who have been my most profound teachers over the years.

Alison Miller, Ph.D. and *Allison Rees, Ph.D.*

Editor's Introduction

Thousands who have read Dr. Miller's and Dr. Rees' regular columns in the magazine *Island Parent* or attended their *LIFE Seminar* workshops over the past 30 years say that their families run much smoother and enjoy greater harmony than they ever did before. With such support and so much successful experience in the field it was inevitable that they would write a book. They did, and here it is. (Actually, it turned out to be two books: Book II, *The Parent-Child Connection*, will soon be available). I feel honored to have been involved in editing both books.

There is no lack of parenting books on the market. Is *Sidestepping the Power Struggle* special? I think it is, for several reasons. Unlike many books on psychology, this one is written in clear, everyday language yet at the same time the authors do justice to the complexity of issues. Also, unlike many books on parenting, *Sidestepping* covers such a wide range of topics that it serves well as a handbook. (To facilitate this kind of use we have included a detailed table of contents and a good index.) For example, if your child's homework is a problem, just look at the index. It will guide you to the relevant pages. Suppose that you are worried about the habits of one of your kids' new friends: look up 'peer group' and it will point you to the right page.

A glance at the table of contents will give you a quick idea as to how much ground this book covers and how useful it will be for you. One great section suggests that you divide issues into "family issues" (in which kids have to obey family rules) and "kid issues" (in which kids are allowed to control things themselves). This simple strategy can solve the common problem of the messy bedroom. It also can solve the problem of homework. What a relief that can be!

Another useful principle (one taught by parent educators long ago but easily forgotten in this generation) is to allow children to experience the natural consequences of their actions; protecting them from reality does not develop strength of character.

There are other things I love about this book. I enjoy the authors' humor and their ability to show (in many anecdotes drawn from their own families) the amusing, human side to parenting situations. I have to chuckle at their many comments on the little surprises and ironies which family life has in store for us. Dr. Rees is well-known for her droll wit and amusing analogies; Dr. Miller has a special gift for hitting the nail on the head and for making the abstract seem concrete.

It helps that both authors have raised their own children (Alison Miller, three; Allison Rees, two) and raised them with flexibility and an eye always open to the possibility that there might be better ways of parenting than what they had learned in their own childhood or in what other parents (and teachers) were doing. What better laboratory than an open-minded, loving family?

Throughout this book you will find guided exercises which will help you to understand the ideas in depth and relate them to your own family situation.

A huge bonus of *Sidestepping* is the many meaty quotations from key thinkers in family studies: Fitzhugh Dodson on transition stages, Jordan and Margaret Paul on using natural consequences, Thomas Gordon on the pitfalls of authoritarian parenting, John Bradshaw on the dysfunctional family, and Rudolf Dreikurs on the ins and outs of rewarding children. There are many others as well, e.g. Bruno Bettelheim, Dorothy C. Briggs, and Stephen Covey.

But this book isn't just about your children. It is also about you. I think you might find that this is the biggest revelation of all. For example, you probably will discover which of the nine personality traits you inherited, where this puts you on a scale of 1 to 10 and, more important, how these inherited traits affect your parenting. You will also see quite clearly what kind of family government prevailed in your family when you were growing up. You might discover that you yourself weren't validated much as a child and that you need above all to learn to validate your child. Or maybe you learned to obey rules and laws essentially out of fear. The authors show you how to go beyond fear and teach your children to motivate themselves with altruism and the Golden Rule.

Whether you have little or a lot to learn, *Sidestepping* will give you many answers. I think this book will help many parents to break out of the old patterns which can be so unproductive and destructive. I have a feeling that *Sidestepping* will change many families so radically that the effects will resonate down through future generations.

Robert Stuart Thomson
Godwin Books
Victoria, BC, Canada
www.godwinbooks.com

Authors' Introduction

Raising human beings is the most important, the most complex, and probably the most difficult job in the world!

Freud said that the first six years of life determine what the adult will be like. Yet people leave these years to chance. We don't have courses in high school on how to be an effective parent. People are expected to have some kind of "parenting instinct" that kicks in automatically. Unfortunately, for many of us it doesn't, especially if our own parents didn't know how. Think how many years the schools put into teaching us the simple, basic skills of reading – doesn't parenting deserve at least that much attention?

Without knowledge, we end up doing what our parents did. If our parents were very skilled and loving, we are fortunate; if they were not skilled and loving we may have a lot of difficulty with our own parenting, through no fault of our own.

We (Alison Miller and Allison Rees) have been developing and teaching our parenting courses, known as *LIFE (Living in Families Effectively) Seminars*, since 1981 – that's 25 years! All the important things we have learned in our journey as parents and as professionals have been incorporated into our two parenting manuals, *Sidestepping the Power Struggle* (this book) and its companion, *The Parent-Child Connection*.

We believe our two books together have all the essential ingredients for parenting success. Our main goal is to help you raise children who can think for themselves and respect the rights of others, living by the Golden Rule ("Treat other people the way you want them to treat you.").

What do you need to reach this goal? First, you need to understand why children behave as they do – their temperament, their stages of development, and the things they respond to. Then you need practical skills in communicating effectively with children, teaching them responsibilities and values, and managing their behavior. Finally, you need ways to deal with yourself and your own emotional reactions to your children. Our books cover all of these issues and more.

We think you will enjoy this book, just as thousands of people have enjoyed our courses over the past 25 years. We hope you will find it not just enjoyable (it is full of humorous stories and cartoons) but also inspiring and encouraging, as you strive to help your children become all that they can be.

If you want to learn more about *LIFE Seminars* or what's in the other book (*The Parent-Child Connection*), see the comments at the end of this book, or go to our website at www.lifeseminars.com.

Alison Miller, Ph.D. and
Allison Rees, Ph.D.
LIFE Seminars
Victoria, BC, Canada
www.lifeseminars.com
May 2007

Our next book:

The Parent-Child Connection, our second book, complements the material in **Sidestepping the Power Struggle.** We believe both books are a must-read for you to master all the essential principles of parenting.

The Parent-Child Connection discusses the parent-child relationship in depth, including bonding, communication, boundaries in the family, handling emotions, and developing self-esteem.

These are just as important as understanding child development and knowing discipline techniques. Even good discipline techniques can be misused if you don't have the relationship skills discussed in **The Parent-Child Connection**.

Table of Contents

Social scientists now generally agree that children are born with at least nine temperament traits. These traits influence behavior and it is easier to parent your children once you are aware of their inherited temperament (and your own inherited temperament, for that matter). Each of the following sections includes comments on the pros and cons of each trait, parenting pointers and some things to think about.

Chapter 2: Tell Me It's a Stage 41
Development of the Child's Self

Perhaps the main goal of any child is to become independent. The road to independence is marked by transition stages (e.g. from preschooler to school-age child) which are usually characterized by challenging behavior (defiance, stubbornness, etc.) This chapter looks at the stages in developing independence, as well as children's learning to handle emotions, learning to recognize others' needs, and sexual development.

Chapter 3: **Act Your Age** 79
Development of the Child's Understanding

Children are both immature and inexperienced in the world. This chapter explores many of the ways they behave because of this immaturity and inexperience: their worries, their insecurities, their difficulty adapting to adult notions of time, their embarrassing candor, their need to explore, their endless questions, their tendency to make messes and their poor memory. If we know what to expect from children, we will be more likely to relax and enjoy them for what they are.

Chapter 4: Taming the Triggers 107
Managing Antecedents of Behavior

Behavior (both our children's and our own) is not only influenced by individual temperament and stage of development. It is also affected by what happens to us in life, both the big upsetting events and the little everyday things. These "triggers" cause problematic behavior and emotional outbursts. If we as parents can detect triggers before they begin to create problems we can prevent many difficulties.

Chapter 5: **The Freedom of Responsibility** ....
Helping Children Develop Responsibility

If your child takes on responsibility he can learn from the natural consequences of his choices, pleasurable or sometimes painful. It is important to know which responsibilities to hand over and when to hand them over. The process is made much easier if you distinguish between "kid issues" and "family issues". Letting your child be in charge of certain things minimizes conflict in the family and helps your child mature and become responsible.

We want our children to grow up into caring, honest adults. This chapter describes the stages of moral development and shows us how to help our children mature beyond either selfishness or blind obedience. Specific problems discussed include counteracting the negative effects of the media, lying, and stealing.

Parents need to set limits on children's behavior, at least regarding family issues, and impose consequences if necessary. But the use of consequences for negative behavior often creates more problems than it solves. Certainly it doesn't foster a relationship of harmony and mutual respect. We discuss alternatives to the use of consequences, as well as the pros and cons of various commonly used consequences: time-outs, grounding, removal of privileges, etc. This chapter explores how and when to use consequences, and how to negotiate them with your child.

And at the back of the book:

- History of the LIFE Seminars
- About *Sidestepping*'s companion book: *The Parent-Child Connection*
- About the production house.

1

I Gotta Be Me!

Understanding your Child's Inborn Temperament

Does your child complain about the toe seam in his tube socks? Do you find that noise or bright lights upset her?   Do your children's voices easily irritate you? Does your child get labeled shy? Do you and your child easily get into shouting matches?

All these behaviors result at least partly from inborn temperament, and you are about to take a huge sigh of relief when you discover that it's not your fault!! These characteristics are inherited, and you aren't responsible for making your child that way.

In this chapter we focus on individual differences in temperament, the master blueprint of all people. Once you understand temperament and figure out where your child and you stand on a scale of 0-to-10 for the nine temperament traits you will appreciate better your child's (and your own) behavior, and your unique strengths and challenges.

This knowledge will help you provide the encouragement and support which your child needs and you will probably view your child in a different way for the rest of your life. It is only when we understand our children and ourselves that we can pause and choose loving behavior rather than reacting with impatience and anger. Understandably, as adults we may find that our own temperament traits are more difficult to identify than our children's; this is not surprising because we have spent so many years adapting to the world.

As you read through this chapter, see whether you can put the pieces together. It takes courage to examine your own temperament but it leads to understanding and tolerance.

1 - The Nine Basic Traits

Each child begins life with a unique set of inherited characteristics. A child's temperament is his basic style, the way in which he approaches life. The *New York Longitudinal Study*, headed by Doctors Stella Chess and Alexander Thomas, began in 1956 to study different behavior traits in individual children over more than 30 years of their lives. Researchers went into a maternity ward and recorded everything possible about the newborn babies there: how often they smiled, how loud they screamed, how much their bodies moved, how often they became hungry, and so on. They then used statistical techniques to find out which of those behaviors tended to occur together in the same infant.

They came up with nine basic ways in which these babies differed. These children were studied right into adulthood, to see how many of the original characteristics of temperament persisted throughout life, and what effect they had on the children's later adjustment and behavior.

Most children continue during later years to show many of the qualities of behavior which they showed as infants. However, two babies who start out very much alike may develop quite differently, depending on how their parents respond to them, and also depending on other influences in their lives such as school, extended family, peers, culture and media.

To help your child develop into the best person he can be, you must become aware of his unique temperament and respond to him as he is, rather than treat all children as if they were the same.

> **Our level of understanding determines our reactions.**

"Children don't belong to us..."

My mother did her best to make us feel unique and worthwhile.
Over and over again, in every way she knew how, she told us that we
didn't need to earn her love. We were loved and valued
(and therefore were lovable and valuable) exactly as we were.
"Children don't belong to us," she used to say. (...) They are little stran-
gers who arrive in our lives and give us the pleasure and duty of caring
for them -- but we don't own them. We help them become who they are."
(Gloria Steinem, *Revolution from Within; A Book of Self-Esteem*, pg. 65).

The Dream & the Reality

I took the kids to Mount Douglas Park for a hike one day... this is a place near where I grew up as a child in Victoria, BC. I had expectations of sharing that wonderful part of my past, showing them the trees I used to climb and all of my favorite spots. I envisioned a special outing with lots of fun and closeness.

We hiked into the heart of the woods when suddenly my son Peter, who was six years old, tripped over a tree root and fell onto his knees. Peter has a low sensory threshold to pain and doesn't do well with unexpected surprises. His immediate reaction was to burst into tears, and then he yelled, "I hate this stupid park, I want to go home". It took some time for the pain to pass, which was unfortunate because we had a long way to go before we were out of the woods.

Moments later my daughter, who was four, tripped over a rock. She cried as I acknowledged her "owies" and the blood trickled down her shin. Then it was over and she was running back down the path, blood still dripping. Meanwhile, Peter was still hobbling along complaining about "this stupid park".

I used my knowledge of temperament to counsel myself and work through my own feelings. Though I was disappointed, and somewhat annoyed that our outing had been spoiled, I didn't react with blame and anger.

Rather than sending a lot of guilt messages and attacking Peter for being a 'killjoy', I found that loving place inside myself where I could have some empathy. I realized that his pain was real and his intense nature and big feelings are just part of who he is. He wasn't looking for attention or trying to ruin our day.

It wasn't the magical outing I had envisioned, but it was memorable! -- *Allison Rees*

'Nine Basic Traits'

1.	Activity Level	How active is the child generally, from an early age?
2.	Distractibility	How easily is the child distracted? Can he pay attention?
3.	Persistence	Does the child stay with something she likes? How persistent or determined is she when she wants something?
4.	Approach / Withdrawal	Does the child have a positive or negative response to new places, people, foods, clothes, or toys?
5.	Adaptability	How does the child deal with transition and change? How long does it take the child to get used to changes in routine?
6.	Emotional Intensity	How much emotional energy does the child put into his/her responses, whether happy or unhappy?
7.	Bodily Regularity	How predictable is the child in his/her patterns of sleep, appetite, bowel habits?
8.	Sensory Sensitivity	How does the child react to sensory stimuli: noise, bright colors, smells, pain, warm weather, tastes, the texture and feel of clothes? Is he easily bothered? Is he easily over-stimulated?
9.	Mood	What is the child's basic mood? Is the child generally happy or unhappy?

Recognizing the Positives

I'm wonderful, you're okay, she's no good

When I was a teenager my friends and I used to play a game with adjectives. The game was interesting because it showed clearly how people talk about other people. A person would take a single quality and use different words to describe this quality in herself, in the person she was talking to, or in a third party. The word used for the self would be positive, the one for the other person would be neutral, and the one for the third party would be negative. Here's an example: "I am verbally fluent, you are talkative, she yammers constantly." Or the opposite side of the same trait: "I am thoughtful, you are quiet, he has nothing to say." -- *Alison Miller*

'The Temperament Game'

This game points out how easy it is to see the negative instead of the positive side of any trait, particularly in other people, especially in our children.

Those of us with poor self-esteem also tend to see our own qualities of temperament in a negative light.

It is important to learn to view each person's temperament positively and help our children and ourselves capitalize on the positive aspects of each trait.

We can view any of the temperament traits, in ourselves or our children, either positively or negatively, as in the table below:

Trait	I (am) ...	You (are) ...	He (is) ...
High Activity Level	Full of energy	Very busy	Exhausting
Low Activity Level	Careful with energy	Slow-moving	Lazy
High Distractibility	Perceptive	Distractible	Inattentive
Low Distractibility	A good concentrator	Non-distractible	Tuned out
High Persistence	Determined	Stubborn	Never lets go
Low Persistence	Flexible	Non-aggressive	Gives up easily
High Caution	Wise	Cautious	Cowardly
Low Caution	Enthusiastic	A risk-taker	Foolhardy
High Adaptability	Spontaneous	Adaptable	Wishy-washy
Low Adaptability	Stand my ground	Firm	Rigid
High Intensity	Passionate	Emotional	An overreactor
Low Intensity	Even-tempered	Calm	Boring
High Regularity	Consistent	Regulated	Inflexible
Low Regularity	Easy-going	Temperamental	Unpredictable
High Sensitivity	Sensitive	Touchy	Hysterical
Low Sensitivity	Unflappable	Normal	Insensitive
Positive Mood	Positive	Optimistic	Phony
Negative Mood	Realistic	Pessimistic	A wet blanket

2 - Activity Level

Highly energetic or physically active children are busy; they have a strong need to move their bodies. They like to do a lot of different things and don't seem to need much down time. It is often surprising to see an active child asleep because five minutes before this, he seemed so awake. Active babies will squirm and kick on the changing table, often making diapering look more like a calf-roping contest at your local rodeo.

Do you think he's normal?

When my younger son Alexander was about a year-and-a-half old, we attended a family picnic with many other families. I sat next to a woman with a very placid little boy who watched everything with nothing moving but his eyes.

Someone gave the kids cookies – and Alexander sprang into action! He ran around faster than the naked eye could see, and stole every cookie from every other kid before they had time to react. The placid little boy still didn't move. His mother and I stared at each other, and asked one another: "Is my child normal?"   -- *Alison Miller*

Do you think he's normal?

Do you think he's normal?

Active children have a harder time making their beds than others do. One very puzzling phenomenon of the active child…how did their blankets end up hanging from the track lighting? Have you ever tried sleeping with an active child? Even the less active ones sleep sideways! It is kind of like going to bed with a blender.

High Activity Level	Variable	Low Activity Level
10 ⟵⟶	5 ⟵⟶	1
♦ moves around a lot, hard on sneakers ♦ can't sit through a meal ♦ staying still is hard work	♦ depends on the activity and interest	♦ body movements slower and more selective ♦ often takes a more passive position in a group, preferring to watch ♦ moves his eyes more than his feet

Understanding High Activity Level

First of all, *acknowledge the trait*, don't fight it! The purpose of this information is to act-knowledge: put your knowledge into action. We often go around blindly reacting to behavior without ever stopping to think why it is there or what the needs are behind it.

An active, energetic child might be more difficult to parent than a quiet child. Energetic kids need to move, get involved, touch, and use their big muscles while learning about their world. Do yourself a favor on that rainy day and stop at the park anyway. When active children are expected to cope with restricted environments without an opportunity to do what comes naturally, they will have more emotional meltdowns. If parents say "NO," to everything, the kids will be unable to follow the rules.

The first few years of school are sometimes challenging for the active child. Remember that the older the child, the easier it will be for him to adapt to social requirements. Always consider the preschool environment carefully: is there lots of outside time for climbing and tricycles? Can he do big pictures using full sweeps with a brush and stand back proudly to admire the color without it having to be anything? Will he only be expected to sit still for short periods of time? Two of my (Alison Miller's) kids regularly got in trouble, one in preschool and one in first grade, for being active when they were supposed to sit still. Do you know that if an active child is told to stop fidgeting in class, he spends so much time trying not to fidget that he can't learn anything? Chewing gum or having molding clay to fidget with can be a big help although chewing gum may not be acceptable in a classroom.

By the age of six you may find that your active child can sit at the dinner table for the entire meal. If not, have him get the ketchup from the fridge! And encourage your active child to help out with household tasks while he's still keen on being involved; he'll love it and it will help him become responsible.

About Hyperactivity and ADHD

Many parents, especially parents of preschool boys, tend to think their children are 'hyperactive'. This usually happens because parents do not realize how active little boys (and sometimes girls) normally are. They can't keep still or concentrate simply because they are little children. Studies have shown that children who live in apartment buildings are labeled 'hyperactive' more often than children who live in houses.

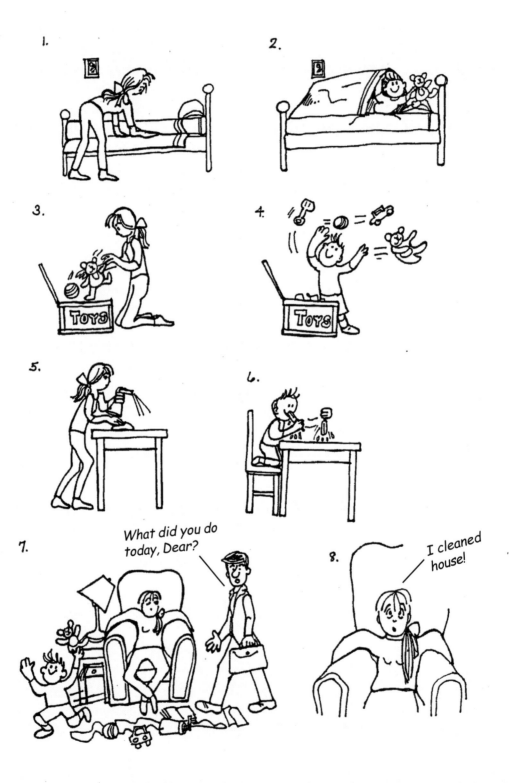

The essence of the problem appears to be a mismatch between the child's ability to keep still, be quiet, and pay attention and the behavior required by the child's environment.

Some children suffer from a condition now known as Attention Deficit Hyperactivity Disorder (ADHD). Studies of these children find that they differ from other children – not necessarily in the amount of body movement, but in the timing of this movement: they move around when they are supposed to be keeping still and paying attention.

Recognizing ADHD

The symptoms of ADHD include:
- difficulty focusing attention
- short attention span
- extreme distractibility
- impulsiveness (not stopping to think)
- not connecting behavior with consequences
- excessive body movement
- low need for sleep
- emotional reactivity

Some children have an Attention Deficit Disorder (ADD) without being very active. And, of course, a child can be highly active without having ADD.

Understanding Low Activity Level

If you have a child rated low on activity level, don't expect her to be able to handle a busy life of activities. She may not be able to handle the pace of swimming, skating, and dance lessons. You may think she is okay because she wants to get into a lot of things but what you will see is a puddle of emotion at the end of the day or week.

A child with a lower activity level will seem easier to parent but there can still be concerns. Often he is seen as lacking motivation when actually, he just needs more down time to re-energize. Please don't label him lazy, and don't let other people do it either!

Every strong trait has a negative and a positive side.

Parents often wonder if their children are normal. The parents of an active child may feel anxious and embarrassed as their child runs around grabbing things and throwing things – but so do the parents of the child who just sits there and seems to be doing nothing! Remember, it's not laziness, it's just the temperament the child was born with.

> ## Parenting Pointers

Active kids need:
√   room to move and lots of activity
√   only short periods of sitting still, until they mature
√   outdoor activities where there aren't a lot of restrictions
      (but the few restrictions are firm and consistent)
√   active parents to keep up with the pace
√   programs that permit the use of hands-on learning and touching

Watch the Messages

Remember that your child's activity level is a part of his wiring. Making negative comments only leaves the child feeling helpless and unaccepted: "Can't you ever sit still?" "You are tiring me out!"

Remember that less active children may not be able to keep up to your level. They need down time and permission to rest. They don't need to hear comments like: "Get up and do something, you lazy slug!"

Apply Your Knowledge

- Where is your child on the activity level scale?
- How does this challenge you?
- If you are the parent of an active child, how do you look after your needs?
- What is the positive side of high activity level?
- What is the positive side of being less active?

---

3 - Distractibility

An easily distractible child has a hard time staying with one thing at a time because she notices everything that is going on around her. She can hear sounds that we can hardly hear. While making a trip to do something, these children get so distracted by what they see that they veer off in an entirely different direction to explore something which has caught their eye. They see what others can't see or simply wouldn't notice, and they do all of this while we are trying to tell them something. It's like having a conversation with an oscillating fan in high gear. Children can have a tough time following through with instructions due to high levels of distractibility. It's not a memory issue, it's an interest issue; these children can remember details that will astound you, and often remind us of things we would prefer to forget. Young children are distractible anyway, and a child who is high on this trait can really be a challenge.

Distractible	Variable	Non-distractible
10 ⟷	**5** ⟷	**1**
♦ notices and responds to many things at once ♦ has difficulty listening because there are so many choices of things to listen to and notice ♦ has no trouble watching TV because the picture changes all the time	♦ can concentrate if he is really interested	♦ the house is on fire and this person is still reading ♦ does not notice the ice cream truck outside because he is working on Lego ♦ concentrates hard and does not get sidetracked by potentially distracting events

Understanding Distractibility

The child with an Attention Deficit Disorder is, of course, the extreme example of the distractible child. But children come with various degrees of distractibility, all the way from the child who is distracted by everything to the child who concentrates so hard that he doesn't hear a thing.

Don't judge your children by how long they can watch TV. Even distractible children easily become hypnotized by TV. Distractible children need calm places to do their homework, with little brother or sister kept out of their room during that time. On the other hand, kids like to be near the family. At our house (Rees's) we often have "ink time" which is just a half hour with no phone, TV or radio; we sit at the table and read, write or draw. This is an inviting atmosphere for doing homework, although we don't strictly set it up for that.

If children understand that distractions make it hard to concentrate, such awareness is half the battle. Noise can be distracting and annoying. One solution is to create some 'white noise' (e.g. turn on a fan) to drown out the irritating sounds. We are amazed at how many distractible children can still study with the music blasting. This is because the music drowns out the other noises which might otherwise distract the child from his work.

> **Extreme traits of any kind can affect self-esteem if we focus on the negative.**

Understanding Non-Distractibility

Let's look at the other extreme, the non-distractible child. He won't allow anything to divert his attention from his homework – or from the novel he's reading. When he is doing it he's really concentrating! This is a plus. Unfortunately, he also can't be distracted from that electric socket when he's crawling towards it, or from his misery if he is crying.

The distractible child won't pay attention to what you're saying because he's noticing everything else. The non-distractible child won't pay attention to what you're saying because he's concentrating, and you didn't get his attention first. So they're alike!

Apply Your Knowledge

- Where do you place each of your children on the Distractibility scale?
- What kinds of challenges does this present?
- Where are you on the distractibility chart? What challenges have you had in your life as a result of being this way?

Watch the Messages

Getting his knapsack...

Just this morning I commented to my son that time was marching on and we would be leaving for school in a couple of minutes. "Great," he said, "I'll go downstairs to my room and get my knapsack". Thirty seconds later I heard the piano. I took a deep breath ... one minute later as the theme from *Star Wars* was being plunked out, I found myself hollering at the top of the stairs like a sick rooster, "Peter! What do you need to be doing right now?" "Sorry, Mom," he said as he ran up the stairs without his knapsack again. I always say, "It's a good thing they're cute!" *-- Allison Rees*

What would your Mom or Dad have said? "Honestly, you would forget your head if it wasn't attached to your shoulders." Sadly, one of the negative labels that is attached to Distractibility is 'stupid'. Even if our parents didn't label us that, the danger still exists that we might internalize the experience and label ourselves. Of course, this trait has nothing to do with intelligence (or lack of it), but if this trait isn't understood, it would be easy to make such a conclusion. The fact is that distractible people aren't thinking less, they are thinking more. They just need to learn to prioritize their thoughts and attention. This takes a lot of maturity and awareness.

As one mother once told us, "Being a distractible adult is tough too. I notice all these things and I need to concentrate that much harder to tune them all out. I am also a lousy listener at times because I am so distracted by things. I really need to focus when it is time for me to be listening, otherwise I will start cleaning my children's faces with 'mother spit' while they are talking because I notice that little tiny speck of spaghetti."

Messages Not to Give: "How many times do I have to tell you to get your socks on?" "Why can't you ever stop what you're doing and pay attention to what I'm saying?" "Look at me when I talk to you!" Try to avoid these kinds of negative messages. Words are weapons, like torpedoes that blow away the child's self-esteem.

Parenting Pitfall: Nagging

Parents say, "If I didn't nag, it wouldn't get done." Acknowledge and accept that distractible children do need more guidance, but there is a big difference between nagging and reminding. A reminder doesn't have the judgment attached to it. It gives the child a chance to think for himself. A reminder can be one word. "Homework!" But remember that body language is a large part of communication so stay as calm and neutral as you can.

Nagging is doing our children's thinking for them. We can get into that habit and slowly create a child who will only learn to dawdle and passively resist any directions or requests. He may become totally dependent on our thinking rather than developing his own abilities.

Parenting Pointers

- make eye contact before you begin talking (this is important for both the distractible and the non-distractible child)
- leave packed bags hanging on a doorknob the night before your child has to go out
- give only a limited number of instructions
- use different media to give messages, like written humorous notes, pictures, skits
- give a distractible child a quiet space to work in, or a constant noise that actually helps him focus
- give a positive suggestion of what to do rather than what not to do

Be creative with your messages.

The Plus Side

Distractible people take everything in, if only partially. They don't get bored because there is so much to see and think about. Take the time to listen to your distractible child. Can you compliment her on her ability to see things or notice things? What other positive qualities does she have?

Take some time to appreciate your non-distractible child. His ability to concentrate and tune everything out is admirable. He can also do his homework in any setting without being distracted by what's going on around him.

Apply Your Knowledge

- How do you react negatively to this trait (do you nag, get angry)?
- How can you work with the challenging aspects of your child's trait?
- What is the positive side of this particular trait? What kind of messages can you give to your child so s/he can feel good about being this way?

---

4 - Persistence and Non-Persistence

Persistence describes the length or duration of a person's focus. A person rated high on this trait will often stay with a job until it is done. This type of person is not one you would want to argue with over silly rules because she will bring you to your knees; she doesn't give up easily. If you, the parent, are also persistent you could have some dynamic power struggles. And two persistent spouses can argue for a very long time about things that aren't worth the effort!

A persistent child will play with one toy for a long time; a non-persistent child will focus only briefly on any one activity before moving on. In an older child, persistence shows up in the length of time the child is able to give to a task and the amount of frustration that she is able to tolerate before giving up.

High Activity Level	Variable	Low Activity Level
10 ⟷	5 ⟷	1
◆ does not give up easily ◆ long attention span ◆ determined	◆ depends on what she is doing	◆ doesn't continue with frustrating tasks ◆ short attention span ◆ spends a short time at each activity

Don't Sweat the Small Stuff

If you have a persistent child, avoid labeling your child stubborn and recognize that persistent children actually go through a grieving period when they let go of something they are involved in. They may try many tactics of negotiation and then get angry before they grieve. Experiencing some disappointment and frustration is hard but learning to cope with negative emotions helps us mature.

Persistent kids need to learn to hear "no" when a "no" really needs to be there. But there may well be an argument, and they may accuse us of being unfair. We need to be able both to listen to them and to stand our ground.

We need to point out the strengths of this trait to our persistent children, and we can present the challenges with humor rather than disapproval. Point out their incredible ability to learn new things with such determination.

When I (Allison Rees) think of my determined daughter, I think of the number of times that I myself have wanted to have my own way, since I too am persistent, and the needless power struggles over things that didn't matter. So often my power struggles could have been avoided if I could have let go and said of my daughter, *"She is her own person. She truly knows what suits her best. My way isn't the only right way. Let it go."*

Apply Your Knowledge

- How persistent is your child (on a scale of 1 to 10)?
- What challenges does this present (if any)?
- How do you disengage from your child's persistence?
- What negative habits does your child's trait bring out in your parenting?

Parenting Pitfall: Arguing and Giving In

Persistent children learn to keep demanding if they discover that their parent's "No!" finally turns into an "Okay, fine then!" When a parent gives in, the behavior gets much worse. We then create the "little lawyer syndrome" – kids who get so used to negotiating that they just can't hear "No." When a parent argues and then gives in, it trains kids to whine or argue longer. So if you *are* going to give in, it would be best to give in right away, instead of teaching her to debate everything that comes up. Save your "No" for times when you really need it and chances are it will be much more respected when such a time comes up.

Ask for time to think about your answer so you can decide whether a "No" is really necessary. If you are persistent too, learn to be flexible and recognize the difference between setting reasonable limits and having to get your own way!

A flexible parent respects the child's ideas and turns his child's persistence into a strength, not a weakness. Letting go of having to win all the time is not about giving in or not respecting limits. A persistent child who understands the reasoning behind limits will be great at respecting them and sticking to the rules.

> **A persistent child needs to have very few limits, but these limits must be consistent or she will push on them until she gets what she wants.**
>

Parenting Pointers

- ◆ Let natural consequences step in when it causes no problems for others and safety isn't involved.
- ◆ Don't be rigid with rules, and avoid overusing "no".
- ◆ Offer lots of choices and discuss important issues ahead of time.
- ◆ Discuss limits and negotiate when feelings are calm rather than during a debate when emotions run high.
- ◆ Give yourself time to think about your answers.
- ◆ If there is a "no" give a brief explanation and then disengage.
- ◆ Accept your child's negative feelings without trying to fix them.
- ◆ Notice when your child is being flexible and show him appreciation.

The Plus Side

Helping Her See the Plus Side

One day my daughter was lying on her bed feeling down about the limits and the squabbles. She recognized that she had a lot more of them than her "sucky" brother. Knowing about persistence and the incredible drive behind it allowed me to step into my child's shoes and say, "Sometimes I guess it feels unfair and I imagine you feel kind of hurt right now." She cried and buried her face in my chest. I went on: "You know, honey, I remember when you were three years old and you wanted to ride a two wheeler. We took you down to the park and watched you fall off your bike 50 times but you didn't give up, and you ended up riding it home. Your determination and drive is going to serve you well." *-- Allison Rees*

The Non-Persistent Child

If your child is **not** persistent, allow him to come and go from tasks because it is difficult for him to stick with things for any length of time. Learning through short repetitions is more effective for these children, and eventually the task will get done. Any time you can lighten the load with humor or some creative twist, *do it!*

Know that as he matures, he will develop the ability to stay with things longer. If your child is not persistent, accept it and don't force him to focus for long periods. Forcing something that is difficult for him will undermine his self-esteem and his confidence.

Give your low-persistence child a break. As he matures he will be able to take on more. Point out to him his admirable ability to be flexible, as that is one of the positive sides to this trait. Give him lots of practice at thinking things through on his own by involving him in decision-making. Give him encouragement for just doing things, rather than for completing them.

Low persistence is not the same thing as distractibility. Think of distractibility as *breadth* of attention (how many things are attended to at once), and persistence as *length* of attention (how long the child focuses on one thing.)

Apply Your Knowledge

- If your child is non-persistent, how can you support her to complete a task that is difficult?
- What positive messages could you use to encourage your child?

Learning Difficulties and Persistence

While some children are low on the scale of persistence and give up easily, be aware of possible learning disabilities. When children give up quickly ask yourself if it is an issue of persistence or ability. Children try hard when they get positive results from their efforts. When children try hard and get nowhere, they become discouraged. Persistence is not enough.

When they are faced with something day after day that feels impossible to them, it takes its toll. They may be told to try harder but trying harder doesn't improve the result. If it did, trying harder would be rewarding. Many of these children are of above average intelligence. Think of how confusing it must be for them to know that they are so smart in some things and yet they continually do poorly in others. They are too young to figure this out on their own. They need your help.

Many children slip through the cracks in our school system. Teachers aren't always able to pinpoint these kinds of challenges. Be an advocate for your child even if you have to insist. If your child is struggling at school and you can't figure out why, talk to the teacher or principal.

The Learning Disabilities Association or your local equivalent can provide you with preliminary questionnaires and information to help you and your child figure out why she is having difficulty. Many children drop out of school because of undiagnosed learning disabilities. They go through school trying so hard, and yet what we ask of them is akin to asking a handicapped person to get out of her wheelchair and walk: it's just not possible. School becomes a tremendously stressful environment. In the end, the child chooses to hang out with other kids who agree that school is uncool. In her eyes, it's better to be bad than stupid.

> **Up to 20% of children have learning disabilities, and many of them are undiagnosed. These children are often accused of not trying hard enough. This is not an issue of persistence but an issue of ability.**
>
>
>
> **The answer isn't more effort from the child, but more effort from parents and teachers. Simple adaptations to the curriculum and the classroom can make a huge difference.**

> **Like adults, children are motivated by success.**
>
> **They try hard when trying hard pays off; they stop trying when they get nowhere.**
>
> **This has nothing to do with persistence.**

5 - Cautiousness

How does your child respond to new situations, people and places: negatively or positively? The child who goes up to strangers in the mall probably has a positive approach to new places, people, and things. Today this trait can have its share of challenges as we try to keep our children safe.

Cautious Approach to New Situations	Variable	Enthusiastic Approach to New Situations
10 ⟵⟶	5	⟵⟶ 1
♦ slow to warm up to new people, places or activities ♦ will get labeled as shy	♦ You guessed it – yes, it depends – she may hang back a bit but then jump in	♦ jumps into new situations quickly ♦ sometimes accused of not thinking before she acts ♦ can act impulsively

A child with a positive response to new situations is generally outgoing rather than shy.

Super-Shopper

My daughter Anna has always been enthusiastic about new situations. As soon as she could walk, trips to the shopping center became hazardous because she would take off and explore the territory, sometimes coming back with interesting objects she had 'found' in the stores. It was quite a challenge to figure out where to return them. Anna would run up and hug strangers whom she liked the look of. As she got older, she was just as enthusiastic about activities. She enrolled herself in everything that was going on in school, then was puzzled when she became exhausted from having taken on too much. If you have an outgoing child, you don't have to worry about her making her way in the world.
-- *Alison Miller*

Understanding a Cautious Approach

The more challenging side of this trait may be the reserved or cautious response to new situations, places, people, or things – or, in more extreme cases, to all of these.

Many adults recognize this trait in themselves and tell us that people interpret them as being snobby. While they aren't hiding behind their mother's skirts any more, they may feel like observing people or places before jumping in.

Getting Used to Things

My son Justin, unlike his sister or his younger brother, is a 'slow warmer-upper', backing off from anything new. When he was about a week old, the public health nurse came for her official visit. I was giving Justin his bath when she turned up. He had only been having

continued on next page ...

baths for a week, and wasn't adjusted to the experience; he howled the entire time! I tried to take it in my stride, wondering what on earth the nurse thought as Justin's yells rang out through the neighborhood.

He was the same throughout his childhood. When he was five, I took him to swim classes and gymnastics lessons but he hung back and barely participated. He wasn't really comfortable in school until about the second grade. When he was 10, a friendly lady greeted Justin at a parents' meeting, and his response was to growl at her!

By his teens, Justin had learned to be outgoing in situations he was familiar with, but I thought he would probably always have some difficulty facing totally new situations because of his combination of high persistence, reserved response to new situations, low adaptability, and intense emotional reactions – all of which led to lots of temper tantrums.

Whatever the source of our personality traits, most of us learn to deal with them with time and support. Justin is now an adult and has established a successful career in another city. He has learned to accept his temperament and to be more comfortable meeting new people and entering new situations. When I was expecting him, I had an image of him as a great big strong and beautiful tree, and I kept that image in mind as I struggled with his temperament. As an adult he is now becoming like that tree.   *-- Alison Miller*

Parenting Pitfall: Push or Pull?

It is easy to introduce an enthusiastic child to new people and activities; the challenge is in protecting the child from things into which he may plunge without thinking of the consequences. The slow warmer-upper, who backs off from new experiences, is more difficult for a parent to handle. He must be given the opportunity to experience new situations without pressure, and to re-experience them until he becomes familiar with them. If a parent gives in to a slow warmer-upper, and allows him to avoid new activities, he will never leave the house! If, instead, the parent forces him to participate, the pressure will make him retreat and balk rather than move forward.

He always screams when I give him a bath because he's only been having baths for a month and he isn't used to them yet ...

Parenting Pointers

◆ Give the slow-to-warm-up child the time he needs to adapt to new situations and allow gradual separation from you.

◆ Let the child know that it is okay to need time to get used to a new person, place or thing, and that you will be there for her.

◆ Discuss how things will look before you go there.

The Plus Side

Remember that every strong trait has a positive and a negative side. The more accepting and patient you are, the more relaxed your child will become in many situations. With support these children can find the courage it takes to face new life experiences.

Apply Your Knowledge

● How cautious is your child?

● If your child is more cautious and slower to warm up to people, places and/or things, what kind of challenges does this present for your child?

● How can you express yourself supportively to your slow-to-warm-up child without labeling the child 'shy' or 'fearful'?

● Children with a positive approach to new situations can be very outgoing. When they are young, trips out to the store can be hazardous as they take off and explore. As they get older they enroll in a lot of activities and can often take on too much. What kinds of tools would be useful for the parent of these children?

6 - Adaptability and Non-Adaptability

Adaptability refers to how easily the child accepts changes, and how long it takes him to become used to new routines. A child who has a hard time with change is sometimes difficult to deal with. A slow-to-adapt child needs a lot of warning about changes. If he expects burgers for dinner and ends up with burritos, you can expect a meltdown.

Transitioning from a play activity to go and eat, getting out of the car, or even changing clothes for different seasons, comes slowly to this child. For a youngster like this, rough transitions can make or break a day, but a wise parent will be alert to the change and plan ahead.

Non-Adaptable	Variable	Adaptable
10 ⟷	5 ⟷	1
◆ Has a hard time with transition (moving from one activity or environment to another). ◆ Doesn't react well to surprises. ◆ Takes a long time to get used to changes.	◆ Depends on the activity.	◆ No problem with transition. ◆ Can skip from one subject, acitvity or environment to another without skipping a beat.

Parenting Pitfall: Forcing Change

Some parents feel hurt when they go to pick up their child after being apart for a few hours or a day, and the child doesn't want to leave whatever he is doing and go with the parent. It's hard not to take it personally when you have been missing him, but if you are familiar with this trait you won't personalize it so much. Dragging the child away while berating him for not wanting to see you doesn't make for a good relationship!

Non-adaptable children also need their parents not to change their living situation without warning, and not to do it without thinking carefully about how long it will take the child to get used to the new routine. Some children adapt fairly easily to a new schedule of eating or sleeping, a new place to live, or a new family member while others don't. They will fuss and complain and refuse to settle down for quite a long time. Obviously, the non-adaptable child is more difficult to deal with. If you have a child like this think very carefully before you make a change in his life. It will probably take at least a few weeks before the child settles down in the routine. Is the change worth two weeks of misery? With a slow-to-adapt child you have to learn patience.

Parenting Pointers

◆ Get into a routine – non-adaptable children do better when they have a routine they can count on. If you aren't a scheduled, organized person this may feel a bit burdensome, but it's worth the effort to sail smoothly through the day.

◆ Talk with your child about what is coming up in the day. Verbally prepare your child for change before it happens. Give your child a calendar so she can see what is coming. When possible, let your child be involved in planning.

◆ Limit the number of transitions in a day.

The Plus Side

Admire your non-adaptable child's love of organization, and hope that when she becomes an adult she will be very reliable as a result of having this trait.

Apply Your Knowledge

- How adaptable is your child?
- Children who have difficulty with change present more challenges. They like to know what to expect and they love to be organized. If your child is like this, how can you support him or her?
- What kind of supportive messages can you express to your child about this trait?

---

7 - Emotional Intensity

An intense behavior is one in which a large amount of energy is used; a mild behavior is one which uses up minimal energy. An intense infant grabs or strains for the spoon to get a mouthful of food she likes; a mild one just opens her mouth. An intense child squirms, makes a rude noise and hits the spoon to reject food; a mild one just closes her mouth or turns her face away. When a response is positive, intensity is wonderful. When it's negative, watch out!

Intense Reactions	Variable	Mild Reactions
10 ⟷	5 ⟷	1
◆ You believe this person when he tells you how he feels. ◆ Could be described as enthusiastic, loud, expressive or lively. ◆ Knee-jerk reactions. ◆ Intense with the positive and the negative.	◆ Intensity of response depends on the situation.	◆ Can be accused of lacking passion. ◆ Has to reassure people that he really does like their gifts. ◆ May seem unemotional but is 'laid back' rather than controlled.

Parenting Pitfall: Intense Parental Reactions

Parents often find an intense child difficult to deal with. She needs calm, firm, patient management without the parent giving in or joining in with the emotional outburst. This can be difficult, especially if you are an intense reactor yourself. An intense child's reaction can tap into the intensity of a parent so that the parent does what comes naturally – yells back! Intense responses come from the speed and strength of reaction of a person's nervous system, and the individual can't change that.

Eat up your dinner, Dear.

I DON'T WANNA EAT MY DINNER!

YOU DON'T HAVE TO! STOP YELLING AT ME!

However, control can come with maturity and conscious effort. It is important to make space for people to feel their emotions; feelings often calm down when they receive attention without being taken personally. (See the chapter on the intelligence of emotions in *The Parent-Child Connection.*)

Emotional intensity runs in families, and intense family members can set each other off. It would of course be wonderful if parents could stay calm and patient while their child is screaming and yelling but in the real world it doesn't usually work that way. Stress from the day can bring out intensity even when the person's trait is variable or mild.

When our children are intense they may bite, kick and scream as toddlers or curse, yell and slam doors when they are older. Many parents feel intimidated by their children's intensity and avoid doing or saying things that might upset them. The result of giving in is a demanding, spoiled and aggressive child who uses his negative intensity and anger to control others. Similarly, intense parents can intimidate their children with aggressive behavior.

Apply Your Knowledge

- Emotionally intense children may be impulsive in their behaviour. They may lash out and feel terrible about themselves afterwards. Younger children will have intense temper tantrums and scare themselves. How can you offer your child reassurance and guidance during these times?
- If you have an intense child and you are intense yourself, be careful not to overreact. How can you *plan ahead* to deal with emotional outbursts in your family?
- Being intense does not mean being aggressive. How can you allow your child to have strong feelings while setting limits on behavior?
- If your child is a mild reactor it is helpful to empower him with assertiveness skills such as speaking up for himself. How can you teach your child to be assertive?

Parenting Pointers

- It is wise to plan ahead or have a family vision to deal with the challenges that come up. If you are an intense adult, don't expect to act like a mild one. Enjoy being intense and enthusiastic, that is who you are. However, being intense is not permission to be aggressive, and being aware of this trait can help us respond to situations rather than reacting to them blindly.
- Manage your own feelings and you will set a good example for your child. Each of the techniques below can be used for your child as well as yourself.
- Get in touch with your feeling vocabulary and use it with the safety net of *"I Statements"*. How much more effective it is to say, "I feel so angry when you do that!" than "You are a ____ jerk!" What a great role model you will make – not just for your family but for the rest of the neighbourhood who will probably hear you. Take responsibility for the words that come out of your mouth. Words can be weapons.
- Time yourself out. Go into the bathroom, turn on all the taps and breathe. You do have a choice to say 'no' to aggression and disengage. You can do this by either dropping a subject or leaving the room if your verbal sparring partner won't stop. Remember that sudden parental disappearance can be shocking to an emotionally-charged child, especially if he's young.
- Try calming activities such as baths, silly putty, reading, humor, cooling down periods, or quiet one-on-one times with your child.
- Teach your children words to label their feelings, and don't punish them for expressing those feelings with passion. They will rarely say in a mild voice, *"I am angry right now,"* and if you get hung up on the volume you are missing an opportunity to listen, learn and love.

♦ Have a "second chance rule". You can say, *"You have just made a major mistake by calling me a _____. You may have a second chance to reword that."* Kids need a second chance to help them choose a different way of communicating their feelings, and the more practice they get, the easier it will come.

♦ Give yourself a second chance too. Don't beat yourself up for not living up to all these things we've suggested; just try again.

The Plus Side

Emotionally intense people can be very lively and enthusiastic. You don't need to do a lot of detective work to know how they are feeling either – they can be pretty quick to let you know. Intense people can be passionate in love, and passionate for causes. They can find great joy in small things. I (Alison Miller) remember counseling a woman who left a calm, rational husband for an intense person who fought with her constantly; she said he made her feel alive.

Intense individuals are sometimes puzzled by others who don't have the same strength of response that they do. They may feel the mild individual is hiding his feelings, when that person is simply being himself. He feels but not with the same force. We have often been grateful for the patience and calm demeanor of a duty person on the schoolyard or a teacher who has that mild reactive personality that our intense children call 'so boring'. A mild person can calm down an intense family and help them resolve conflicts and see reason.

Apply Your Knowledge

- What is the positive side of being intense?
- What is the positive side of being a mild reactor?
- What kind of positive messages can you give your child about his or her trait?

8 - Body Regularity and Irregularity

Children and adults differ in the degree of rhythm or regularity with which their bodies function. Some have 'built-in alarm clocks' – they wake at the same time every morning and fall asleep at the same time every night. This regularity can also apply to hunger and toileting.

Ten o'clock, time to put her on the potty. I save a lot of diapers by watching the time.

Regular	Variable	Irregular
10 ⟷	5 ⟷	1
◆ Gets hungry and tired at predictable times and doesn't take well to a change in schedule.	◆ Pretty regular but can be flexible when he needs to be (i.e. missing a nap won't be a crisis).	◆ Rarely gets hungry, tired or sleepy at the same time every day. ◆ Can be flexible with routines.

Do you know anyone you can set a clock to? He eats three square meals a day and reserves the bathroom for 7:00 a.m. every morning. If your child is like this then getting him to bed, toilet training, and feeding are probably not a huge challenge when you follow everyday routines. But if you travel and have to change your schedule, watch out! Adults or children whose bodies are regular have typical sleepy times of the day and can really suffer when their schedules are interrupted.

My Precise Brain

I wake up each morning, weekday or weekend, at precisely 6:57 a.m. I have a sleepy period right after lunch, and I managed to fall asleep in classes from Grade 11 right through university. My brain 'switches off' at 10 p.m. no matter whether I'm in bed, watching a movie, or at a party. I would like to bend my schedule to accommodate more variety, but my body won't let me! -- *Alison Miller*

The Irregular Child

And if he cries there's usually a good reason for it. He's probably hungry, or thirsty, or tired. Or lonely and needing a little attention, or frustrated or bored. Or maybe he's soiled his diaper. Or he could have a tummy ache. But don't worry about it, he might not cry at all ...

If you have an irregular child, you may find that your child resists structure and routine, causing challenges with bedtime and mealtime. Life just doesn't have that predictable flow that can keep the household calm, and you may need to consider paying babysitters more to make up for the uncertainties they have to deal with.

Irregular adults also need to be aware of their own temperament; then they can consider the needs of others who may need more structure and routine.

Apply Your Knowledge

- Where do you place your children on the scale of regularity? Regular children can be easier to parent when they are younger. They are more predictable and you know what to expect.
- Irregular children present more challenges around mealtime, toilet training and bedtime. If your child is irregular how does this challenge you?
- Irregular children won't be tired at the same time every night and as they get older they might be tucking you in! How can you exercise your boundaries while respecting this trait in your child?

Parenting Pitfall: Mismatched Parents and Kids

Problems can emerge in families if the individual differences among the family members in terms of regularity are not taken into account. If you are not a regular or rhythmical person yourself, be aware that your child may be, and you will have to adapt to her, because she cannot adapt to you.

As a parent you will have to provide meals when the children need them, not when you are hungry, and so on. If you are a regular person, and your children are irregular, you will have to work out some compromises which will allow you to keep your sanity despite your children's unpredictability.

Dealing with Meal Time and Bedtime

Bedtime

♦ **Leave enough time.**

- If bedtime is 8:00 p.m., start the teeth and toilet routine no later than 7:30 p.m. Let them know that if they can get all their nightly chores done (brushing teeth, using the toilet, etc.), then whatever time is left over before 8:00 p.m. is for stories or talking.

- Talking in a whisper emphasizes quiet or sleepy time. Planning to keep your voice to a whisper through the night also stops you from yelling when your kids wake you up at 2:00 a.m.!

- Your regular child may already be asleep when you shut the door, while your irregular child may be ready to do somersaults off the bed.

♦ **Have a firm rule in place.**

- *"You don't have to go to sleep, you can look at some books or listen to a story tape, but you must stay in your room and preferably on your bed."*

- The consequence if children dawdle is, of course, losing *some* (not all) story time, and that time is usually very special to a child. When your children are younger, you may need to allow more time for getting ready.

♦ **Have a special routine.**

- The routine of the story or bedtime talk is very important for a child's sense of being loved. Make sure you leave enough time so that this can happen every day. We believe a bedtime story is a child's right, not a privilege, so it shouldn't be denied as a consequence of behavior. Children always need to feel they are loved and that they belong.

- Before you begin reading, ask your children if there is anything they need before they settle in for the night. Massage can relax any child (or adult). Give her something to look forward to that will relieve tension.

- Just because your child is reading on his own and wearing bigger shoes than you doesn't mean you can't still have that special story time. Older children prefer books with chapters; choose ones you enjoy too and it will be something you can really look forward to. One word of caution – if your child reads chapter books to you while you are lying on the bed, you will probably fall asleep!

♦ **Respect your own bedtime boundaries.**

- The principle behind the bedtime rule (ritual) is that while you're respecting your child's bodily need to sleep or not to sleep, you are also respecting your need to relax and have some time to yourself. Being gentle yet firm about this boundary assures her that you mean what you say.

♦ **Teen bedtime.**

• With teens you are going to have to face some serious facts. There is a good chance they will be tucking you in at night, especially if you are regular and get tired at 9:30 or 10:00 p.m. every night. Kids start wanting to set their own bedtimes at about age 11. For a while they will stay up too late but eventually they will figure out that this makes them tired and that going to bed at a reasonable hour will be beneficial.

• By the time they have reached this point, they will need to know the procedure for being the last one to bed. A list of To Do's is a great idea – check locks, all lights out, etc. No, you don't tell them to brush their teeth and have a pee any more.

Meals

♦ **Timing – Let Them Listen to Their Bodies.**

• Irregular children probably won't want to eat during regular mealtimes because they have been eating throughout the day as their bodies tell them to. Don't fret; people who are in touch with their bodies are usually very healthy! It is important to learn to eat when you are hungry and stop when you are full. Many adults are trying to learn how to do this! There is some recent evidence that specific diets (particularly weight-loss diets) are frequently unsuccessful and can possibly lead (if followed poorly) to dangerous health consequences. Nutritionists are encouraging people to let their bodies tell them whether they are hungry or full.

♦ **Snacks.**

• Many doctors and nutritionists believe that it's a lot healthier to eat small amounts of food frequently (e.g. six small meals daily) rather than stuffing oneself three times a day and starving in between. Your children are actually doing the healthy thing when they want to eat several times a day. However, to avoid cooking all day long, teach your children how to open the fridge door and find their own snacks. Have fruits and veggies cut up every morning so they can help themselves from a snack drawer that is within reach. Keep plastic cups down low with some easy-pour containers in the fridge or a water dispenser nearby.

♦ **Who is responsible for children eating well?**

• Take yourself out of the picture so that your children can listen to their bodies. They need to respect the little voice inside their head (or tummy). It won't lie to them. Our job as parents is to provide healthy food in a pleasant environment and the rest is their business, not ours. Avoid using food as a reward or a punishment. Try not to comment on how much food they eat at the table; remember it is none of your business (you can't hear the little voice!). If they don't eat all their dinner, wrap it up; they may want it later.

9 - Sensory Sensitivity

We have at least five senses: sight, hearing, smell, taste, and touch. Some people are much more sensitive than others to sensory stimuli. Children with high sensory sensitivity notice all kinds of things that are perceived through their senses and feel some of them intensely. They can't sleep through noise. They hate being in wet diapers. They notice the taste of their food and may dislike many foods. They react strongly to pain.

A parent with high sensitivity will understand what their sensitive kids are going through but a parent who is less sensitive may be shocked to discover that their kids aren't faking it or looking for attention when they complain about small things like the seam in their socks. A child can't do anything about the degree of sensory sensitivity he was born with, so it's important for parents to understand this rather than try unsuccessfully to change it.

Children with lower sensory sensitivity are easier on parents. They don't care how their clothes feel, they can fall asleep and stay asleep in the middle of a noisy party in a bright room, and they will eat anything. They don't even mind going to the dentist. However, when they discover music, watch out, especially if you, the parent, have high sensory sensitivity.

Highly Sensitive	Variable	Less Sensitive
10 ⟵⟶	5 ⟵⟶	1
◆ Sensitive to even very low levels of light, noise and discomfort. ◆ Some children are sensitive to the emotions of others.	◆ Sometimes sensitive, or sensitive in one area but not another.	◆ Can tolerate lots of noise, light, etc. ◆ Does not notice environmental details.

Daggers and Shrieking Whistles

My son Peter had a serious tone as he told me about his day. He began by pointing to the little metal lace grommets on his shoes. He said, "See these metal rims, Mom? They are like daggers digging in my feet." I squinted hard trying to imagine how these tiny things could even make their way into a conversation. After some discussion of the daggers, he went on to tell me that the smell in his lunch kit almost made him sick and he couldn't even think about eating the sandwich which also had this horrible smell (though all I could smell was a Dad's cookie). He also had a tough time getting his journal finished because two of the girls in his class were chatting and their voices were like shrieking whistles.

-- Allison Rees

Sensitive adults have a much harder time listening to their children bickering, the rap music blaring from their rooms, and the whining from the youngsters. They will react to it and become exhausted from it. If you are a sensitive individual with children you may want to consider earplugs.

Parenting Pitfall:
Disbelieving Your Child's Experience

No, she wasn't a drama queen, she was sensitive!

I (Allison Rees) listened to a mom complain about her seven-year-old daughter. Her daughter had a school performance with her dance club. Mom delivered her daughter's skirt along with a slip and shirt. When her daughter saw the slip that mom brought she burst into tears explaining that she couldn't wear it, that it itched and hurt and it would take away from her performance. I asked the mom whether the girl had a history of being sensitive to lights, smells, feelings and so on. Her reply was: "Yeah, she is a real drama queen, anything for attention." My heart sank because right there I knew that this girl's feelings and needs were not being met or accepted with regard to this area of her life. I hoped that the girl's mother could begin to understand her daughter's sensitivity.

-- Allison Rees

Parenting Pointers

♦ **Work with the senses.**

Work with the senses, not against them. Aromatherapy, soft lighting and pleasant sounds could help both you and your children. Water can be very soothing; if your child is old enough let him soak in a warm tub while you make dinner. Or, try massaging your children before bed in front of a heater or fire place; a hot water bottle wrapped in a soft towel is great to cuddle. Sometimes children enjoy a swatch of velvet to touch when they are tired. In other words, as sensitive as they can be negatively is as sensitive as they can be positively. Being sensitive makes some things in life hard to bear but it also increases the enjoyment one gets from life's pleasures.

> **Provide positive experiences that rekindle energy for the sensitive souls in your life whether they be your children, your spouse, your friends, or yourself!**

♦ **Be patient regarding food.**
Sensitive kids will often be picky eaters. If you think their feet are sensitive, get a load of their tongues! That pancake will feel like lizard skin if it is overcooked. They will be put off by smells and textures, hot and cold, dry or moist .... aarrrgghhh! Be patient. They will cook for you one day and it will be absolutely perfect. Be aware that sometimes kids' food dislikes reflect foods they are allergic to and do what is necessary to check that out.

♦ **Give a sensitive child time to refuel.**
Find a closet and put a cushion on the floor. Put a little sign on the door that says 'Refueling Station'. You could even get fancy and have some soothing music ready to go. Perhaps a flashlight would be handy as well in case they are afraid of the dark. Sensitive people need a special alone place where they can go and refuel if they need to. However, it might not sound good if you say that you spend time in a closet, so you may want to be careful how you describe it. Of course this is not for little kids – the isolation might frighten them.

Apply Your Knowledge

- How sensitive is each of your children?
- If you rated a child as sensitive does he complain about the seam in his tube socks and the labels in the back of the T-shirts? What else?
- Does she become over-stimulated or drained at the mall or in the classroom?
- Sensitive children really feel things and if they are intense as well it may sound as if they have seriously injured themselves when they get a paper cut. Can you accept that this is real and know they aren't faking it?
- If you are a sensitive adult your children's noises may be intolerable to you but acceptable to a less sensitive adult. How can you state your needs as a parent and yet manage reasonable expectations of your children?
- Sensitive people also respond positively to pleasant sights, sounds and touch. What kinds of sensory experience are pleasing to your child?
- Children with a low sensitivity to sound and light can sleep through a party. Sensitive children can hear a clock ticking at the other end of the house. What strategies can you come up with to keep your sensitive child comfortable?

10 - Positive or Negative Mood

Do you know someone who tends to see the world in a more serious or pessimistic way? You know, the person who sees the glass half empty instead of half full? The researchers of the *New York Longitudinal Study* (1956 to 1986) found that newborn babies vary considerably in the quality of their mood. Some are usually in a positive mood and spend most of their time smiling, burbling and cooing. Others are usually in a negative mood and frequently fuss and cry. Most, of course, are in between, having variable moods.

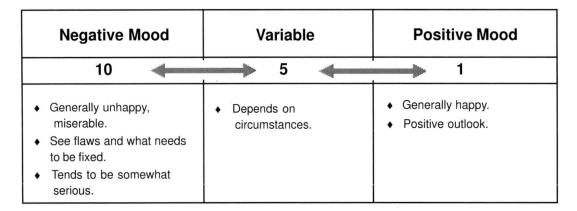

Negative Mood	Variable	Positive Mood
10	5	1
♦ Generally unhappy, miserable. ♦ See flaws and what needs to be fixed. ♦ Tends to be somewhat serious.	♦ Depends on circumstances.	♦ Generally happy. ♦ Positive outlook.

Parenting Pitfall: Overreacting

Parents often find it difficult to accept a child of negative mood without blaming either themselves or the child. Negative moods can be catching too – have you ever felt grumpy after talking with a grumpy sales clerk or bank teller?

Parenting Pointers

A child of negative mood needs calm, matter-of-fact, pleasant management without her parents overreacting to her mood. Role model a healthy thinking style by avoiding the three P's as outlined by Dr. Martin Seligman, a leading child psychologist:

♦ **Personal.**
  We need to learn to take things impersonally instead of personally.

♦ **Permanent.**
  When times are tough we need to see that it's a temporary situation, not a permanent one.

♦ **Pervasive.**
  It doesn't mean that every aspect of our life is affected when we have a problem with a friend or school work. These are isolated situations rather than pervasive ones.

Children need a feeling vocabulary that they can refer to and use with a parent who listens to them and accepts them. It doesn't mean we need to take their feelings on. It's important to have healthy emotional boundaries in place.

Apply Your Knowledge

- Rate the negativity of your child's usual mood (from 1 to 10).
- If your child is fairly serious or negative about life experiences how can you deal effectively with his outlook on life?

Whose fault is the baby's bad mood?

People certainly like to find explanations. When my younger son Alexander was a couple of weeks old, I took him out with me to a meeting. After the first half hour, he began to cry and fuss. I nursed him. No response. The woman sitting next to me, a social worker, told me off. "You're giving in to him far too much; that's why he's so fussy." Alexander continued to cry. The woman had to leave the meeting early and was replaced by a man who happened to be a psychologist. He watched the same thing happen. "Oh, how lovely," he said. "You're so aware of the little guy's needs. He'll grow up very well-adjusted."

Alexander didn't stop crying all evening. It was the only time he ever went through a period like that. It appeared that the problem may have been a stomach upset because I had been eating broccoli. Alexander didn't turn out to be a child of a generally negative mood, thank goodness. But the incident made me aware of how quick people are to judge our parenting by the quality of our children's moods. Of course, we do have considerable power to make our children happy or unhappy. But certain children, and most children at certain times, are negative no matter what we do. -- *Alison Miller*

Other people are going to judge our children for temperament and personality traits they were born with. And they're going to judge us, the parents, for not making our kids instantly different! We need to learn to accept that this will happen and to continue accepting our children as they are, while helping them learn to live effectively in a world which can be very judgmental.

11 - Temperament, Life Experience and Personality

Even though we come into the world with a basic temperament, life experience has a huge influence on our later personality. While our basic temperament does not change, new characteristics come into existence over time. Some of these may be learned but others are inborn and don't show up until a certain age. Everyone has a unique personality, with strengths and weaknesses. If you realize that someone functions in a particular way then you can make allowances, compensate for your personal disposition, and welcome those who function differently.

Apply Your Knowledge

- Once you know the nine basic temperament traits, does it help you to see your child as a unique human being?

The combination of traits that we reviewed can show up differently in every person. A person can be intense and sensitive. Someone else can be distractible and persistent. Sometimes when these traits come together they make a person introverted or extroverted.

This is my class project! It's a photocopy of a dead mouse Dad found in his shoe! He wore it for two weeks -- thought it was a Dr. Scholl's insole until it started to smell. Actually, we thought the smell was his own feet....

An **extrovert** is:
- outgoing, personable, easy to get along with
- happy-go-lucky, bold, and energetic
- adventurous
- a person who prefers to be with groups.

An **introvert**:
- prefers to be alone and to have fewer friends
- may be more oriented to things and ideas than to people
- is more self-sufficient
- does not enjoy noisy groups
- does not need as much stimulation

You and your family members may be neither. Some people come out exactly in the middle while others are more extreme. Either way, getting to know yourself and your child can only enhance self-esteem and your relationship.

Personality Clashes in the Family

The individual temperaments and personalities of family members affect those they live with. Two intense people may have passionate fights. A sensitive person may react to the music of a less sensitive family member. A regular parent may be run ragged by an irregular child. We call it a 'personality clash' when two people can't stand each other.

Sometimes the clash is because these two people are alike (e.g. intense and sensitive); sometimes it's because they're different and they can't understand what makes the other person tick. Even when our personality clashes with that of our child, they always need our unconditional love.

Temperament and Expectations

Appropriate expectations can go a long way towards avoiding power struggles. Use your knowledge and understanding of your child's temperament to keep your expectations appropriate for your child's unique self. Help others to understand her and advocate for her needs.

Apply Your Knowledge

- Which particular temperamental characteristics of your children do you have difficulty accepting?
- Do you have a deeper understanding of your family interactions as a result of understanding each person's individual temperament?
- Individual temperaments and personalities of family members interact within the family. Sometimes we have difficulty with those who are different, and sometimes we have difficulty with those who are like us because we don't like those traits in ourselves. How much conflict do differences or similarities in temperament create in your family?

This chapter has summarized nine basic traits of temperament which people are born with. Understanding our children's basic genetic makeup helps us parent each child according to his or her needs. It also helps us understand ourselves and why we react as we do to other family members.

A Look at Family Temperament Traits

This table is designed to help you to see how you perceive your family's temperament traits. Remember that your ratings reflect your own temperament and perceptions — what seems high to you might not seem high to another person. Completing this chart may give you some insight into the personalities in your family and their relationships with other family members. You may find two members who are alike and perhaps clash at times, or members who get along well because their temperaments complement each other.

How to use this chart: Rate each person from 1 to 10 on each trait. Use 10 when you think the person high; 1 when you think the person is low; and somewhere in between to reflect medium, medium high, and medium low.

Color Tip: For a more visual presentation, color the highs in red, the mediums with yellow, and lows in blue.

Names of Family Members:					
Activity Level					
Distractibility					
Persistence					
Approach (10) Withdrawal (0)					
Adaptability					
Emotional Intensity					
Bodily Regularity					
Sensory Sensitivity					
Mood					

Further Reading

Chess, Stella and Thomas, Alexander. *Know Your Child.*
New York: Basic Books, 1987.
Chess and Thomas were behind the *New York Longitudinal Study*
as mentioned on p.34.

Kurcinka, Mary. *Raising Your Spirited Child.*
New York: Harper Collins, 1991.

Turecki, Stanley.   *The Difficult Child.*
New York: Bantam, 2000.

Zimbardo, Philip. *The Shy Child.*
New York: McGraw Hill, 1981.

2

Tell Me It's a Stage:
Development of the Child's Self

This chapter and the next will give you a good sense of what's normal for your child's age so that you can stop worrying and enjoy your child for the child she is without expecting her to act like an adult. With a basic understanding of child development you will know which of your child's so-called problem behaviors are just part of being a child rather than indications of deeper trouble.

In this chapter we look at four areas of children's development:

1. Their need to develop independence and take charge of their own lives.
2. Their difficulty in handling their emotions.
3. Their self-centeredness (egocentricity).
4. Their developing sexuality.

On their way to independence kids go through 'transition stages' during which they seem to oppose everything we say. In this chapter you will find some tips on how to handle these difficult times; it is not easy to keep your cool when your child is feeling overwhelmed. All kids are self-centered. It is wise to accept that they are this way and focus on teaching them how to gradually develop some awareness of other people's needs. Sexuality is a huge problem in today's society; we have suggestions on how to talk to your kids about it.

Understanding the stages of children's development helps us to provide love, fairness and a healthy framework of limits so that they can move forward confidently with their self-esteem intact.

1 - Developing Independence

It can be a shock when our children start asserting themselves as they struggle to become independent. A child who was sweet and cooperative one day can suddenly become completely defiant, resistant and even aggressive the next. And just when we think our child has had enough of us, he regresses, clings and shows incredible insecurity.

Could this be a stage? When we parents are aware of the steps and stages toward maturing and independence, it changes our reaction to our children. We learn to respond with fairness and love rather than with anger. We need to understand "what normal is" rather than trying to change or fix behavior.

Maturing is not a one-way street, even for adults. For example, a person who has worked hard to establish new personal boundaries experiences times of strength and independence as she exercises her newly found boundaries, but often slips back a little when she feels insecure or needs reassurance.

Children too grow by "two steps forward, one step backward." At one point I (Alison Miller) had a

The Hulk Returns

It was a beautiful sunny day. I took my two-year-old son to the beach. I still have the pictures. He wore his little red baseball cap and little high top sneakers. He was so cute! We had a snack and then went to the swings. There were other moms with their children enjoying the day. A couple of them had been to a presentation I had given on Positive Discipline at their pre-school.

Finally, it was time to leave. After a little warning I went to pull my son out of the swing. My sweet little boy went absolutely crazy. He arched his body in that special way kids do when they don't want to be picked up and started screaming. Now everyone was watching. "What would the great parenting teacher do?" Well, with all the strength I had, I lifted him from that swing, his body writhing. He grabbed onto my face with both hands and bit my nose. Latched onto my nose, he hung from my body as we made our way to the parking lot. I wrestled him into his car seat, and once again his back arched. It was like straddling and tying up a calf. I strapped him in and shut the door.

Then I smiled and waved to the sympathetic onlookers, wondering, "What do you think of me so far?" Looking in the car mirror, I could see scratches on my face and a nose with perfect teeth marks indented into the flesh. Looking further back into the mirror, I saw him. The Hulk! He cooed and smiled at me and said, "I love you, Momma".

If someone had told me at this time that it was just a stage, my first impulse would have been to slap them. After that, through trembling lips, I would ask, "How long does it last?"
-- *Allison Rees*

three-year-old son insisting on eating with a knife and fork, while my eight-year-old ate with his fingers. The younger one was trying to be mature, while the older one was asserting his right to still be "little".

Pass salt pease, Mommy.

Transition Stages

Although the development of independence continues without a break from birth to adulthood, there appear to be certain phases that are particularly hard on parents. In these phases the child changes from one kind of being (e.g. a baby) to another kind (e.g. a preschooler), and the transition causes some emotional upset, in both the child and the parents! Dr. Fitzhugh Dodson calls these stages "transition stages" (see chart on next page).

Real power for parents lies in their ability to empower children, not control them and make them mind. How easy that is to say, how difficult it can be to do. We say we want our children to be responsible, resourceful, resilient, loving individuals who know how to think, not just what to think. However, we often find ourselves teaching them what to think based on what we think. From the time our children are toddlers we can hear ourselves saying to them, "Think for yourself. Don't forget your coat and mittens." (...) "If you had put your shoes in one place, we wouldn't be looking for them now." "How many times do I have to tell you to think for yourself?" Many kids spend the first years of their adult life trying to figure out how to think for themselves, because they had learned so well what we think and rarely got the opportunity to practice how to think.

-- Barbara Coloroso, *Kids Are Worth It*, p.74.

Transition Stages in Childhood

Transition	Change	Age (Years)
1st	Baby to Preschooler	1 - 2
2nd	Preschooler to School-age Child	4 - 5
3rd	Child to Teenager	11 - 14
4th	Teenager to Adult	17 - 25+

The Struggle for Independence

The following signs indicate that your child is struggling for more independence:

- feeling negative or resistant
- changing her mind constantly
- refusing help
- showing stubbornness
- arguing, showing defiance and talking back
- criticizing parents
- shutting out family members
- doing things to irritate you

I had a huge fight with my son about what music he could listen to on the stereo. I was ready for this when he was a teenager, but now ....

How old is your son?

Three.

Many people feel their child is the only one who acts this way! When we conduct parenting courses we often hear people say how great it is to realize they aren't alone. It is nice to know that you aren't doing everything wrong just because your child behaves as he does.

Children Resist Directions

When a child feels resistant she refuses to do anything you want her to do! Whether it is using the toilet or eating a meal you have just prepared, her resistance to you feels like the Great Wall of China!

So Why Did She Ask Me?

When my daughter was nine she asked me if I liked her pants zipped at the bottom (they were zip flares) or unzipped. Pleased that she asked, I gave her my honest opinion. "Unzipped looks kind of cool." She immediately zipped them up and walked out the front door. We can only hope that our teens practice that same kind of resistance with peer pressure. *-- Allison Rees*

Apply Your Knowledge

When children are struggling for independence small things can become power struggles. They may change their minds constantly. They may ask for your advice only to reject it.

● Do you recognize any of this? Take some space to write about some of your experiences.
● Do you remember doing this as a child or teenager?

Children Change Their Minds

Children constantly change their minds as they struggle hard for independence. Decisions don't come easily and there is little commitment to what they do decide.

The toddler will change his mind from juice to milk and back to juice, ending the frustration with a tantrum. Give young children a simple choice between two alternatives (e.g. concerning drinks or clothing) and then insist they stay with what they choose.

As abstract thinking develops in the teen years children often present arguments about everything: politics, how best to set up a tent, or any number of other things. But they won't be able to make simple decisions like whether to put ketchup on a grilled cheese sandwich. It can be a bit of a surprise to hear your independent teen asking for help with these simple kinds of decisions.

This can happen at any age; adults still do it! Making a decision can be very complicated. Do not engage in a power struggle because you may end up joining your child with a temper tantrum of your own. I wonder how juice and milk taste mixed together?

Children Refuse Help

I can do it myself!

I just watched my friend walk down my front stairs with his two-year-old boy. Of course the two-year-old was crying because he didn't want to leave. After carrying Junior down the stairs, my friend put him down to continue his walk to their car.

Junior would have nothing to do with that walk until he climbed back up the stairs and went down himself! "I can do it myself!" was his motto.   -- *Allison Rees*

If your child is persistent (see Chapter 1), you will be standing for a long time watching him attempt to do up his own shoelaces. You could view this as a good time for your child to learn new things. If you try to help, he pushes you away. What is important is not having it done but learning to master the task. You may see many emotional meltdowns based on pure frustration. Prepare ahead and try to take more time for the usual practical things such as putting on clothing or shoes.

This behavior of pulling away continues as children get older. Such behavior is healthy – it means your child is growing up. If children didn't declare independence this way we would probably keep doing things for them long beyond the point where it's needed. Be welcoming when they fall back into dependence at times.

Don't Take It Personally

Your child's refusal of help is a rejection, but it is healthy and it is a rejection of his younger self more than it is of you, so don't over-react. See it as positive and develop the parenting wisdom to stop, breathe deeply, and accept that it is designed by nature. Children really, really want to grow up and do things themselves, unless they've had experiences which make them afraid of this.

Although your teen has many challenges to face, she's likely to staunchly refuse your help. She really doesn't want to let you in right now. After all, what could you possibly know at your antiquated age? You are an adult, one of 'them', and the only people who really mean anything in the world or have any brains are her friends. It is difficult for adults to understand the subtle pressures of a teen's social world, which feels to her like her entire world.

This is where you get fired as your child's general contractor and hope that you will get hired back on as a consultant! Feel privileged if she lets you in, and don't blow the opportunity to hear her by lecturing or giving advice. That is what adults often do, and kids don't want advice unless they ask for it (and even then, they will probably reject it).

If a teen needs adult help, often an outside adult is a much safer place to share a part of himself – perhaps a *cool* aunt or uncle, a teacher or counselor, or an older friend whom he can confide in. What's important is that it isn't Mom or Dad! Teens know their parents are too emotionally involved or too anxious to be able to act as resources to help them make decisions. Also, they don't want to worry or disappoint their parents. Allow them to have their outside adult consultants – it doesn't mean you're fired, just that they're growing up.

It's hard to let go and let your teen manage things you know you could handle better. It's hard to let her face the consequences of her mistakes. But it's really important to do so. That doesn't mean you should never intervene. But unless there's a serious danger, it pays to let your teenager make her own decisions and experience the consequences. We will discuss this further in Chapter 5.

Children Become Stubborn and Defiant

"No, I don't want to and you can't make me!" Suddenly any idea that comes from the parent is cause for a great debate. It seems as if the most simple requests become major power struggles. Whether it is a young toddler refusing to get into the car seat or an older child battling about clothes, it all boils down to becoming an independent self. Does this mean *selfish*? Not at all. A child who doesn't go through this healthy kind of separating doesn't develop a self – *a sense of who he is*, what he likes, what makes him tick, and how he feels about things. Without a self you can't have self-esteem. We have treated many adults who have never developed a self because their parents tried so hard to squeeze them into a mold rather than allowing them to develop independence.

Many adults are unable to stand up for their rights because they were punished and shamed for saying "no". Disallowing "no" teaches kids that to be loved and accepted they have to please others by saying "yes" to experiences they don't feel good about.

Preschoolers can be blunt. Have you been called a *weenie-head* lately? How about *pooh-pooh pants*? It's a little embarrassing when you drop your child off at preschool and he says, *"Go away, butt head!"* Yes, this is normal behavior! And so is physical defiance like biting, hitting, and kicking. But try to convince the other parents who haven't gone through this yet with their little darlings or the grandparents who have forgotten what preschool kids are really like – they're sure you have somehow created this by your bad parenting.

Teens are so good at talking back they don't even have to use words. Their body language is amazing! The rolling of the eyes, the curl of the lip – all those wonderful non-verbal messages that say, *"Give me a break and get out of my life!"* – at least for an hour until they need something like money, a ride, or a letter excusing them from gym.

Their words are even worse. Teens' swearing is a way of separating from you because chances are you don't use the same lingo (although it is amazing how contagious it is!). Express your concern about swearing from your own sensitivities rather than judging your child as rude. If you say, *"Don't be so rude, how dare you talk like that,"* you will hear it again, fairly soon. Instead, if you can explain how you feel when you hear certain words, she may listen. *"When I was growing up that word was used to belittle women. I feel hurt and angry when I hear it even though I understand it may have a different meaning for you."*

You really do need to ignore some of it though. There is a difference between cursing about something as opposed to cursing at somebody. When your child swears at you he is crossing a major boundary, and you have a right to say, *"Not okay!"* But if swearing isn't directed at anybody and is done under the breath, it's probably better to ignore it.

However, if swearing becomes a habit and your teen doesn't understand that swearing is best curtailed around adults, you might want to address it. I (Allison Rees) got tired of hearing the word "bastard" 50 times a day in the peace of my own home. My daughter didn't even notice when she was using this wonderful word. I explained my need for peace and my concern about how she would be perceived by others if she spoke this way (especially in front of adults). We agreed that I could point out when she was using the word. When I first started doing this she was unaware that she had even said the word. A number of times, she didn't believe me! Eventually she became conscious of the word and it petered out but it was replaced by other words before her habit of swearing improved.

If you swear, be prepared to hear it from your kids. Some people are comfortable with swearing but kids need to learn that others may not be. We parents go through a stage of changing our habits when our kids are really young. When they are babies, we aren't that concerned about our language. Once they start talking, we pay a little more attention and start sounding like Julie Andrews in *The Sound of Music*.

Arguing with parents is common during transition stages. Sometimes disagreeing will be non-verbal, especially when a teen (or even a preschooler) discovers something that really bugs his parent. This kind of thing is a necessary part of the child or teenager becoming an independent person. Doing whatever the parent doesn't want isn't true independence, of course. It's what might be called "counter-dependence". It's still a reaction against feeling controlled by what the parent wants or likes.

The fact that a child does this doesn't mean you shouldn't have any boundaries or limits. We will discuss this more in Chapter 7: Love, Limits and Consequences, as well as in our other book, *The Parent-Child Connection* (in the chapter on Family Matters: Interactions in the Family System).

Children Shut Parents Out

New behaviors in the teen years include your child shutting you out of many areas of her life. She will become closed-mouthed about her life, and insist that you keep out of her room and mind your own business. She will refuse to attend family outings or to be seen with parents and younger brothers and sisters.

No Power in Her Life

When my daughter at 14 refused to let me see a book of poems that she had handed in to her English teacher (whom she criticized constantly), I felt hurt, and asked her why I couldn't see them when Mrs. C. had. "Because Mrs. C. has no power in my life," she replied. In order to become her own person, she needed to reduce my power in her life – even though she loved and generally respected me. She needed to feel increasingly that her life was not her family's but her own.

Now she's about to turn 33 – and she finally gave me a book of her poetry! I guess she's grown up. -- *Alison Miller*

When Friends are Over, I'm Chopped Liver

When my daughter was six, she would roll her eyes whenever I made a request of some kind. At first, I felt like doing the martyr thing: "After all the things I do for you, you have the nerve to make those faces just because I make a simple request." Then I realized that she was trying to be independent and show that she had her own ideas. Especially when her friends were nearby!

When I took a closer look at my own behavior, I had been treating my daughter as if she were younger than her age. Her behavior (the rolling of the eyes) was trying to give me a message: "Let go, Mom, give me a chance. I'm growing up – are you paying attention to that?" I decided to ignore the behavior once I understood it. -- *Allison Rees*

Apply Your Knowledge

- Stubbornness, defiance and talking back are signs of developing independence. How does your child try to assert himself?
- Do you remember struggling for independence when you were growing up?
- How do you feel when your child behaves this way?
- Why does this important part of growing up create so many problems?

Children Try to Change the Rules

During the teens, anything you want your child to do is up for debate. Be prepared for her to 'act smart' and stop discussing issues with you. Be very specific with your limits because a teen who is looking to push them will find a loophole.

Children can be incredibly creative at turning a "No" into a "Yes". This is especially true if it is a question of restricting them from doing what 'all the other kids' are doing. Their need to fit in with peers will often make the rules change when they walk out the front door. Do you remember making a few adjustments to your clothes when you went out at that age?

Oh wow! Where'd you get the blue eyeshadow? I thought your parents didn't allow you to wear makeup.

They don't let me wear makeup. But they never said anything about pool cue chalk!

Apply Your Knowledge

- While our young children might embarrass us when they are messy and loud, they grow up into young teens who are embarrassed by our appearance and behavior. How did you feel as a young teen?
- When kids go through stages of pushing limits and trying to become independent they find lots of things to argue about and they do things to irritate you. What limits is your child pushing, and what arguments does he or she create?
- Are there any power struggles that you can walk away from?

The Cat Years

I just realized that while children are dogs –
loyal and affectionate – teenagers are cats.
It's so easy to be a dog owner. You feed it, train it,
boss it around. It puts its head on your knee and
gazes at you as if you were a Rembrandt painting.
It bounds indoors with enthusiasm when you call it.

Then, around age 13, your adoring little puppy turns into a big old cat.
When you tell it to come inside, it looks amazed, as if wondering who died
and made you emperor. Instead of dogging your doorstep, it disappears.
You won't see it again until it gets hungry – then it pauses on its sprint
through the kitchen long enough to turn its nose up at whatever you're
serving. When you reach out to ruffle its head, in that old affectionate
gesture, it twists away from you, then gives you a blank stare, as if
trying to remember where it has seen you before.

You, not realizing that the dog is now a cat, think something must be
desperately wrong with it. It seems so antisocial, so distant, sort of
depressed. It won't go on family outings. Since you're the one who raised
it, taught it to fetch and sit and stay on command, you assume that you did
something wrong. Flooded with guilt and fear, you redouble your efforts to
make your pet behave.

Only now you're dealing with a cat, so everything that worked before now
produces the opposite of the desired result. Call it, and it runs away. Tell
it to sit, and it jumps on the counter. The more you go toward it, wringing
your hands, the more it moves away.

Instead of continuing to act like a dog owner, you can learn to behave like a
cat owner. Put a dish of food near the door, and let it come to you. But
remember that a cat needs your help and your affection, too. Sit still, and it
will come, seeking that warm, comforting lap it has not entirely forgotten.
Be there to open the door for it.

One day, your grown-up child will walk into the kitchen, give you a big kiss,
and say, "You've been on your feet all day. Let me get those dishes for
you." Then you'll realize that your cat is a dog again.

Source Unknown

The Fear of Independence: Babyish Behavior

Janie's a bit dependent right now.

So far we have discussed your child taking "two steps forward" on the road to independence. But there's also the "one step backward." It can come as a shock when your five-year-old suddenly decides to wear diapers again, talk baby talk and cry when you leave him with a sitter. He wants you to cuddle him like a baby and in the night will creep into your bed when you are too tired to move. If you have a new baby, your older child may start acting like a baby again – or it may happen even if there isn't a baby in the family.

It's hard for kids to face the new challenges of growing up, and sometimes they need to regress and feel that you still love them as you did when they were babies. This happens especially when the child is under stress, often from a new developmental challenge like dealing with a baby sister, learning to talk, starting elementary school or starting high school.

The following signs indicate that although your child is growing into new independence, he is also afraid of the responsibilities that go with it:
- needing parents at night
- crying when parents leave
- whining "You do it for me!"
- self-criticism
- touchiness
- babyish behavior

Often around the age of 1½ or 2 years, many children begin needing their parents through the night. If this is happening to you, you are not alone. Many parents confess that their young ones sleep with them or wake up every two hours. All of our children did this from time to time, especially if they felt insecure or sick. Each time they got sick we had to wean them from our beds again. If your kids try to come into your bed at night, don't make a big deal about it when they're little. Just accept it, and encourage them to sleep on their own again when they're ready.

Young children can become very upset when you leave them (see information in Chapter 3 about separation anxiety). Listen to your children's worries, reassure them, then leave anyway, though for only short periods when they're very young. They need to learn that you will come back; they'll never learn this if you never leave. The cartoon illustrates what often happens: once the parent is gone, the child is happy again.

Growing up is scary business and it isn't unusual for a 12-year-old to say so. More often she won't say anything but will act in childish and fearful ways, criticizing herself and doubting her ability to do things. She might feel easily misunderstood and find it impossible to handle criticism. She will ask you to drive her places she could get to herself, or will ask you how to do her homework. She will hang around doing nothing, whining or complaining when you are trying to get work done – but won't actually ask you to do anything with her. She's too old to ask you directly to look after her, but that's what it's all about.

> **"Such a situation is like always having swum with a life jacket that you believed was part of you, only to discover that it's removable. This awareness immediately creates anxiety, especially if you are not so sure you can swim."**
> **– *Dorothy Corkille Briggs***

It helps to accept the child's behavior and realize that independence comes through this slow backward and forward movement. Let him behave less maturely at times; you aren't spoiling the child. You don't have to give in completely, but you do need to accept what's going on. Your child just needs to know that you are there for him when he's scared about growing up. When you go with the flow a little, he will become more secure and then take another step forward. Acceptance brings security! Your child will not stay dependent forever.

The Second Diaper Stage

At four my daughter wanted to wear diapers again. She had an allowance and I figured by the time she saved enough money for Pampers, she would be over it. No! She came to me with $25 asking if that was enough. At that moment I wanted to say, "No, diapers cost $1,000!" but my good conscience wouldn't let me. My daughter didn't want to use the diapers; she just wanted to wear them. So I took her to the mall with her $25. Before going to the drugstore, I made sure to take her through a great big toy store first. "You could have this nice doll or one of these neat games," I said. "Nope, I want diapers!" She had enough money to buy diapers and a bottle. After all those years of breast-feeding!

My husband came home from work and there was our daughter standing at the front door to meet him wearing only a diaper with a bottle hanging out of her mouth. "Tell me this is a stage!" he said. And it was a stage, one that lasted about six months! She loved her diapers and actually confessed to her closest friend that she was a closet diaper wearer. She didn't go to the bathroom in them. They just represented a certain security that she needed at that time. *-- Allison Rees*

Apply Your Knowledge

- Young children cry when their parents leave, cling to them, and climb into their bed at night. Have you gone through this with your child? How did you deal with it at the time? How might you like to deal with it now?
- You may notice children who can do things for themselves wanting you to feed them, dress them, give them a bottle, and so on, especially when a younger child or new baby is around. They say they can't do things that you've seen them do before. How have you dealt with this? How would you deal with it now?

Apply Your Knowledge

- Teens are a little more subtle in their fear of growing up. They will criticize themselves, feel misunderstood, put off doing things they don't have confidence about, ask you to drive them places, or ask you to help with homework when they can do it themselves. Have you seen this in your children or other teens you know? How have you dealt with this? How would you deal with it now?

Working Through Transition Stages

Growing up is a scary business. Once it's done, you can't go back. Adults often yearn to be children again – to be free of all the responsibilities we now have to handle and to have someone look after us. Why shouldn't kids sometimes feel the same way? When, through their behavior, they express these fears of growing up, you need to accept the feelings, although you don't have to give in to the demands. If you are responsive both to your child's desire for more independence and to his desire for more protection, he will appreciate you in the long run.

But remember – you won't always be able to please him, particularly since he doesn't always know what he wants, and at times he needs to oppose you just to feel that he is a separate and independent human being.

During a transition stage, it is helpful to avoid getting into power struggles with your child by minimizing your rules and demands. Remembering that it is a stage will help you ignore a lot of the contradictory behaviors as you observe the underlying struggle for independence.

Dr. Fitzhugh Dodson, who introduced the idea of transition stages, says that during a transition stage you must:

1) **Minimize your rules.**
Minimizing rules means you don't have a hundred things your two-year-old isn't allowed to touch, and your teenager doesn't have to ask permission every time she wants to go out, as the guidelines about where and when have been made clear.

2) **Be consistent with the rules you have.**
Consistency means your child knows it's useless to try to talk you out of fair and reasonable limits. (See Chapter 7)

3)   Ignore your child's verbal flak.

Ignoring is difficult but quite possible if you recognize your child is in a transition stage. Ignoring helps you to avoid power struggles and hurt feelings, and it discourages further mouthing off by not rewarding it with attention. (See Chapter 5)

4)   Be positive.

This is really important for your own and your children's self-esteem. Talking to a pleasant, positive person can make anyone feel better, including an argumentative child.

5)   Spend one-on-one time with your child.

Believe it or not, even teenagers want to spend time with their parents, especially one child with one parent alone, doing something the child enjoys. For little kids it may be playing a game, doing a puzzle, or reading. For teens it may be shopping or driving.

6)   "Roll with the punches!"

This means we need to accept the existence of transition stages, acknowledge that stage-related rebellious behavior will happen, try not to take it personally, and get through these stages by knowing they won't last forever!

Apply Your Knowledge

- Which of the six points have you tried, and how did it work out?
- Have you tried anything else that seemed to be effective?

---

2 - Extracurricular Activities: Sports, Music, Leisure

We frequently hear from parents who are upset that their children want to drop out of extracurricular activities such as music lessons, dancing, or sports. Some parents think they should make their children stick it out for a year or more and finish whatever activity they started. But how can a child really know what she likes until she has tried it? Is it fair to make her spend so much time and effort on something she was just exploring to see whether or not she'd like it?

Children already have to go to school and accept the discipline of attending classes and doing homework. They have to learn the subjects in the curriculum whether they like them or not. Isn't that enough discipline for a developing mind? Extra-curricular activities are meant to be optional – activities which children explore and continue with if they enjoy them.

Everyone has certain natural abilities and potential interests. Usually our interests are closely related to our abilities – we like to do what we are good at. Sometimes, however, the two don't coincide. We may be good at something, such as mathematics, but don't enjoy it. Or we may love doing something, such as dancing, but are not good at it. We have to live our lives in our own bodies, with our own abilities and interests, and it makes good sense to explore those abilities and interests in childhood.

Childhood is a time for exploration and for learning basic skills. By trying different things in childhood we learn what we like and don't like, and what we are good at or not so good at. If we are encouraged to try many things and not be judged on the outcome, we will find those activities which can give us pleasure for the rest of our lives. I (Alison Miller) know a young woman who spent her childhood being pressured by a coach to practice her sport and become a world champion athlete. All her spare time was spent in training. Now in her 20s, she has no idea what she wants to do in life because she never got the chance to try many things and find out what she liked.

When a child begins a new activity it helps if he can make a commitment for a limited period of time. That period should be measured in days or weeks, not months. It's not wise to go out and buy expensive musical or sports equipment, and then resent your child for not wanting to use it. Let him try things for short periods with a minimal commitment then gradually increase the length of commitment as he gets older and the required skill level increases.

One of the purposes of enrolling your child in extracurricular activities is to teach her that her interests and abilities matter, and that it is okay for her to consult her own feelings when deciding how she wants to spend her time and her life. This is a very important lesson. A child becomes an individual self by exploring various opportunities and discovering what he or she likes and dislikes, as well as what he or she is good at. Until at least age 10, a child should still be exploring, and should have plenty of opportunities to look into new interests, and change his mind if he discovers that he really doesn't like something he has enrolled in.

Even in the teens and adulthood, a person should not have to make a long-term commitment to something he is just exploring. If you force a child to continue in an activity that he doesn't enjoy, you are teaching him that his own feelings and preferences don't matter, that it isn't okay for him to like what he likes; he must subdue his own feelings and act out of 'duty' and do what others say he should do. This damages his self-esteem, his ability to be independent, and his ability to use his own feelings as a guide to what is good and fulfilling for him.

Some limits must be set. If allowed to choose their own activities, some kids will choose to spend all their time playing video games or watching television rather than exploring other options. Parents need to limit TV and video games and help their children find stimulating activities, preferably things they can do together.

Age is a factor in another way. Time feels much longer for a very young child; a six-month course is an eternity. When a child is introduced to a new activity, courses should be brief. Look out for programs which require a year-long commitment and prepayment; your child might decide to quit and you don't want to have to pay for services that you're not going to use.

If you don't have much money, rent rather than buy expensive equipment such as musical instruments. Buy only when you know your child really likes this activity. Otherwise you may end up blaming your child unfairly for your financial losses. The time for making commitments and following through with them is after the child's talents and interests have been discovered.

After about age 10, if your child already knows through previous explorations what an activity is like, it is appropriate for him to be asked to make a commitment for the duration of a course, and you may also put out money to back up your child's commitment.

What about team sports? It is fair to expect that if a child joins a team, he will continue throughout the team's season of play. It is a useful learning experience for a child to be part of a team in which he has to work together with others. But still, children will not like all sports equally. It's worth allowing them to try several different sports to see which they do like rather than enrolling them in a particular sport and then expecting them to continue in it for several years.

How do you determine what your child really likes or doesn't like? Don't go by how he feels on the very first day. If your child comes home the first day from an activity and says he loves it, it could be an initial enthusiasm based on an entertaining teacher or on the presence of friends. This could wear off soon. Both my (Alison Miller's) sons and my (Allison Rees') son went through this with the martial arts, and we were stuck with useless uniforms which had cost a lot. A child must continue liking an activity for some time before you can consider it an important interest. Also, if your child dislikes something, make sure it isn't the teacher rather than the activity that he doesn't like.

If your child is not enjoying an activity, ask her why, without judging her. I (Alison Miller) dropped out of piano at the age of seven because my teacher, who was blind, kept stretching my hands farther than they could go, and it hurt. It didn't occur to me to tell my parents about this problem. I think I would have loved piano and become really good at it if I'd told my parents and they'd enrolled me with a different teacher. Some kids drop out for other reasons: bullies in the class or an inept teacher, rather than because they dislike the activity itself. A different class or teacher might totally change the picture.

Scheduled learning activities aside, kids need time just to be kids – to play board games and imaginative games and just hang out with friends and relax. Children develop their creativity and their social skills in these unscheduled times. Play is probably the most important activity for a child of any age – make sure your child has time for it.

Be aware of your own unfulfilled ambitions so that you don't impose them on your child. Just because you always wanted to dance and didn't get to doesn't mean that she will love dancing. Children really like to please their parents, so it is very important that you encourage your daughter to follow her heart rather than do what you think might be right for her. She is her own unique person and if you support her in trusting her own feelings she will find enjoyable activities which will last all her life.

We (Alison Miller and Allison Rees) have counseled many adults who don't know what they like, how they want to spend their leisure time, and even what they want to do for a living, because they learned in childhood that they must put their own preferences aside and do what they were told. In some cases they have spent many years getting trained for a profession which they don't like in order to fulfill their parents' ambitions for them. Childhood is for figuring out who we are and what we like, not for being made into what our parents want. Let's honor our children by giving them many different opportunities so that they can select the activities which are fulfilling to them.

Apply Your Knowledge

- How did your parents select your extracurricular activities when you were a child?
- Did it give you an opportunity to explore your interests and abilities? Why or why not?
- Are your children happy with the activities they are presently involved in? Why or why not?

3 - *Children's Problems with Feelings*

Feelings are very complicated for most people, especially young children. They don't have the vocabulary to express themselves, and many feelings are difficult to identify.

Children have various problems with their emotions, such as:
♦   not knowing what is the matter
♦   identifying feelings incorrectly
♦   hurting others physically
♦   hurting others verbally
♦   wanting something right now
♦   temper tantrums
♦   moodiness, moping and sulking
♦   touchiness

Identifying Feelings

Children are often unable to figure out what they are really feeling. Even such basic feelings as hunger or fatigue are difficult to comprehend.

Am I Hungry, Tired or Angry?

My daughter would often get the feeling of 'hungry' and 'tired' confused. She would insist that she was hungry so I would make her a sandwich and prop her up on a stool. Ten minutes later I would come back expecting to see her finishing up, but instead she would be face down asleep in her sandwich. It took her a while to stop calling that tired feeling hungry. In the meantime, the family went through a lot of peanut butter.
-- Allison Rees

My son Alex went through a stage of saying he was hungry whenever he had a feeling of any kind. Then he learned that sometimes he was actually angry. The 'mad' stage came next. Every feeling was called 'mad'. He just didn't have the words for all the different emotions. *-- Alison Miller*

It helps to name the feeling which you think your young child is experiencing, so that he learns what each of the different emotions is called. Name your own emotions, too. This is no different from naming objects or actions, something most parents do automatically when their child is learning language. The child will learn to associate her own body sensations with the names of the feelings which describe them, and will also learn to connect those names with other people's facial expressions and tone of voice. (See the chapter on The Intelligence of Emotions in *The Parent-Child Connection* for more information about feelings.)

Apply Your Knowledge

- Do you notice a change in your child's behavior when she or he is hungry and tired?
- Children are unable to identify many of their feelings. As they get older they become better at identifying more complex emotions. How can you help your child identify his or her feelings?

Tantrums and Blow-Ups

Did you know it isn't terribly uncommon for a toddler to have up to six temper tantrums a day? They don't have the words or the knowledge to describe their feelings, and that can be very frustrating. It is up to us as parents to identify their needs as much as we can. The difficulty is that a child becomes his emotion. His entire body takes it on and he doesn't have the maturity to wait for things or practice patience. Retail stores know this only too well and actually depend on the demands of a child to make a sale.

Put it by the checkout where the little kids will see it . . . .

Dealing with Tantrums

♦ Model ways to handle anger and frustration.
♦ Catch your child being calm and express appreciation.
♦ Catch the pot bubbling before the lid blows off.
♦ Sometimes ignoring tantrums helps.
♦ If it is about not getting something, stand your ground and know your child needs to learn he can't always have his own way.
♦ Forget the tantrum when it is over and don't hold it against him.

Apply Your Knowledge

● How does your child react to frustration?
● Which approach seems to help your child?
● How can you deal with your own feelings of frustration during these challenging times we live in?

Helping Teenagers Understand Their Feelings

By middle childhood kids have learned to delay gratification to some extent. But they don't have either the emotional vocabulary or the power of self-control, so they may say *"I hate you"* rather than *"I'm angry with you"*. Sex hormones come into play around age 11 so moodiness and moping can be present without the child even knowing why.

The moodiness and the pronouncements of *"life sucks"* or *"I hate my life"* are really hard to decipher. Is there really a cause for concern? Symptoms of teenagers' moodiness include rarely smiling, acting annoyed when parents try to talk, expressing boredom, and never showing any signs of joy. Their speech may be mumbled or monotone.

Teens are often just as puzzled by their own moods as their parents are. They may still not be experienced enough to analyze what's bothering them. There are so many stressful things to deal with: bodily changes, hormones, dating problems, school, peer pressure, and parental expectations. Feelings can be very intense.

Try to remember that this isn't about you. Don't criticize or judge your child for his behavior. Brush up on your communication skills. When kids know they can talk to their parents without hearing the typical responses of advice giving and lecturing, they are more likely to open up.

One good way for parents to help children understand their feelings is for parents to talk about their own feelings in ways that don't blame the child for the parent's feelings or present her with things that are too complex for her to understand. Seeing that parents also struggle with their own feelings might make this process less threatening for a child. (We will discuss this further in the chapter on The Intelligence of Emotions in *The Parent-Child Connection*.)

Paternal Love

I remember one night when I was about 16, I was overcome with affection for my father. I saw him sitting there in his chair and I awkwardly blurted out, "I love you, Dad." He was so shocked he didn't know what to do. He immediately reached into his back pocket to pull out his wallet, asking me if I needed any money. That was his way of saying "I love you too." Imagine the surprise the poor man must have felt when I came up with that in the middle of my teen years (being Scottish didn't help). *-- Allison Rees*

When Is It Depression?

You don't discipline teens for depression. You get them help, the sooner the better. Keep an eye out for these symptoms:

☐ persistent feelings of sadness
☐ excessive unexplained fatigue
☐ loss of appetite
☐ inability to get a good night's sleep
☐ pervasive anxiety
☐ poor concentration
☐ inability to derive pleasure from normally enjoyable activities
☐ lack of friends or interest in friends
☐ suicidal thoughts
☐ reckless behavior

> **Feelings are to be accepted and expressed.**
>
>
>
> **Behavior is to be guided.**

The teens are difficult years even if you aren't depressed. Do you remember what it felt like to be a teen? Support your teens. Love them. One mother reflected how excited she feels when her teen does confide in her. She said, *"I try to be cool and calm and ho-hum about it, but really I am thrilled."* Keep yourself open for them without engulfing them. Touch them as you pass by rather than insisting on a hug. Don't force affection on them or perceive it as rejection when you don't get it.

Many adults still handle their feelings like children. They ignore their feelings and yet experience resentment and anger from doing this. Or they have childish outbursts.

The woman in the cartoon is being unassertive, building up emotions and then unloading them onto her cat. Unfortunately, many parents do this with their children. Unless we can learn how to recognize our own emotions, control our behavior, and act on the situations causing the feelings, we are vulnerable to this kind of 'feeling dump', and our families can suffer.

(The chapter on The Intelligence of Emotions in *The Parent-Child Connection* will help you to understand emotions and handle them in a healthy way.)

65

Apply Your Knowledge

- Have other people blamed you for your children's normal childish emotional immaturity?
- Do your kids have difficulty knowing what they feel?
- Moodiness, moping, sulking and temper tantrums are typical ways for children to express their feelings. Do your children do this? How do you handle it?
- What are the dangers of ignoring, dismissing or shaming a child's feelings?
- How can parents accept their children's feelings while dealing with difficult behavior?

4 - Children's Egocentricity (Self-Centeredness)

Gradually, as we mature we discover that other people have feelings and needs like we do. The child below is too young and immature to realize that his yelling could be making mom's headache worse. He is trying to help!

Realizing that other people have feelings and needs just like we do is an important part of maturing and caring for others. Many adults have not reached this kind of awareness. Can you recall a time when you became more aware of other people being a "me" like yourself? Most adults have learned to behave as if they think other people are as important as they are, even though they often feel that they aren't!

Egocentric Behaviors

Little Sarah honestly assumes that she is the center of the universe and that you are there for her convenience. That's why she always waits to ask her important questions until you're on the telephone (long distance), or have guests visiting. When she was one year old, she shared her possessions very nicely with other kids – until, at two, she suddenly realized that when the other child had a toy, she didn't have it! Now she kicks up a dreadful fuss when she's expected to share. Little Willy hugs the cat so hard that the cat avoids him whenever possible. These are quite normal behaviors for an egocentric preschool child.

It comes as a shock to children when they learn that the world doesn't revolve around them. As parents we need to manage their very normal egocentric behaviors as they mature into empathic individuals. In the meantime, though, you can expect children to:

- demand undue attention
- refuse to share
- be cruel to animals
- be cruel to people
- provoke and bug
- fight and argue
- participate in group cruelty to those who are different

It is important for children to be centered on self. In many ways, it is unhealthy for a child to be overly concerned with the feelings of others. Children need to understand and explore their own feelings first. Without going through this process, how can they truly feel empathy for anyone else? They may only learn how to *act nice* rather than understand why they need to treat others with kindness. Or they may not develop a good sense of self, especially if they have to take care of their parents' feelings rather than their own.

Developing a deeper understanding of why one should treat others with respect takes time, but it is the basis of true morality. It comes from understanding what it is to feel and need. Parents can help children develop true caring for others by helping them imagine what it's like to be the other person. See Chapter 6 for more details.

Apply Your Knowledge

- What have you noticed about your child's inability to see others' points of view?
- Of all of the undesirable behaviors your child shows, which are due to egocentricity?
- It takes all of childhood and then some to see others as 'a self like myself'. Have you expected too much from your child in this regard? What would you do differently now?

Protect Your Pets

Many parents are frightened by their young child's aggression toward the family pet. Small animals need to be protected from young children.

It's those poor old cats and dogs that can really take a beating. If a child is constantly being reprimanded for teasing the family pet, the negative attention may affect the child and poison the family atmosphere. Protect the animal when you can't supervise play and keep them separate. Set up several 10-minute periods per day to show the child how to touch the animal, and praise him when he uses gentle touching.

Slowly give the child more responsibility such as brushing, but stay by his side, praising him and patting his back for being so gentle. Usually, by the time a child is about five, he is able to understand that other creatures can feel pain.

Teaching Children to Protect Themselves without Aggression (Growling, Snarling and Biting)

We often see children being aggressive on the playground, and sometimes we wonder how to handle it. It's important to recognize that there's a difference between *pretending* to be aggressive (as when playing good guys vs. bad guys) and actually *being* aggressive with intent to do harm. You can allow more leeway in play than in everyday behavior. A child who is threatened by another child pretending to be a 'bad guy' won't really be scared or hurt (providing the 'bad guy' doesn't really hit him).

It's pretty well impossible to avoid good guy-bad guy play, especially with little boys. They will do it anyway, no matter what toys they are given or denied. However, you will find there's less "good guy-bad guy" play if your child watches less TV and plays fewer video games with this theme. It's important to teach our kids that no one is fully a good guy or a bad guy. This may confuse them at first, but over time it's an important lesson to learn.

When a child is aggressive he is often just protecting his personal boundaries. Animals set their boundaries through growls and snarls. An animal is vicious if it actually bites, not if it just growls a warning. Yet we expect our children not to give these warnings. Shouldn't children feel free to growl and snarl a little? They need permission to be able to tell other kids to back off and leave them alone.

Real aggression often comes out when a child is angry and doesn't know how to express it and set boundaries with another child. For example, one child may 'bug' and provoke another until the other child lashes out. It's important to teach your child to use words to express what he feels or wants: "Don't touch my stuff," "Don't make faces at me," and so on. We need to coach our children how to express themselves verbally so that they don't need to resort to physical threats and violence.

It isn't enough for a child who is being provoked to make wimpy statements like "Please don't do that." or "That hurts my feelings." These just invite further bugging or bullying. A child needs to be able to give the verbal equivalent of a growl or a snarl. This can be done without damaging anyone's self-esteem.

What's not okay? Threatening with weapons (other than in what is clearly play). Physically assaulting another child when he hasn't attacked you physically. Remember that physical assaults like kicking, biting, pinching and hitting often happen when the child has overwhelming feelings and doesn't know what to say. Giving your child some strong words to use can make a physical attack quite unnecessary.

What about physical retaliation if someone does attack you? I think this needs to be kept as an option – kids need to be able to defend themselves. Martial arts training can help a child know when this is necessary, and how to do it in a way that is defensive, not hurtful.

Dealing with Behavior Designed to Get a Reaction

We have already mentioned swearing in this chapter. It can be a wonderful way for a preschooler (or a teen) to get a reaction from people.

Oh, those magic words!

I once worked in a group home where a four-year-old girl lived. Once, as I was supervising her washing her hands before dinner, the little girl began singing "Ficky-f_cky, ficky-f_cky," while watching me closely. I realized that the child was testing my reaction to a 'magic word' so I ignored her and gradually watched her face fall as she got no reaction. This was just innocent experimentation. -- *Alison Miller*

Both of us experienced our children at three or four hitting, pinching or kicking us. There is no fast way to get a child through this stage of development.

Parents may not like this but it is normal. Our task is to teach our child empathy, by explaining the way others feel, without hurting our own child in the process.

Parents don't get hurt, do they?

When my eldest son was about five, he would come up and hit me for no apparent reason. He wasn't angry at me, he was just experimenting. I would hold out my hand as if I were about to slap him and ask him, "May I hit you?" He'd look very surprised and say "NO!" I'd ask, "Why not?" "Because it would hurt!" Then I asked him, "Does it hurt me if you hit me?" He replied, "No – o – o," more slowly, thinking about it. -- *Alison Miller*

A child who hits a parent or a pet without even being angry may be testing to see whether other creatures feel pain. This is a step towards developing empathy. If parents become angry at their children for this behavior, they can damage their children's self-esteem. Children can't help being immature, and if we accept them and teach them patiently, they gradually develop into mature individuals who care about others.

Apply Your Knowledge

- When our children hurt others in their attempts to get a reaction, how can we teach them that other people (and animals) have feelings too?

Teaching Empathy

Many children learn to behave in socially acceptable ways without developing a deeper understanding of people's feelings. They are not truly caring; they just know how they are expected to behave. If parents try to shape a child's behavior through reward or punishment without helping the child mature in understanding how others feel, she may become obedient. But the same child who blindly obeys her parents will later blindly obey her peers. Developing empathy is more important than learning socially acceptable behavior because in the peer group socially acceptable behavior might include cruelty to others.

Annie, why are you walking home with 'big-ears Bobby' instead of us?

Mom said I had to, so you wouldn't throw any more rocks at him ...

But I think it would be okay if you kicked him instead.

Apply Your Knowledge

- Children can be cruel. They pick on any unique aspect of a person and make fun of it. Unfortunately group cruelty is also a normal part of childhood. Can you remember experiencing group cruelty as either part of the group or the one being singled out?
- What would you say to your child if he were a victim of this kind of cruelty?
- What would you say to your child if he were engaging in this kind of cruelty?

My Child's Self-Development

Use this table to determine what signs your child shows of the struggle for independence, grappling with emotions, and learning to understand others. Check off the behaviors you recognize in your child or teen.

Symptoms of the Fear of Independence

- ☐ needing parents at night
- ☐ crying when parents leave
- ☐ 'you do it for me'
- ☐ self-criticism
- ☐ touchiness
- ☐ babyish behavior

Symptoms of the Struggle for Independence

- ☐ negativism
- ☐ changing his mind
- ☐ refusing help
- ☐ stubbornness
- ☐ defiance and talking back
- ☐ criticizing parents
- ☐ shutting out family members
- ☐ doing things to irritate you
- ☐ arguing

Egocentric Behaviors

- ☐ demanding undue attention
- ☐ refusing to share
- ☐ cruelty to animals
- ☐ cruelty to people
- ☐ provoking and 'bugging'
- ☐ fighting and arguing
- ☐ group cruelty to those who are different

Children's Problems with Feelings

- ☐ not knowing what is the matter
- ☐ identifying feelings incorrectly
- ☐ hurting others physically
- ☐ hurting others verbally
- ☐ wanting something right now
- ☐ temper tantrums
- ☐ moodiness, moping and sulking
- ☐ touchiness

5 - Sexual Development

Masturbation

Many little kids discover that it feels good when they rub their private parts either with their hands or against things. It's also normal for children who have experienced this kind of feeling to show curiosity about one another's bodies and want to look or touch.

With most kids, this kind of behavior is a normal, innocent exploration of good bodily feelings and it will develop later into the capacity for sexual pleasure. It is very important for us adults not to make them feel guilty about this. If sexual feelings become associated with shame and sex becomes 'dirty', then kids will think of it as something illicit which has to be explored behind others' backs, rather than something good which can eventually be shared with a person you love.

If you find a child 'humping' or rubbing himself, just tell him that these kinds of body feelings are private, and suggest he do it in his room rather than in public with other people around. That's enough. If he's doing it in a situation where there aren't others around, (e. g. while watching TV at home), and you see him, I suggest you ignore it. If you find two or more children exploring their bodies together, this is the time for a little talk about 'private parts' and what 'private' means, without shaming them. You might want to get a book about bodies and read it to the children. One of our favorites is *A Very Touching Book* which has hilarious illustrations of naked bodies and can be used to prevent unwanted touching as well as to teach about body parts.

Many children get into the habit of exploring each other's bodies (for example, 'playing doctor') in a way that becomes obsessive. Sometimes there is bullying involved even if the children are the same age. If your children seem to be going through an exploratory stage with their friends (around ages four to nine), make sure you provide gentle, inconspicuous supervision to ensure that the sexual exploration doesn't become obsessive or involve one child forcing another child to do things he doesn't want to do.

Sexual Abuse

There's a difference between this innocent exploration of body feelings and the behavior of a child who has been sexually abused. Sexually abused children often act out with other children in ways which imitate what has been done to them.

This goes beyond just 'You show me yours and I'll show you mine'. If you see children mimicking oral sex, for example, this deserves further investigation, because the idea of oral sex doesn't occur to them spontaneously. This suggests that some adult may have done this to them. The same applies if a child corners another child and forces him into sexual play which the other child doesn't really want.

An adult needs to ask each child individually and kindly about their experiences both with one another and previously. Remember that sexual abusers often make threats about bad things which will happen if the child discloses, so be sure to be gentle and emphasize that you are able to keep the child safe from anything he's afraid of.

There's an in-between situation in which a child has observed sexual behavior which she doesn't understand, either in person or on TV, and is imitating what she has seen. I (Alison Miller) remember a little girl who was imitating sexual intercourse with her dolls. Everyone was very concerned that she might have been sexually abused, even though she did not appear emotionally disturbed. In the play therapy room, I casually asked her whether she'd seen anyone do this, and she said, "Oh yes, when the babysitter's boyfriend comes over." That was of course inappropriate behavior on their part but it was not abuse directed at the child.

Television and the Internet now give children the opportunity to view sexual behavior which they are not ready to understand. Computers pop up ads for sexual perversities. A computer program that denies access to these sites is a good idea if your child is old enough to use the Internet. It's also a good idea to monitor which TV shows your child watches. It's not that children should be unaware of all adult sexual behavior, only that so much of what the media show is perverted and counter-productive to developing healthy attitudes towards sex.

As much as possible we want our children's exposure to sexuality to be healthy and in the context of loving relationships. There is a time when we need to let them watch the other stuff, but only after they have had an opportunity to develop positive values in the realm of sexuality.

Sexual Information

It's good for children to get as much accurate information as they want about sexuality as early as possible. It takes the mystery out of it and leaves them less vulnerable to inaccurate information coming from peers. My (Alison Miller's) younger son was born when my older son was about to enter kindergarten, and my older son told his entire kindergarten class all about it, from conception to birth. The teacher told us about it, and added, "I didn't stop him because it was all accurate." At this age kids have no natural shame about all these things; shame comes later when sexuality is made sordid and weird by the media and the peer group – and sometimes by parents.

Let's give kids the truth, told in a loving way, when they are very young. Teach them the right names for body parts, describe what happens, and then they can answer other kids' misinformation with accurate information. This also helps in sexual abuse prevention. There are very good books you can read to children on this subject (see references at the end of this chapter).

Answer any questions your child asks clearly and accurately in language he can understand. It is we rather than our children who are embarrassed by this subject. Kids will just accept what we tell them and feel relieved that they now understand. It is important to do this before they reach their teens.

> ### Apply Your Knowledge
> • Does your child have sufficient sexual information to satisfy his curiosity? What else do you need to provide?

Understanding the Opposite Sex

Right now Western society is pushing sexual behavior to a younger and younger age, long before kids are able to deal with its emotional repercussions. Young girls don't understand sexuality, in particular male sexuality. The TV role models for young girls dress in sexually provocative ways, so it's common for girls themselves to do this without necessarily realizing its effect. Teenage boys don't understand female sexuality; they are overwhelmed by the combination of seductive clothing and hormones, so feel constantly 'turned on'. Many boys and men assume that girls who dress certain ways are 'asking for' sexual involvement when the girls are just trying to look 'pretty'. Even if they know the girls aren't wanting sex, they are likely to think about having it with them.

Male sexual response is very different from female sexual response. Men respond with instant sexual arousal to visual stimuli, and if a girl or woman dresses in a way that emphasizes her body contours, most men will be 'turned on'. Women, on the other hand, respond more to touch and to emotional intimacy. Neither gender understands these differences very well.

I (Alison Miller) learned this one summer in my youth when I was working at a camp in which the camp cook (who was both married and unattractive) pursued me constantly in a lecherous manner. After I made it clear I was not interested, he sat me down and gave me a lecture about all the little things I did (clothing, the way I sat, etc.) which made him sexually aroused. I had no idea at all, and I found it absolutely disgusting that he could look at me in this way. Like most young women, I was enjoying being attractive and admired. I was not advertising my availability. I didn't even know he was thinking about sex.

Unfortunately, many guys don't understand this about girls. They assume that girls' sexuality works just like their own. Portrayals of female sexuality in the media also give this impression. To complicate matters, guys are still expected to be the ones to approach a girl to see if she is interested. Girls with low self-esteem often feel that they have to "put out" sexually just to be accepted. At present in North America we have an epidemic of anonymous oral sex among young teens and pre-teens; girls think they have to engage in this boy-pleasing behavior to be 'cool'. We need to teach them that they own their own bodies and don't owe boys anything. And we need to teach boys to respect girls' ownership of their own bodies and not misinterpret girls' attractive clothing or pleasant smiles to mean they want instant sex!

Girls want to be accepted in their peer groups, and often this means dressing like everyone else. By the time they reach their teens, they should probably feel free to choose what they wear. Their need for social acceptance is very great, and fighting them about their dress will only result in power struggles. However, a little education about guys will help them make wiser decisions.

The same thing goes for boys. Boys need to learn that girls' sexuality works somewhat differently from their own. They need to learn to consider girls' feelings and needs. Many young men wonder why their wives or partners don't enjoy sex, when the truth is that they have never even learned how their female partners' bodies work!

At present our understanding of sexuality is undergoing a huge revision: effective birth control has removed the pregnancy risk from sexual activity and many conflicting value systems have surfaced.

There is for most people a relationship between sex and emotional intimacy which is difficult to avoid. Our culture increasingly tolerates and even encourages sexual activity in the early teens, long before kids are ready to handle the emotional side of being sexually active. North American society currently supports a kind of male sexuality that is totally self-interested and does not involve emotional intimacy. This short-changes everyone, especially men and boys. Boys don't understand that their own sexuality is connected with emotions and with attachment. They follow the cultural role models of being a 'stud' (the female equivalent is unfortunately a 'slut'), and then are confused when attachment needs kick in, resulting in jealousy and other extreme emotions.

I (Alison Miller) once counseled a young man who played in a rock band. He would wake up the morning after a concert with a girl whose name he didn't know, and instantly want to marry her! Now not all guys have this reaction, but in general, young teens who engage in casual sex, or sex in relationships that last only a few weeks, find themselves on an emotional roller coaster even worse than the one they were on from just being teenagers.

Research shows that most of the girls don't actually enjoy the sex – they just think they have to do it to please their boyfriends or to follow the peer group. The boys enjoy it – but are confused about relationships. We are now seeing teens in counseling who are so afraid of the peer pressure about casual sex and drugs and alcohol (which often go together) that they don't want to attend school! We need to raise children, boys and girls, who will go against the crowd, refuse to be blindly pressured into behaving like everyone else, and will stand up for a healthier view of sexuality than our society currently provides.

Apply Your Knowledge

- If you have a teenage or pre-teen daughter, have you educated her about male sexuality so that she can make wise decisions about her dress and behavior?
- If you have a teenage or pre-teen boy, have you provided help for him in handling his sexual feelings and impulses, and have you helped him understand girls?

In summary of this chapter, a child or a teen is immature in her ability to be independent, in her ability to manage her feelings, in her awareness of others as persons, and in her understanding of her own and others' sexuality. Many behaviors which are problematic for parents arise from this immaturity. While we wouldn't tolerate such behavior in an adult, we know it is quite normal for a child or teenager. Its presence does not indicate something is wrong with the child; it just indicates that she is a child.

Pay attention to your thinking. If you take your children's behavior personally or think your child is doing things just to bug you, you will feel resentful. Can you catch your thoughts and change gears? For example, "My son doesn't hear his loudness. He is frustrated and he just needs to calm down. I need to calm down, not take it seriously, breathe."

Apply Your Knowledge

- Can you remember going through any of these stages as a child yourself? If so, how does this change your perspective (if at all)?
- Many people feel guilty about having experienced certain normal behaviors and emotions in their childhood. Can you remember things that you felt unnecessary shame or guilt about as a child? Do you still feel this way about these things?

Further Reading

Ayers, Lauren. *Teenage Girls: A Parent's Survival Manual.*
New York: Crossroad, 1994

Bayard, R. T. *How to Deal with Your Acting-up Teenager.*
Markham, Ontario: Fitzhenry and Whiteside, 1998

Dodson, Fitzhugh. *How To Parent.*
Scarborough, Ontario: New American Library of Canada, 1978

Gurian, Michael. *A Fine Young Man. (Raising Boys)*
New York: Tarcher/Putnam, 1998

Hickling, Meg. *Speaking of Sex.*
Kelowna, British Columbia: Northstone, 1996

Hindman, Jan and Novak, Tom. *A Very Touching Book.*
New York: McClure-Hindman, 1998

Mackoff, Barbara. *Growing a Girl.*
New York: Dell, 1996

Snyderman Nancy. *Girl in the Mirror (Raising Teen Girls).*
New York: Hyperion, 2002

3

Act Your Age:
Development of the Child's Understanding

If we don't know how normal children act and think, we parents may overreact to normal child behaviors, and try to make our children change things they are unable to change until they're older. This chapter helps us understand what it's like to be a child. Children's brains are not fully developed, even when they can talk a blue streak and even when they are teenagers. Often we expect them to be able to perform intellectual tasks which they just can't do, such as pay attention for long periods, understand priorities, keep things in order, think in abstractions, and remember what they've been told.

Not only are kids' brains immature, but they lack experience in the world. They don't know how things and people work. Children, however, are wired for learning. They are intensely curious about everything, especially when they're very young. They pick up language much faster than adults, and they explore their surroundings with enthusiasm.

Much of children's upsetting behavior is simply the result of their immature brain, their lack of experience in the world, and their intense desire to learn. Children's ignorance of the world leads to worries and insecurities, as well as to explorations which can be dangerous. Their cognitive immaturity leads to their difficulty in adapting to adult notions of time, a tendency to make messes which they are unable to clean up, and what seems to us like poor memory. How they embarass us sometimes with the candor of their questions! Yet if we can understand how children's brains work, we will be more likely to relax and enjoy them for what they are.

Jason was two. He had temper tantrums about three times a day. His parents were at their wits' end. Mom wondered whether he'd turn out like Uncle Rufus, who was in jail. How did she and her husband manage to produce such a monster? Is it something they did, or did he just inherit some bad genes?

They came to our parenting course to learn whether there was anything they could do to "fix" Jason before it was too late. They attended a small discussion group with eight to 10 other parents of two-year-olds. And lo and behold, almost everyone in their group had the same problem (except one superior lady who had a two-year-old angel for her first child and didn't know yet that her next one would turn out to be a holy terror at that age!). They discovered, with shock and relief, that temper tantrums are normal behavior at two and that if handled appropriately will be outgrown.

Discussion was similar among the group of parents of five-year-olds. Quite a few of the kids still wet their beds. Most of them couldn't remember more than one instruction at a time. And among the parents of 11-year-olds, the mothers were discovering that their daughters all sassed them back. The parents of teens weren't so surprised – they had already been told that adolescence was a 'stage'. But what a relief just to share your frustrations with other people who were going through the same thing, and share and learn some ideas about dealing with these normal problems of child development.

Many of the problems we experience with our children come simply from their immaturity. Let's face it, children (including teens) are immature – and why shouldn't they be, frustrating though it is for us? In this chapter we consider the child's immaturity in terms of understanding the world and developing and using his intellectual capacity.

1 - Learning to Understand the World

A baby comes equipped with full human potential, but with almost no knowledge about the world. Her understanding develops only as she interacts with the world around her. She has a tremendous desire to discover what the world is all about. The combination of her lack of experience and her curiosity can cause a great deal of frustration for parents.

Children Have Mistaken Ideas

A baby has to figure out where one object ends and another begins – and where one word ends and another begins. We've probably all had this experience with words, when listening to a foreign language. But a baby has it with everything! Imagine how difficult this is when some things change their shape because they move.

The baby also has to figure out which objects are alive and which aren't. How many possibilities does she discard along the way? Are moving things all alive? Are warm things all alive? Are things that make noises all alive? It is difficult for us to imagine how little our children really understand. Often parents assume their children know or understand things that they couldn't possibly know. This is especially true as children get older, become mobile, and start to explore. They don't know what a mess is or why it is a problem. Why do the adults around them get so upset by fingerprints on walls or stains on a carpet? What is a stain?

First Love

When my daughter Anna was about eight months old, she had a love affair with the refrigerator. She would bounce in the kitchen doorway in her Jolly Jumper, and would smile and laugh and talk to the gigantic old white fridge.

I couldn't figure out what she saw in it until I put myself in the baby's shoes.

The fridge was probably one of the few things in life that Anna could figure out – it was always in the same place, totally different from its surroundings, never moving or talking or changing shape, a certainty in a world of constant change.

Anna knew where it started and where it ended; it was stable and quite different from people who presented different views to her as they moved across the kitchen. *-- Alison Miller*

Creativity

My daughter Emily didn't know the difference between paper and carpeting in her toddler years. Unfortunately it was the brand new wall-to-wall carpet that she decided to draw on with my bright pink lipstick! I was horrified when I saw the mess but realized that if I reacted too strongly, Emily would be confused and scared. I had Emily help me clean it up and explained the difference between carpeting and paper! *-- Allison Rees*

Television can really add to confusion as kids try to decipher reality from fantasy on the screen. What would really happen if that person fell off a roof — would they really get up and shake off the dirt and not be hurt? Do teddy bears and dolls really talk? Kids form mistaken hypotheses all the time, and too often we're unaware of it. Sometimes we can detect it, as when they obviously use a word incorrectly. Sometimes we can't. Children hear words with similar sounds and find it easy to get their meaning confused, especially if they are words which they don't hear often when they're with their friends.

In the learning process kids go from knowing nothing to taking in tons of information every day. While they learn at a tremendous rate, they are still bound to make mistakes. The cartoon below shows the immature ideas of children at two different ages about money.

Of course you can afford to buy me a mini-bike, Dad, you just go to the bank and get some money from the machine.

Of course you can afford to send me to Harvard, Dad. You just bought Jerry a mini-bike.

Money doesn't grow on trees any more

"According to a survey conducted by the Hong Kong Institute, 30 percent of kindergarten children in Hong Kong believe their parents' salary is paid out by bank machines. While 70 percent did understand the connection between work and pay cheques, three out of 10 children thought their parents could simply go to the ATM to get all the money they need."
-- *The Asia Post*

Workers trying to help teens who have become pregnant have learned that one of their most important needs is sex education. One girl disclosed in counseling that she believed she couldn't be pregnant because she was not having her menstrual period when she had intercourse. She was engaging in risky sexual behavior on the basis of distorted information. Teens also tend to spread information quickly throughout their peer networks. This can be fine if the information is accurate but when it comes to subjects such as sex, the information is often incorrect.

Modern Contraception

I recently interviewed a sexual health educator on my radio show. I learned that many intelligent teenagers actually thought a certain popular soda drink lowered a male's sperm count and therefore was an effective birth control method. They thought if the guys drank a glass of this pop before having sex, the gals couldn't get pregnant!

-- Allison Rees

Parenting Pointers

♦ Don't assume a child understands an idea just because he or she can say the word for it.

♦ Ask kids questions about their understanding of things if you suspect they may not fully grasp something.

♦ Accept their immaturity.

♦ Be open to explaining concepts that we take for granted.

Apply Your Knowledge

● Think about some of the mistaken ideas your child has had about the world or the way things work.

● Remember your own misinterpretations as a child regarding complex issues such as money or sex?

2 - Children Embarrass Their Parents

Kids don't know instinctively what is and isn't okay to do or say in public. Their lack of understanding and experience can cause parents some embarrassment.

Today, we are trying to be open to discussing body parts and teaching our children about sex. We do this because we know it will actually help protect our children from shame and abuse. However, this has had some repercussions for parents because children can express that openness with a very loud, clear voice in public places!

Preschool Geography

When my daughter was three I took her to the food fair at our local mall. We exchanged small talk with an elderly gentleman at the next table. When we got up to leave my daughter looked at him very seriously and said, "Excuse me, do you have a penis or a vagina?" He looked at her calmly and said, "Yes, I have been back East but I didn't stop in Regina." *-- Allison Rees*

... and I used the word properly too...

When I was just learning to talk, a church minister came to visit, and I dropped something out of my high chair and screamed, "Bugger!". I knew it was what you say in those situations, but I didn't know that there were some people you aren't supposed to say it in front of, or that our society has different rules for what adults and children are allowed to say. *-- Alison Miller*

Sometimes it isn't the words that are embarrassing to us; it's the way a child expresses what he sees without using the discretion that an adult would. Often a parent's embarrassment gets in the way of his understanding what is really going on for his child. It can be especially difficult if these kinds of behaviors were forbidden when he was growing up. The stress of having to be well-behaved as a child can create similar kinds of stress-related emotions in him as he parents his own children.

You may feel embarrassed by your child's lack of knowledge, but wait until she is a teenager! Then she will be embarrassed by your lack of knowledge – of the way 'people' (that is, teenagers) dress, the music 'people' like, and so on. Teenagers are at a stage of development in which it is important for them to show how much they know about the world. They are almost ready to venture out into that world, so they need to feel confident and capable. One way in which they show this rather fragile confidence is by showing how much more worldly-wise they are than their old-fashioned parents. It is hard in this situation to remember that in many ways they are still inexperienced, and need help and information from us.

The same teen who informs us that we just don't know how to dress, and that 'people' never behave as we do, doesn't know how to make exploratory phone calls about matters vital to her future. Fortunately, we don't mind it, since we learned long ago that foolishness is part of the human condition.

Parenting Pointers

♦ Don't let your embarrassment make you react negatively to your child, who probably won't understand.

♦ Avoid judging or labeling your child.

♦ Don't withdraw your affection or approval.

♦ Make a gentle request: "If you want to say something about somebody, please tell me in private where they can't hear."

♦ Be tolerant of your child's lack of social knowledge.

♦ Ask thoughtful, open questions suitable to your child's age:
  - "How do you feel when you hear people swearing?"
  - "I am wondering if that lady might have felt hurt when she heard you describe her as fat. What do you think?"
  - "Do you know what those words mean?"
  - "Can you remember someone saying something that hurt you?"
  - "Do you think other people have the same kinds of feelings you do?"

Apply Your Knowledge

● Can you recall a time when your child has embarrassed you?

● How do you deal with your own uncomfortable feelings during those embarrassing moments? Do you assume your child is testing the limits or trying to embarrass you?

● Can you remember a time when your parents were embarrassed by something you did or said when you didn't know it was inappropriate?

● How can we slowly teach children to understand how their words or behaviors make other people feel without shaming them?

3 - Children Explore and Take Risks

Children's lack of experience plus their curiosity to test and try new things often spells danger, whether it is a toddler climbing on table-tops, a nine-year-old playing with matches, or a teen experimenting with drugs. The curiosity drive is healthy and normal: without it, they would remain dependent on us all their lives! But the combination of the child's strong need to explore and discover, and her ignorance of what the world is about, what is safe or unsafe, creates plenty of problems for parents. It's normal for little children to get into everything. But sometimes adults don't understand this.

It isn't so bad when your child is too young to move around. But once she can get around, watch out! The most difficult period is the period from about 10 months to three years, when the child has the capacity to get around, but has no idea about safety. Another difficult period in this regard is adolescence, when the child becomes mobile not just in the home but in the world. Parents go through a lot of sleepless nights worrying about exploring teenagers.

Just Tell Her to Stop

When my daughter was a year old, my brother and his new Japanese wife moved to town. Auntie Yukiko had all kinds of beautiful little Japanese ornaments – some even made musical sounds. Anna was entranced. She just couldn't stop touching when she was told not to touch. My brother and his wife thought Anna must be badly brought up. But strangely enough, when they had their own baby a few years later they had to use a gate to keep him away from the ornaments.   -- *Alison Miller*

You just can't expect a child under five to have the self-control to refrain from touching and taking apart things that are within reach. It's unfair to the child to say "No" all the time. Better to put things where the child can't get at them, preferably where she can't see them either (or you'll tempt her to climb).

There's always at least one parent in our parenting courses who swears his child never touches anything she isn't supposed to touch. This is usually stated with pride, and the implication that other children should be as well-trained. We worry about that child who doesn't touch. It is abnormal for a child not to have a tremendous drive to explore. There are differences in activity level, of course, and some children explore with their eyes before they test reality with their bodies. But inhibiting a child's curiosity (usually through punishment) can interfere with the child's development of intelligence and independence.

Curiosity and exploration not only create anxiety in parents, they also cause frustrations. Many explorations produce messes. Kids mix up all the jigsaw puzzles. An 18-month-old can trash a room in about 10 minutes.

Aunt Enid, have you seen my bug collection?

Older children make messes when cooking or taking on a project and leaving their related articles lying around. This is okay if it's just homework books or dishes but can be awful if it means some ugly, hairy bug escaped from their science experiment jar.

Parenting Pointers

- ◆ Toddlers need lots of supervision and dangerous goods need to be locked away.
- ◆ Children should be supervised while they learn how to handle situations that are new (like lighting matches or riding a bus) rather than being told they shouldn't do these things.
- ◆ Teenagers need ongoing education about sex, relationships, drugs and other life issues. However dismissively they act, more sinks in than you might think.
- ◆ Except for dangerous behaviors, allow your children to make mistakes; this is a part of the learning process.
- ◆ Move gradually from protection, to supervision, then to freedom (see Chapter 5).
- ◆ Allow your children to question. Give explanations and talk about subjects openly while inviting questions.
- ◆ Praise the child's new learning and ask him questions about what he is learning.

Apply Your Knowledge

- ● How does your child test the limits of safety? Why do you think your child does this?

- ● How can you give your child sufficient opportunities to explore safely, without making her afraid of the world?

4 - Children Have Fears and Worries

Parents are often puzzled by their children's fears. It's frustrating, and you feel helpless when your little boy is afraid of monsters, or of the dark, or of dreams. Saying "Monsters don't exist," or "It was only a dream" sometimes doesn't seem to help. And to an adult, who long ago put behind him that world of magic and strangeness, sometimes a child's fears seem ridiculous.

Unrealistic Fears

Imagine yourself being a child. There is a lot you don't know about the world. You watch a lot of television and you regularly see monsters on the screen. You don't know that they are any less real than other things you see there. How do you know that people and animals on the TV screen aren't right there in the room with you? How do you know they won't jump out of the screen? Even if you have been told that there's no danger, fears are irrational emotional reactions and it takes time and life experience to really know that the lion won't jump out of the television.

Dreams too take up a significant part of your life, and how are you as a child to know that these strange experiences, which don't make sense and can be terrifying, are any less real than the things which happen in daylight?

There are no such things as monsters. There is nothing to be scared of.

> ### The Furnace Monster
>
> When my daughter was four, she told me that she used to lie awake at night listening to the monster breathe. "What does it sound like?", I asked. She demonstrated with a loud sighing noise. "Oh Anna, that's the furnace!" In a tiny scared voice she asked: "W-what's a furnace?"
>
> I took her to the furnace room, showed her the furnace, and explained that it heated the house by blowing warm air through it and that's what she was hearing. If she hadn't told me about the monster, I never would have known that she was terrified every night.
> -- *Alison Miller*

Attending to a child's fears means attending to his needs. This tells him that he matters and that you care. If a child is scolded or told he is being ridiculous or silly he may learn to conceal his fears, but they won't go away. To really help a child with his fears, a parent needs to be patient, listening to the child and comforting him.

It is important not to ridicule the child's fears. We also need to repeat, perhaps more than once, the real-life explanation for what is bothering the child while accepting the child's feelings of terror or anxiety. Sometimes it can help for the parent to enter the child's imaginative world and converse with the 'monster' or use 'monster spray' to get rid of it.

Realistic Fears

Children also develop some fears which are quite rational – of pain, of death, and of nuclear war or terrorism, for example. What do we do about these? These fears affect us quite differently than the irrational ones do, because we ourselves have no answers and no good explanations for these things. We have learned to live with the constant possibility of these things occurring by putting them out of our minds. The healthy way to cope with these possibilities is to do all we can (within reason) to prevent them, and then just stop thinking about them. Adults too are helpless in the face of the unexpected. We just don't like to think about it.

It is a great shock for a child to learn about the reality of death and pain; it shakes the security of his world. He already feels helpless a lot of time, and he relies on adults, especially his parents, to reassure him that the world is really a safe place. A parent can help a child to cope with monsters, the dark, and dreams, but when it comes to the real dangers in life a parent can only be of limited help.

We can stress the fact that accidents happen very rarely. This is important information for a child. We can explain that death is a natural process that usually happens in old age, and only rarely happens to a young person or animal. Without lying to a child, we can nevertheless let him know how rarely these awful things happen to anyone like him or us. We can also stress the fact that safety precautions make these things less likely to happen; this will help the child feel some control over them.

Avoid lying to your children. If you tell him that the injection won't hurt, and then it does hurt, you undermine his faith that all the other things you tell him about his safety are true. Euphemisms such as "You'll feel a little pinch" are not helpful, although saying "This'll hurt like hell" is no better! Tell him instead that it will probably hurt a little but it will prevent him getting a sickness that would hurt a lot more, and it will be over soon. Tell him that you know he is strong enough and brave enough to handle it. This way you build up his confidence for facing the things in life which he will have to face.

Older children and teens often take more seriously than parents the threats to our lives and our world from pollution, destruction of the environment, global warming, smoking, and other humanly created evils. They may be right! In our need to go on living with the reality that these things exist and do damage to people, we learn to block them out of our minds. This blocking prevents our taking positive action. We can be thankful for the positive energy and realistic vision of young people who often see these things for what they are, and handle their fear by creative action.

Children often misunderstand the real dangers in the world. They think some things are dangerous when they aren't (like the furnace monster). And they think other things are not dangerous when they are (e.g. drinking cleaning fluids from the kitchen cupboard). It is important that we help them understand the realities.

Sometimes children are expressing fears about something which is not the real source of their anxiety, because the real source is too scary to talk about. We need to be sensitive to underlying problems which the child can't put into words or is afraid to mention. For example, if you and your spouse have an argument, your child may be afraid you will divorce.

Parenting Pointers

♦ Say things like:
"It sounds like this is really scary for you."
"If I believed in monsters I would feel frightened too."
"You have a wonderful imagination and sometimes it imagines scary things."
"What do you need to feel better?"
"When I was younger I believed in monsters too. Now I know they don't exist in that way."
♦ Spend time listening without interrupting or trying to change your child's feelings.
♦ Give children facts and truth at an age-appropriate level. Be real and avoid sugar-coating the truth.
♦ Give them any honest assurance that you can.
♦ Stay calm yourself and model an optimistic outlook.
♦ Turn to your spiritual beliefs.
♦ Teach the child relaxation skills such as breathing, meditation, yoga, positive imaging, or comforting daily rituals.

- If necessary, distract the child by moving on to other subjects, telling a story, or engaging in an activity which will take his mind off his fear.
- Use humor and make light of the situation if it doesn't put the child down.
- Create a story or fantasy of how the child overcomes the monster or scary situation.
- Increase physical exercise if possible when anxiety is running high.
- Pay attention to anxiety which may point to some real issues, e.g. marital conflict which could lead to separation or divorce.

Apply Your Knowledge

- What kinds of unrealistic or irrational fear has your child experienced?

- What kinds of irrational fear do you remember having when you were young?

- It is important for children to be taken seriously even if their fears are irrational. How can you take your child's feelings and concerns seriously while assuring him that his fears won't come true?

- Children can also develop fears of things which could possibly happen, like death, divorce, and car accidents. What realistic fears has your child had? How have you dealt with these?

Separation Anxiety

Many parents consult us about separation anxiety because their children are going through periods of being afraid that they will be separated from them.

Infants' Need for Attachment. Separation anxiety is usual in infancy and even in the preschool years. Very young children are not yet able to imagine where the parent is when he or she isn't with them. That's why they scream and cling to your leg when you leave. If a parent is away for a long time it's as though they've lost that parent. This is why it isn't a good idea to take a holiday and leave your children when they are under four years of age. A young child in joint custody should have very short periods of separation from the primary parent, and if both parents are primary, should go back and forth quite often.

Hearing About Scary Events.   When a child six to nine years old suffers from separation anxiety, the most likely cause is something the child has seen or heard which has led him to believe something bad could happen when he is separated from his parents. Examples:

♦   seeing natural disasters on the news with the suggestion
    that it could happen here
♦   hearing statistics on car accidents
♦   knowing a child who has been taken into foster care
♦   hearing about a child or a parent who died
♦   hearing about someone who abandoned his/her children
♦   watching a frightening movie or TV show in which something
    happened to a child while separated from his parents
♦   hearing parents argue and fearing divorce
♦   a bad dream

We adults have become used to hearing about dangerous events, and most of the time we are able to put them in perspective. We know that even though earthquakes and fatal car accidents happen, they are rare. We know that movies and TV shows and dreams aren't real, and that they contain much more violence than real life does. We know that most people die of diseases of old age, quite quietly. We know that serial killers do not lurk behind every tree. We know that arguments don't mean divorce, and that divorce doesn't usually mean that the child loses a parent. Children, however, don't know about statistics, and in their attempts to make sense of the world they base their ideas about safety on what they see and hear – which means the media, especially television.

Watch what your child watches on television. Decide what might frighten her. Be aware that sometimes there are frightening commercials in the middle of wholesome shows.   If you watch with your child, you can help her understand anything which gives false ideas about the world.

Traumatic Experiences

Sometimes a child's separation anxiety arises from some traumatic experience which has actually happened to that child. If you have a child with a lot of anxiety, you need to do some detective work to find out what has happened or what he thinks might happen. It could be a number of things: a scary movie, seeing another child hurt, a dream he has taken literally, hearing about abducted children on the news, actually being hurt by bullies, being sexually abused by a babysitter or a friend's parents.

It is possible that something has actually happened to your child, something that he isn't telling you about. If he doesn't come up with any other reason for the separation anxiety, ask him directly whether something has happened to him that makes him afraid to be apart from you. Sometimes kids just don't tell their parents these kinds of things even though the parents may want them to. I (Alison Miller) remember having a babysitter who locked my brother in his bedroom all evening and made out on the couch with her boyfriend, with me watching. It never occurred to me to tell, even though I was very uncomfortable with the situation. I think I just assumed my parents would know about things like this, but of course they didn't. Before you leave your children with a sitter, a relative, etc. make it clear that you expect them to tell you if anything happens which makes them feel uncomfortable. If a child seems particularly uncomfortable with a certain adult, ask about it.

You can't discount the possibility that your child has actually been abused. It is common for sexual abusers, for example, to threaten to harm the child's parents if the child discloses. Watch and see if there is anyone in particular whom your child wants to avoid. If there is, take it seriously and try to find out more about why he doesn't like this person. If he's evasive even though you ask gently, you have cause for concern. Maybe threats have been made; maybe your child feels like it's all his fault and you'll be mad at him for what happened. On the other hand, it's best not to assume too readily that your child has been abused. Most separation anxiety is related to more common causes.

Fear of Growing Up

Children often become fearful and clingy as they approach new life challenges. Beginning school or a new level of school, moving to a new neighborhood and having to make friends, approaching puberty and noticing body changes, entering a new social group – all these things can create fear. The child fears she won't be able to negotiate the new challenges. She needs encouragement and help in handling the new situation, whatever it is, and she needs to be closer to you at such times.

Listening to Your Child

When you find out what the problem is, you can take steps to remedy it. Your first step is to listen. When you're in a nice, relaxed situation with your child (e.g. after you read her a story), ask her if she's worried about anything, and what she thinks might happen if she's separated from you. Also ask her whether she has scary dreams, and see whether they contain any clue to what is wrong. If she's reluctant to talk, assure her that you can keep both you and her safe if you know what the problem is, and that you won't be angry at her for anything she says or anything she has done. If she can't tell you, let her know that it's okay for her to tell you in any way she likes, such as a story or a picture, and give her a chance to express herself in these other ways. It's possible that your child just doesn't know the source of her fear. In this case, you may want to ask her about specific things that you suspect might be the problem, and see whether they ring a bell for her.

Helping Your Child Deal with Fears

If your child does tell you what he is worried about, you can help him understand that situation, giving statistics on how often it happens, and so forth – and reassure him about his own and your safety. If he worries about you dying, for example, listen very attentively to what he is worried about, then reassure him that the vast majority of people don't die until they're old. Take whatever he says very seriously, and don't scoff at his fears. The media are so full of murders and violence that children often get a distorted idea of what the risks actually are. Of course, if your son has had a real trauma (bullying or abuse), his feelings from that need to be addressed and the situation needs to be stopped. If your child appears not to know what is bothering him, or knows but is reluctant to talk about it, you may need to take him to a professional counselor who can help him express his concerns.

Once you know the source of the problem, and have removed any potential dangers, don't just give in to your child's separation anxiety. He needs to know that you can leave him somewhere, that both of you will be safe, and that you will return. He will never gain that security unless you do.

For the time being, however, you need to coddle your child a little. Spend more time with him, reassure him, phone him to let him know that you and everyone else are okay when he's away from you. Develop a soothing bedtime routine, if you don't already have one, and get him a night light. However, don't allow your child to distort your life so that it becomes really abnormal. He still needs to go to school, and you still need to attend to your regular activities. Otherwise he can become chronically fearful. With time and a normal life, your child's anxiety will lessen if you explain the realities of the situation to him and address any real dangers. If necessary, he can be equipped with a cell phone so he can check on your whereabouts from time to time.

You can teach your child strategies for mastering anxiety. He can have a 'worry time' in which he tells his worries to you or to a pet or a stuffed animal. If you're religious, your child can learn to name each of his worries and give them over to a loving God.

Or if you aren't religious, he can imagine a superhero helping him and being there with him. You can plan specific strategies with your child for coping with each separation situation as it comes up.

Apply Your Knowledge

- Do you have a child who has suffered from separation anxiety? How can you find out what's causing it?
- How can you help your child overcome his separation anxiety?

---

5 - Intellectual Development

Children Say Things That Aren't True

Another puzzling behavior which comes from a child's lack of life experience is telling untruths. This occurs most noticeably around ages four to six, but should begin to disappear after that if handled wisely by parents.

A little child doesn't know the meaning of speaking the truth. He will exaggerate or make up stories to impress people, since he gets lots of attention for these stories.

He will also say what he thinks you want to hear. And he will tell lies to keep out of trouble. You can ask him where the ice cream went, when the evidence is all over his face, and he will say he doesn't know, or blame the cat.

The cat ate the ice cream!

The Brilliant Baby

I remember one occasion on which my older son at five punctured his sister's camping air mattress several times as he experimented with the scissors. He told me that the baby (who wasn't yet able to crawl) did it. He knew he'd be in trouble if he told the truth, so he came up with what he thought was a reasonable explanation for the holes in the mattress. *-- Alison Miller*

As soon as the little child makes up a few stories which are far from the reality of what happened, he finds out that adults don't like him to lie. But he is confused about what a lie is, and also about what's wrong with lying.

What is a lie? You tell the child that a lie is saying something which isn't true. He interrupts you while you're reading his bedtime story to ask whether the story is a lie, and if it is, isn't it wrong? He accuses you of lying when the TV show you promised to watch with him is pre-empted by the hockey game. The notion of a lie is actually quite complicated – it's hard to explain to a young child the meaning of 'intent to deceive'. It takes a certain amount of understanding and intellect.

Time for the Cosby Show.

You lied! The Cosby Show is not on. Just a stupid football game.

A child's perspective is egocentric: he can only see things from his own viewpoint, and from this viewpoint it just makes sense to lie, as he gets attention and stays out of trouble this way. The story of the "Boy Who Cried Wolf" teaches a child the long-term consequences of telling untruths. Young children who lie are not 'selfish' or 'bad'; they are just normal children who are not yet mature enough to recognize how others may feel. (See Telling the Truth, in Chapter 6.)

Usually by age eight children are old enough to know what a lie is, and why it is wrong. If they lie it is usually for other reasons, such as to protect their privacy or to avoid punishment. This kind of lying needs to be handled differently: remove the circumstances that make it necessary for the child to lie in the first place.

Sometimes children lie about their accomplishments, saying they can read or can ride a bicycle when they can't, in an attempt to raise their self-esteem. Ensuring that children get significant positive attention and sincere feedback for positive behaviors, achievements, and efforts can make a difference.

Parenting Pointers

- Don't overreact – stay calm and know that this too is normal.
- If you have a young child who gets lost in fantasy, gently ask if she is telling a story or say, "Sounds like you are telling me a story, great!!"
- Avoid labeling your child a liar.
- Praise your child for telling the truth, even if he did something wrong.
- Avoid using harsh punishment or stating disapproval of the child.
- Make it easy for your child to express his needs and be assertive.
- Let him know it is okay to make a mistake.
- Set an example of honesty.

Apply Your Knowledge

- Has your child ever told lies? Think of an example.
- The concept of lying is a hard one to understand. How can you explain it?
- Do you remember lying as a child? Why did you do it?
- Sometimes older children might lie to avoid disappointing their parents or getting into trouble. How can parents make it comfortable for their child to tell the truth?

Children Ask Lots of Questions

Sometimes a child's insatiable curiosity can wear you down. You get tired of answering "Why?" questions all day long. But think what a wonderful thing this curiosity is. It's the motivating force behind all learning. Children are full of enthusiasm and creativity; if we don't squelch it, it will be their greatest resource in life. Let's respect both our children's lack of knowledge and their curiosity, and help satisfy their need to understand the world they live in.

We need, however, to distinguish between questions which represent true curiosity, and those which are designed to put off bedtime or chores. It's easy for a parent to get confused about this. One general guideline is: if the child has already been told the answer clearly, then he isn't really curious – for example, you've just given your child three reasons why it's bedtime, and he asks "Why?"

Older children often will not ask questions when they need to, because they don't like to admit their ignorance. We need to be sensitive to areas in which they may lack knowledge, and take the initiative by offering them ways to obtain the information they need.

While a child's curiosity is natural, it's equally natural for a parent to feel frustrated by the constant questioning. Time for yourself, away from children, can help you renew your patience by acknowledging your own needs. This is also good modeling for the child.

Parenting Pointers

♦ Sometimes you can ask a question back – "What do you think?"
♦ Help your child look up the answer at the library, in an encyclopedia or on the Internet.
♦ Take the opportunity to learn with your child. Your own enthusiasm for learning is an important example.
♦ Take time for yourself so you won't become too frustrated with your child's questions.

Apply Your Knowledge

● Do you take time to answer your child's questions or help him find the answers?
● Can you tell the difference between curiosity and limit-testing questions?

Children Forget Instructions

It is very difficult to set exact age guidelines for the development of the various thinking skills. The situation is complicated by the fact that children differ in their inborn intellectual abilities, and also in the speed of their development. The best thing for a parent to do is to recognize that kids often have problems in these areas simply

Have you put on your shoes yet, Jimmy?

because they are immature (that is, not yet adults). Once your child is in school, problems will show up if he is unable to keep up with other children. Generally teachers know what kids are capable of in their grade.

Difficulties in remembering instructions are most pronounced in the preschool years, and gradually decline with age. Preschool children have difficulty maintaining their attention on a task or even on a conversation for any length of time. They are easily distracted. They can't remember what you asked them to do, especially if you gave them more than one instruction. A lecture does no good because they tune out – their attention span just isn't that long.

And, by adult standards, they never seem to focus on what is important. That's because they don't yet have the capacity to sort the important from the unimportant: this takes abstracting ability, as well as the life experience to teach what matters and what doesn't.

Inability to focus on what is important combined with not having an adult understanding of time, creates many stressful times for parents, especially in the morning when trying to leave the house.

How can you simplify your requests so that your child can remember them?

Apply Your Knowledge

- Does your child get distracted easily?
- How can you work with your child's limitations when you make requests?
- A normal child isn't able to hold all aspects of a situation in his mind, so he makes decisions according to whatever is in his mind at the moment.
- What kinds of impulsive behavior does your child indulge in?
- Does she choose play over responsibilities?
- Healthy children want to have fun. How can we respect this need while setting limits?

Children Don't Understand Time

Young children don't have the concept of time as organized by the clock. It takes a long time for children to learn about time, and until they do it seems to take forever getting dressed, eating and so on.

Nagging and threats usually don't help. Saying "when you are dressed you may eat" can be quite helpful. But it is important for the parent to accept the child's limitations in managing time, and simply allot more time to get through the routine tasks that an adult could do in a flash if the child weren't holding him up.

Because children live in the present, parents have considerable difficulty when they expect their children to plan ahead. Children don't yet have a clear idea of how their present actions will affect the future. Since they don't understand time, they find it hard to anticipate how long various things will take. Children can only focus on one aspect of a situation at a time: they cannot think about the present and the future as well.

Dinner will be in fifteen minutes!

Parenting Pointers

♦ Keep instructions limited and make a clear, positive request.

♦ Draw pictures of instructions or write them down.

♦ Expect things to take time and allow sufficient time to do them.

♦ Give one-word reminders.

♦ Plan ahead and plan fewer trips.

♦ Use a timer for young children.

♦ Take time to participate in your children's interests even when doing this interrupts your routine.

♦ Use a chart to help them with their self-care routines.

♦ Avoid nagging older children and let them experience some natural consequences.

Apply Your Knowledge

● What challenges are presented because your child doesn't understand time?

● How can you deal with the challenges that this brings into daily life?

● How can you help your child plan ahead or work with time?

Children Say Thoughts Out Loud

You bad girl! You ate the chocolate chips. Are you ever in BIG trouble now!

It is sometimes irritating for parents to have to listen to a young child saying all of her thoughts out loud. This has been studied by psychologists, and appears to mark the beginning of thinking in words: a child at this age finds it hard to think silently, and finds it easier if she vocalizes her thoughts. This tendency is outgrown by five or six. The 'out loud' stage is necessary for a child to develop thinking skills.

Children Make Messes They Can't Clean Up

Room cleanup is often a major bone of contention between parents and children. It's important to realize that while a little kid can put all his toys into a bin or bucket, he just doesn't have the categorizing ability to separate the Lego pieces from the blocks and the puzzle pieces. He also doesn't see the entire messy room: his thinking is still centered, meaning he can only focus his attention on one part of a situation at a time. He will clean up part of the room and not even notice the other parts which are still messy. This does not indicate laziness, just normal childhood immaturity. And we can't do anything about immaturity except wait for our children to grow up, encourage them, and model maturity.

Many of these difficulties persist into older childhood and even adolescence, although they gradually improve. An older child loses things frequently. Older children also have difficulties managing their time and planning ahead. Basically, children only learn a cognitive skill when the tasks they are called on to do require it and when they are developmentally ready to learn it. This means that we must require them to take on a task only when they are ready, and then we must be prepared for plenty of goofing up during the learning period.

Teenagers' cognitive immaturity is hard to see, but it's there. There is a cooperation game in which each of five individuals has a puzzle to complete and is given a set of puzzle pieces. The rule is that you can only give away pieces which you see that another person needs; you can't ask for pieces which you need. Groups of adults typically solve this game in about 10 minutes. When teenagers play the game, they give up after about 45 minutes! You'd never know from looking at them and listening to them that they are so unable to focus on the whole picture – but this is the way they are. The frontal lobes of the brain have yet to become active. This is one reason why teens are sometimes bad drivers.

Apply Your Knowledge

- Normal children don't see an entire messy room; they can only focus on one part of a situation at a time. Because of this, they lose things and they only clean up part of the room. Do you see this in your child?
- Children's brains aren't developed enough for them to know how to put things together, even though they love to take them apart! How do you deal with your children making messes?
- How can we have realistic expectations of our children when it comes to cleaning up?

How We Learn

The following chart shows all the things children have to master in childhood in terms of their ability to think. No wonder they can't remember two instructions in a row, or know what's most important to do at any moment.

Receive Information	Organize Information	Express Information
Watch	Organize in space	Speak
Listen	See patterns	Move
Touch	Put things in order	Write
Taste	Categorize	Draw
Smell	Sort important from unimportant	Manipulate Objects
Pay Attention	Remember	
	Use logic	

6 - Dealing with Children's Limitations

Although children have limitations, some children have more difficulty than others. Unfortunately, we live in a society which tends to think that everyone should try to be equally talented in every area and that all children should develop at the same rate. In our schools children are divided into same-age classes, and are compared in their achievements with others of the same age. The reality is that children do not all have the same abilities and do not all develop at exactly the same rate. Some children take longer than others to develop skills in receiving, organizing and expressing information. And some only develop these skills partially. 'Normal' is a big range!

One child in seven cannot learn adequately in a regular classroom. These children have been defined as 'learning-disabled'. The Ministry of Education in British Columbia (Canada) defines a learning disability as a difficulty in one or more of the following areas: oral expression, listening comprehension, written expression, reading and mathematics. These areas reflect what the school system tries to teach. They do not by any means reflect all the areas of ability a child may have. And of course, many abilities that are extremely useful in life are not taught or used in school.

Children who don't excel or develop quickly in the abilities stressed in school get labeled simply by being singled out for special attention by teachers. Sometimes other children call them stupid, losers, and other nasty names.

Children whose scholastic abilities are uneven (high in some areas, low in others) tend to be treated as if they are lazy or misbehaving when they don't turn in a uniformly good performance.

In addition, there are the 'gifted' children, those who are particularly good at the abilities emphasized in school. One might expect that they would have it easy. But they are often expected to always achieve academically with no time to relax and enjoy other areas of life. They are often not allowed to just be children. They learn that the part of themselves valued by adults is their ability to perform on tests and be 'smart', so it's easy for them to develop in a one-sided manner.

We parents need to recognize and appreciate the strengths our children do have rather than those we wish they had. It is important for us to recognize the areas in which our children may be out of step with regard to society's expectations. But we do need to accept them as they are, get them the special help they need to make it through school, and develop their areas of strength, rather than insisting they be like everyone else.

Apply Your Knowledge

- How can we help children feel confident and good about themselves despite their limitations?
- Can you think of a situation in which you were frustrated by your child's developmental limitations? How did you deal with it? How would you deal with it now?
- How can we teach children that they are loved and accepted for who they are?

Further Reading

Ames, Louise B. and Ilg, Frances have written a series of books describing children's development at various ages, e.g. *"Is your child in the wrong grade?"* and *"Your five year old"*.

Caplan, Frank. *The First Twelve Months of Life. The Second Twelve Months of Life.*
    New York: Random House, 1982

Leach, Penelope. *Your Baby and Child – From Birth to Age Five.*
    New York: Knopf, 1989

4
Taming the Triggers:
Managing Antecedents of Behavior

Kids don't just act, they react. And so do parents. We are all profoundly affected by what happens to us in life, and both the major events in our life and the everyday challenges can create behavior patterns in both kids and parents. Things in the environment which provoke behavior are technically called 'antecedents'. A simpler word is 'triggers'. Many things can trigger both problematic behavior and emotional outbursts in our children and sometimes ourselves. If we parents can detect triggers before they begin to create problems we can prevent many difficulties.

In this chapter we teach you how to track down the environmental sources of your children's behavior. Certain common situations such as getting out of the house in the morning, rushed mealtimes, or shopping, almost inevitably provoke difficult behavior. We provide you with ways to anticipate this and handle these situations.

The behaviors of parents and other family members can provoke misbehavior in children. Does this ring a bell?: "Why do you always choose to be obnoxious when I'm having a bad day?" It's important that we notice how we are behaving with our children rather than just punishing them for the misbehaviors we may have triggered through our own insensitivity or preoccupation.

Parents fighting can upset children. Sometimes it's just our busyness which leads our kids to misbehave; they do it to get our attention. When this happens we need to slow down and spend some time with them. If we identify and remove the triggers to misbehavior, both we and our children will be happier.

Things outside the home, such as school pressure or relationships, can upset children and lead them to misbehave at home. The same goes for major life events such as a new baby or pet, a parent returning to work, a new school, a change of residence, a parental separation, or the loss of a pet or loved one. It is important to recognize these major life changes and help your children to handle them.

1 - Triggers (Antecedents)

An important question for parents to ask themselves is: "When did the behavior start?" Think of anything that happened at the start of or shortly before the behavior. It may not be obvious at first, but sometimes the answer is very clear: "Oh – that is right around the time that my child's favorite baby-sitter moved away!" Or "It only happens when he plays with Johnny," or "It's right before dinner time."

In this chapter we will only consider the antecedents which trigger a child's unwanted behavior to occur. We will look at consequences in chapters to come. Many parents rush to apply consequences – positive and negative – to behavior, and then are surprised when it doesn't work. It often doesn't work because nothing has been done about the antecedents and they have such a powerful effect that the child isn't able to think about what will happen later.

Triggers

- ◆ Time of year, month, week or day
- ◆ Presence of temptation
- ◆ Events
- ◆ Others people's behavior

2 - Triggering Times

Time of Year

Many people (adults and children) feel 'down' in the wintertime. Seasonal Affective Disorder (SAD) can affect people quite strongly. Getting out on bright days as much as possible can help. It might help to buy a light box and spend some time each day under it.

Holidays, anniversaries, and birthdays can also cause old pain to resurface, especially if a loved one passed away recently or if these times remind us of painful childhood memories. For example, people who grew up with alcoholic parents often become stressed around Christmas time, because it was a major drinking season and this led to family fights and tension when they were children. Children who have experienced loss and trauma can suffer from 'anniversary effects' just like adults.

Time of the Month

At least 60 percent of all women suffer from PMS (pre-menstrual syndrome). While there are lots of different symptoms of PMS, many women report a feeling of dissatisfaction and tension as their cycle builds up to their period. Typically this happens a few days before their period begins until about the second day of the period itself. Some researchers think men also have monthly cycles which are more difficult to detect.

Women with PMS may notice their symptoms worsen in the fall when the days get shorter. Many symptoms of PMS are similar to the symptoms associated with SAD (seasonal affective disorder) and if you suffer from both, it can be a difficult time of year. (Add the onset of the holiday season and whoopee – let the good times roll!)

Teenage girls, like their mothers, can suffer from PMS, but it is unlikely that they will know what's wrong when the symptoms come on. Receiving understanding and guidance from a mother or a caring older female can help.

Time of the Week

Certain events happen predictably on certain days of the week, and your child's behavior may be directly related to these events. He may be tired the day he gets up at 5:00 a.m. for hockey practice. She may be in a bad mood the day she has the teacher she hates. Parents who work all week may be exhausted on Friday night. If we know that family members will have reactions on certain days, we can plan for these and not add to their stress.

Time of Day - Mornings

Are you one of those people who bounce out of bed with a smile on your face two seconds after the alarm? Do you blurt out cheerful good mornings to those tired souls around you? Well, that is really nice, but would you please remember that many people take about 30 minutes to wind up to your speed! Because of that, lots of people hit their snooze buttons a good four or five times before getting up. Family combinations of morning folk and night owls make mornings tough for many families.

Children are no different from adults and they don't have the option of a caffeine kick-start! Many parents report their children being really cranky in the morning. When neither parents nor kids are morning people, cheerful mornings can be a huge effort. Be sympathetic and be aware of how difficult it is for them to say or do the "right thing". A glass of juice right beside the bed, downed first thing, can help improve a child's mood in about 10 minutes.

Getting Kids Out of the House:

People find that tension mounts in the morning and again just before their evening meal. This is because of fatigue and hunger. It is especially tough with younger children because parents are often tired from being awakened during the night. In the morning, the little darling may decide that today is the day he will learn to tie his shoes. Nobody can leave until he has done it himself. Pick him up and he will scream and refuse to get in the car! Breathe deeply! Families in which both parents, or the only parent, have to go to work in the morning are more stressed in the mornings than families with one parent at home.

Teenagers won't get out of bed and by the time they do, they have 10 minutes to get ready and go, which is a problem when they need at least an hour to do their hair. Younger children get distracted by any number of things which are far more interesting than putting on their coat and shoes.

While we can't change schools and workplaces to start at 10:00 a.m. (which would be much more civilized), we can acknowledge that the morning is a time of tension and try to make it less stressful. One important way to do this is to have everyone get up earlier so things won't be so rushed. Kids don't have the same sense of time as adults and can't keep focused on tasks the way we can (see Chapter 3).

Planning Ahead:

Have your child choose her clothes the night before and have her get dressed first thing in the morning. We know some parents who got so frustrated with the morning struggles that they dressed their kids the night before and let them sleep in their school clothes. Hey, if it works, who cares about a few wrinkles?

When-Then:

When-Then is a negotiating tool that has been around for a long time. It's also called Grandma's Rule! Let children know they can do whatever it is they're asking to do once they have done what they need to do:
♦   When you get dressed, then we will read this book.
♦   When you are ready, then you can watch your show.
♦   When the veins pop out of the side of my head, then you need to run to the car.

Apply Your Knowledge

- Think of some examples you could use in your family:

When_____,

   then _____.

When_____,

   then _____.

When_____,

   then _____.

One father in our course said that when he was completing a task that his teenagers weren't willing to help him complete he would say, "When I get this kitchen finished, then I can drive you to your friends' place. If you help me, it will help you too."

Recognizing Positive Behavior:

At 8:00 a.m. it is tough to find positive behavior! When things do go smoothly call attention to it. It is a nice reminder that it is entirely possible. Being specific in your comments will ensure that the kids know exactly what they did right:

"You got out of bed on time this morning and had some time to play. I had time to dry my hair, and we all got out on time. What a great start to the day!"

Allowing Natural Consequences:

Letting natural consequences work for you means not being overly involved with the process or the outcome. It is a way of handing an issue over to the child and letting him come to a decision based on his own reasoning.

If the children end up going to preschool in their pajamas, they may decide, eventually, and for their own reasons, that it would be better to dress. They may not care if they wear pyjamas but they may care about missing out on outside activities because they aren't properly dressed. Work with your child's caregiver about how the natural consequences will play out. Usually a simple explanation of what you are trying to do is enough to gain her support.

You may worry about what other people (parents or caregivers) might think of you if you let your child go to preschool in pyjamas, or carry him screaming out of the grocery store instead of giving him a treat. It's hard not to give in to the desire for approval. But know that you're not being a 'bad parent' by letting your child suffer minor natural consequences, and the gain in your child's sense of responsibility will be worth it, no matter what other people think.

What is okay for some children can be totally devastating for others. Never force issues by making a child walk into a school or out of the house in pyjamas as punishment after they have asked to get dressed. That is a huge boundary violation. Just have the clothes available and keep your lips pressed tightly together.

See Chapter 5 (The Freedom of Responsibility) for more information on natural consequences, when to use them and when not to use them.

Using Logical Consequences:

Logical consequences (See Chapter 7) are consequences which parents impose in response to children's behavior. They can be positive or negative, but are most effective when they are positive.

What logical consequence can you come up with for getting ready in the morning?
- Younger kids can earn a trip to the park (there would be time if they got ready faster).
- School age kids could stay up an extra 15 minutes in the evening.
- Teenagers could get a ride to school (and if they aren't ready, they have to walk).

Making Your Feet Listen to Your Mouth:

I (Allison Rees) find the most effective action is to let the kids know I am going out to the van after a five-minute warning. When five minutes are up, I go to the van, and I sit in the van until I see them flying out of the house. The point is that I am taking action instead of nagging. Now they believe me when I say five minutes.

Too often parents give warnings rather than letting their bodies take action. Avoid reasoning with a toddler at the park about why you have to leave. Instead, start walking while you talk. It sounds so obvious, but we need to make our body language work for us.

We have seen parents tell their children that it is time to leave and then engage in another 15 minutes' conversation with somebody else before they actually go. The child is standing there bored to tears, then goes back to playing. Then mom or dad yells to "hurry up" when they do decide to go – how frustrating for the child!

Hungry Times

When it comes to hunger, the simple fact is kids and adults are often grumpy when they are hungry! Why do you think we call dinner time 'arsenic hour' or 'crazy hour'? Some parents make kids wait up to an hour while they prepare dinner even though the kids are really hungry. By the time dinner comes around, the children can be unbearable and everybody suffers.

"The Arsenic Hour"

Healthy snacks make great appetizers. Instead of having their salad at mealtime, why not let kids have carrot sticks, celery or cucumbers as a snack before their meal? Most children are grazers and do better with lots of snacks rather than big meals. Picking your child up at school or from the daycare can be a much more pleasant experience when you come equipped with food.

The Perfect Little Boy

When my son Justin was about three, I worked part-time and he went to an in-home daycare. The daycare provider said he was a "perfect little boy," referring to his ideal behavior in the daycare home.

However, on the way home he inevitably had a temper tantrum. We had to pick up his sister and while walking up the stairs to the house he would rage at me no matter what I did: whether I walked up the stairs ahead of him, beside him, or behind him. I could never do it right! This went on until one day I had a brilliant idea. I realized he was hungry. I asked his daycare provider to give Justin a snack just before I picked him up. The tantrums vanished!

-- Alison Miller

Adults are not much different from children – we can't run on empty. Having a snack before you pick up your kids from school or daycare is a great idea for you too.

Apply Your Knowledge

- Is there a particular time of day when your child's behavior is more difficult?
- Is transition difficult for your child? If transition times are hard how could you help your child deal with them?
- Mealtime can be stressful for many families. Everybody is hungry. This can be a huge trigger to negative behavior for all concerned. How does your child react to hunger? How could you plan ahead for these difficult times?
- Fatigue also has a strong effect on behavior. If there is a typical time of day when your child is cranky, could your child be tired?
- Parents of young children are often sleep-deprived. Are you getting enough sleep? Does this cause any conflict with your child or partner?

The Mealtime Blues

Mealtime is one of the most stressful times of the day. It is a time when a lot of old belief systems create problems. Many parents expect their young children to sit still at the table and eat all their food. We also bribe them with dessert so that they'll eat what they're given, even ignoring their body signals that they've had enough. Then they say they only have 'room' for ice cream but no room for broccoli!

All too often our coercive mealtime parenting results in kids who sit at the table with their mouths tightly shut, refusing everything but dessert. The table can be the scene of a battle night after night. There are many beliefs at work that can keep us in horrible power struggles.

False Beliefs about Children & Meals

- ♦ Children should be able to sit still at the table before the age of seven.
- ♦ Children should eat when we tell them to.
- ♦ They must finish their food.
- ♦ Dessert is a reward for eating.
- ♦ Children can't decide for themselves about their own hunger or fullness.

How much is enough?:

Nursing babies aren't told how much to eat, or forced to keep nursing when they have had enough. They know exactly how much their bodies need. As soon as babies start eating solids served in measurable amounts, the parents somehow assume that responsibility.

We have watched parents chase their children with two-hour-old hot dogs asking them to take one more bite. Yes, we know that if they don't eat much at a meal they get hungry later and want to eat between meals. But, as mentioned earlier, grazing is healthy. Especially for children, who have small stomachs. Don't make an issue about how much! Serve small amounts and remember that children, when not forced, will choose a healthy balance for themselves. Your job is to provide the food but their responsibility is to eat it. Trust them: they won't starve themselves.

How long should they sit?:

A lot depends on the child's activity level and of course his age. Allowing children to leave the table after a short period of time doesn't teach them poor table manners. Children under three can't sit still for more than a couple of minutes. You may end up eating separately or at different times when they are very young. As they get a little older they will begin to be able to sit for short periods of time. They will be more likely to sit if they are also part of preparing the meal or setting the table. If, however, sitting at the dinner table is a tense experience, this process will take longer. Keep it pleasant and they will want to join you when they are old enough.

With older children you can insist that conversation be respectful at the table. This means no behavior that violates boundaries, such as fighting or talking about green slugs, poop or butts. If they choose to fight or disrespect boundaries, they can take their food elsewhere. Maybe you have an area where you can eat peacefully if this happens. Kids won't like it but taking action and protecting your needs is important.

Many parents use mealtimes to talk with one another about adult issues. This is boring for the children and a sure-fire recipe for producing fidgety children! Respect for all family members requires that conversation topics at mealtime be of interest to all — children and adults.

Food Fads:

Problems will arise during the toddler years when a child's appetite drops with his growth rate. Parents see their child eating less and begin to worry if he's eating enough. Most kids go through stages when they only want one thing to eat. This is normal and it does pass. Don't make a big deal about it.

Sensitivities and Allergies:

Be aware of the possibility of food sensitivities and allergies. The best way to discover whether your child is allergic to something is to remove suspect foods and then slowly re-introduce them into the child's diet. Food allergies can create changes in your child's behavior. Kids sometimes dislike foods they are allergic to, and sometimes (and this is the case with 'addictive allergies') they crave them.

Creative Meals:

Variety is the spice of life, and a little creativity sometimes helps introduce new foods to your children. We (the Rees family) used to set up a tablecloth on the living room floor and have picnics in front of the fireplace. Putting a variety of foods on their plates in small amounts can keep mealtime interesting while introducing new tastes.

Mealtime Help:

- Let children help select the dinner menu.
- Make food attractive and serve small amounts so you aren't stressed over wasted food.
- Let the child serve his own dinner onto his plate.
- Avoid commenting on how much your children are eating. Keep your eyes off their plates!
- Teach children about nutrition so they can make healthy, informed decisions.
- Don't reward a child for eating or punish a child for not eating.
- Avoid using food (including dessert) as a reward or withholding it as a punishment.
- If you know she doesn't like the food, give her a simple alternative, like a sandwich, or let her make it and clean up the mess herself if she is old enough.
- Have the child clear his plate and put it in the dishwasher so you don't have to judge his consumption.
- Remember that serious eating disorders can develop out of parent-child power struggles about eating, so stay out of these struggles whenever possible.
- Let him cook! And the sooner, the better! A child who is involved in cooking is less likely to be a picky eater.

Encourage Self-Help:

- Keep a container of freshly chopped veggies and fruit in the fridge so your children can help themselves throughout the day.
- Have plastic glasses in a bottom drawer and an easy-to-pour container of juice in the fridge.
- Teach kids how to cook and let them prepare meals for the family. Increase their skills as they grow older. (Be prepared to eat some weird stuff.)
- If a child is stuck on one food, tell her she can have it three times that week and let her plan the weekly menu. (Be prepared to eat noodles for breakfast.)
- Allow him to listen to his body and respect his inner voice. That voice can be trusted.

Apply Your Knowledge

- What needs to be changed in the way you handle mealtimes with your children?

---

3 - Tempting Triggers

Certain places offer temptations which kids (and sometimes adults) find hard to resist. Temptations can be outside the home (notably when you're shopping) or inside the home (candy, liquor, cigarettes, television).

Apply Your Knowledge

● Is there a particular location where your child's behavior seems worse?
● How can you plan ahead to avoid this situation?

Shopping with Kids

Shopping trips are full of triggers, especially for very young children. Unless you have to, we don't think it's a good idea to take them along when you shop. They have short attention spans, and they want to touch or play with everything they see. I (Alison Miller) remember taking my daughter into a pottery shop when she was about two, and the wise owner said: "She thinks with her hands." If any normal child isn't allowed to touch things she sees, she becomes frustrated. If this goes on for more than five or 10 minutes, the child won't be able to control her emotions and will start demanding, crying, or having a tantrum.

Children also tire easily, and can't take more than about half an hour of shopping. Get a sitter, shop when your child's in school or preschool, get your spouse to look after the kids, or trade babysitting with a friend so you can shop without having to deal with a whining and crying child. If you have to take a child food shopping, make sure the child's tummy is full before you leave, and take a healthy snack along with you.

For adult shopping (such as for your own clothes or furniture), never take a child along, period! For food shopping, tell the child at the start of the trip that she will get a specific kind of treat at the end of the trip if she cooperates and doesn't whine for things. For a child young enough to sit in the buggy, take along a toy to play with. For an older child, ask her to get the food you suggest off the shelves, so she can feel involved in the shopping. If the child starts to whine for a specific item, remind her that she will get her reward at the end only if she cooperates. Make sure you do buy some things your child wants, such as interesting cereals. Don't spend time chatting with friends; get your shopping done as fast as possible so you won't exceed your child's attention span.

If you're shopping for children's clothes, take only one child at a time. Make sure that the shopping trip is going to be short and to the point. Choose one store with a good variety, or a group of stores close together. Take your child's opinion of the clothes seriously and don't buy something she hates. We have heard countless adults in therapy complaining that their mother never respected their choice of clothing. Yes, you may know that the coat you buy needs to be warm, but she may know that it needs to be something she won't get teased about. Make an agreement before you leave that whatever you buy needs to be something acceptable to both of you (a win-win solution). This is a good opportunity to teach your child the art of negotiation, and the value of money. If you can't find something suitable on this trip, go home and plan another trip. If you keep shopping for more than half an hour, you are asking for whining and tantrums.

If you are shopping with your child's money for a gift, or helping your child spend her allowance, plan ahead together as to what kinds of items to buy. If there are certain things you will not allow her to buy (such as guns or junk food), make this clear before you go shopping. If you are using your money rather than your child's money, make your price limit clear before you shop. Then go directly to an area where the items available are within your child's price range. Children will feel frustrated if they spend time in the expensive areas of a toy store and can't buy anything. Help your child figure out how much money she has, and what combinations of things she can buy with that money. Then respect her choices, within the limits you have set.

Store Checkouts:

Talk about temptation! One parent wrote to our website (www.lifeseminars.com): "My kids are driving me up the wall. Whenever I go shopping, they keep at me: 'Mom, can you buy me that? Mom, can you buy me that?' I feel like screaming at them. Don't they understand that I can't afford to buy them everything in the store?" She voiced what many parents feel, especially in the Christmas season when toys and candy are everywhere, and a shopping trip can turn a little child into a whining nag or a screeching banshee.

Children don't understand that you can't afford to buy them everything. It will take them years to understand money, and why an adult who can take $100 out of the bank machine can't produce $100 the same way to buy them a doll or an action figure. You can't expect them to understand or to resist the pull of all the fascinating things they see, or to be able to sit still or walk quietly with you for an hour while you buy things which don't interest them.

Store merchandisers are highly trained professionals whose goal is to get us to leave our money at the store. Those large, colorful bags of candy are placed at the checkout with full knowledge that your children are going to bring you to your knees. If you are going through a difficult stage with your child, you might be wise to avoid these places until he matures a little.

Of course it isn't fair to market to young children but it's routinely done. A couple of years ago, one of our local stores designed Kid Friendly aisles. Instead of candy, they started displaying expensive books and Mickey Mouse calculators. I (Allison Rees) complained to the head person but I think he figured I was just another neurotic parent with a spoiled child. These temptations are really tough on our little ones, who aren't old enough to resist, as well as on us parents.

Don't take kids grocery shopping when they're hungry. A well-fed kid is much less likely to scream for candy at the checkout than a hungry and tired one. If the 'gimme's' are an issue, you need to plan ahead.

To Buy or Not to Buy:

Impulse purchases can lead to high expectations. We often buy kids things we shouldn't either when we're in a really good mood or when we're too tired to face an argument. Guilt can also make us give in too much. One mother called in to a radio show which I (Allison Rees) was co-hosting complaining that her son had very expensive taste. She let guilt push her buttons because she felt she hadn't given him the great life she had wanted to. Her guilt was an antecedent to her own lack of discipline. Don't let guilt or a good mood become an antecedent to indulgence. It doesn't hurt kids to go without things.

With teens, you probably don't have to worry too much because they won't want to be seen with you in a mall anyway. Chances are if you are there together, it's to buy them something. They may need a new pair of running shoes but maybe they don't need the expensive model. Discuss this ahead of time and have them contribute if they want the fancier brand. Distinguish between needs and wants. Be prepared and clear about finances with your teens.

Apply Your Knowledge

- What do you need to change in the way you shop with your children to make it more pleasant for you and them?
- Can you prepare your child ahead of time and have a positive consequence in place to follow a successful trip?

Alcohol, Cigarettes and Drugs

There is some likelihood that your kids will experiment a little. If your child is going through an experimental stage, don't leave things lying around. Lock up the liquor and get rid of any other temptations.

While locking doors in our loving homes sounds rigid and controlling, we have found that installing locks can actually help our teens deal with temptation. I (Allison Rees) remember stealing my dad's cigarettes when I was 16. I really used to wonder why he'd leave them out on the counter when he went to work. Was he doing me a favor? I was just glad that I didn't like his brand of cigarettes too much; otherwise the temptation would have been that much bigger. A 16-year-old girl in counseling said she actually suggested to her dad that he lock up his liquor, because her friends pressured her to steal it when they were over. When he suggested she just "say no" she burst into tears, believing he wasn't willing to give her support. As much as teens want trust, they also want help resisting temptation.

Junk Food

A father in our parenting class complained about his son demanding junk food. We asked the obvious question about whether there was junk food in the house and, if so, who it was for. The man's wife answered that she would occasionally buy cookies or sweets and her husband would immediately eat as many as he could. Like the father, the child was triggered into craving junk food by seeing it, but the child at least was polite enough to ask for it!

Mother unwittingly launches Al on his 'life of crime'.

- What kinds of temptations does your child find irresistible?
- What kinds of items do you keep out of reach or sight?
- Do you remember these kinds of temptations when you were young?

4 - Triggering Events

A New Baby

The birth of a new baby is a major stressor for kids. Faber & Mazlish suggest looking at the child's experience as comparable to what you'd feel if your husband brought home a new wife and asked you to share your clothes with her, love her, and be happy about it.

There are many ways to alleviate the tension of bringing home a new baby. See what works for your family. Depending on your child's age, it may take some time for him to understand the impact of the new arrival on his life.

I don't wanna baby. Take him back.

The fun starts when your child realizes he has to share his mommy and daddy – forever, and that the baby can't be taken back to the baby store. It gets more difficult when the baby starts to walk and gets into his things.

Accepting your child's feelings, spending one-on-one time with him, and including him while caring for the baby are all helpful ways of reducing the stress.

A New Pet

Disappointment

My daughter went through a difficult time emotionally when she was four. When I sat down to track when the behavior started, it was clearly the same time that we brought home our new puppy dog, Rosie. How could this be? Emily wanted this dog so badly. When I thought more about it, the dog got tons of attention and Emily was constantly being told to be gentle with her. I hadn't realized that Emily felt upstaged by the dog. It all made sense when I looked back. *-- Allison Rees*

Returning to Work

One mother complained about her child's negative behavior coming on suddenly. We traced it back to the triggering event and this turned out be her return to work. This child went to a nice daycare but Mom was a little nervous. It was simply that the child missed her; there was no mistreatment going on.

This didn't mean that Mom needed to quit her job, but by identifying the behavior, she was able to work around it. We set up two times of the day for phone appointments so at 10:00 a.m. and at 2:00 p.m. she and her child would talk. She also gave her child a picture of herself (a picture only a child could love!). She made a habit of putting jokes and funny pictures in the child's lunch box.

Keep it light and let your child know that you are okay too. If your child feels that you are missing her, she may become anxious and have difficulty separating from you.

Beginning School

Maybe they're tougher than we think...

An at-home mother decided to put her four-year-old son in part-time preschool so that she could study for a course she was taking as well as give the little boy a positive social experience. But each day when they got to the entrance to the preschool, Mom began to feel misgivings. What if he wasn't looked after properly there? What if he missed her? The little boy would sense his mother's uneasiness, become worried, and cry. When he cried, she would stay around, and he would continue crying until she took him home.

Finally the preschool said they couldn't hold the space any longer, and insisted that Mom leave her son there or allow another child to take his place. Mom reluctantly and sadly left him there. The moment she was out of the boy's sight, he was fine. -- *Alison Miller*

School Relationships

Does the teacher understand?

My daughter Anna had a first-grade teacher who was in her first year of teaching. She thought six-year-olds should be able to sit still in their desks from 9 a.m. till 3 p.m. My daughter came home each day feeling she was a failure because she liked to run around and socialize rather than sit still all day. Five years later my son Justin had a well-liked first-grade teacher who really stressed oral participation in a French Immersion program. Justin was a slow-to-warm-up child who wouldn't speak up in class. He came out of that class feeling he must be stupid. Fortunately in second grade both children had a warm, loving, understanding teacher who helped rebuild their self-esteem. -- *Alison Miller*

A poor teacher or just a 'bad fit' between teacher and child can cause a child considerable anxiety. Other school problems which can trigger anxiety in children include bullying, exclusion by peers, and conflict in friendships. Bullying is a major problem for many children, as is peer pressure. We have known teens who refused to attend school because they couldn't handle the peer pressure.

It can get fairly complicated, especially if a child is also worried about things at home. Pinpointing where the behavior is coming from is the first step in resolving it.

A Change of Residence

A change of residence is one event which frequently is much more disturbing to a child than to his parents. A child's sense of self is embedded in his surroundings. A move takes away his friends, school, home, bedroom, and frequently many of his possessions. He feels he has lost a large part of himself and has to go through a grieving process before he can re-adjust to the new surroundings.

It is important for parents to be conscious of just how disruptive a move can be to a child. A move is particularly upsetting when the child is very young and has not yet developed to the point of understanding that the people and places he has left still exist.

Losses and Deaths

Children can be even more upset about deaths and losses than adults are. They don't really understand what has happened, and often no one bothers to give them explanations. When a family member, classmate, or pet dies, it's really important that a child has a chance to express her feelings and ask her questions. I (Alison Miller) have counseled adults still grieving at age 50 for the loss of a father in childhood, and they still had only a child's understanding of what had happened. At the time the parent died, nobody paid attention to what the child was going through. There are some excellent books on helping children cope with grief and loss, and the topic is too big to discuss in depth here.

Children tend to be literal about death. If they see a coffin being lowered into the ground, they may think the person or animal inside is feeling unable to breathe or is conscious in the dark – or if it is a cremation, that the person feels the heat of the fire. They need to be told that the person is no longer in his body and can't feel anything that the body goes through.

If a pet needs to be put down, it's important that the parents explain the process and help the child understand why it needs to happen, for example: "Because Rover's or Fluffy's body isn't working properly any more and he's in a lot of pain which can't be stopped." Parents also need to explain that Rover or Fluffy will no longer be in their body and won't feel pain any more. Make sure that the child knows that the animal will not feel anything that happens in the body if it is buried or cremated. Don't use the term 'going to sleep' because it can lead the child to fear sleep, thinking it can lead to death.

Hidden Triggering Events

If a child suddenly starts to misbehave it is wise for parents to look for an event that they may not know about. We have had several people tell us that their parents took them for psychiatric care when they were children because their behavior was so bad – and they were at the time being abused by a relative or a baby-sitter. Abuse, trouble with peers at school, an unreasonable new teacher, the death of a relative or a pet, a friend moving away, a new step-parent – all these changes in a child's life can upset him and affect his behavior for the worse.

If a parent discovers the event which is the antecedent of the behavior, it may or may not be possible to correct it. Even if the event is past and can't be corrected, it can be acknowledged. Step-parents can learn to relate to a child in a way which makes their integration into the family smooth rather than difficult. Whether or not the situation can be changed, it is important to recognize the feelings the child is experiencing, and to validate those feelings and help the child express them in an appropriate manner.

Oh no, not again!

Jason's parents consulted me because at age three, his behavior had suddenly become impossible. He was having daily temper tantrums and refusing to leave the house when his parents wanted to take him out. I asked what had changed in his life recently. The only thing was that his grandmother, whom he loved, was visiting. I asked what had happened the last time his grandmother visited. That turned out to be the time the family was about to move. Grandma had looked after Jason while his parents packed up everything he owned and they moved across the country and lived in a hotel room for three months before they got their own home again. Grandma's arrival had signaled to Jason that they might be going to move again and he'd have to live in a strange place without his familiar bed or toys. Once we had it figured out, Jason's parents told him that Grandma was just visiting, she would go back to her own home soon, and they were not moving again. His behavior immediately became manageable again. -- *Alison Miller*

Apply Your Knowledge

- Think of a problematic behavior of your child that came on suddenly. Can you think of anything that happened just before the behavior started?
- What experiences has your child had which could have caused her stress?
- How can you help your child cope with this stress?

5 - Other People Can Be Triggers

What Family Members Do

The family (Dad, Mom, 10-year-old Julie and six-year-old sister Krista) are having dinner. Dad is eating like a pig: grabbing food, reaching across other people's plates, and chewing with his mouth open. As he does this, he is giving orders to Mom to get things for him and to discipline Julie for her poor eating habits, which are directly copied from Dad's. Krista is kicking Julie under the table, while complaining about Julie's eating habits and remarking on how good she herself is being. Mom is scurrying around trying to please everyone, responding positively to Krista who is showing off. Finally, in response to extreme provocation, Julie hits Krista. Dad gets up and screams at Julie, "Get to your room and stay there!"

Why do you think Julie hit Krista? You might have done the same thing in the same situation. The behavior of each family member contributed to provoking her outburst. And, in addition, it was probably a relief for Julie to be sent to her room.

Although obvious from the outside, it is much more difficult to figure out the reasons for our own family members' behavior, since we are part of the situation in which they occur. We also tend to regard the behavior as belonging entirely to the person, rather than looking at the aspects of the situation which helped to cause the behavior.

Now that you have analyzed why Julie hit Krista, what would you do to change such behavior in the future? Many parents would try to solve the problem by punishing, but experience tells us that it just wouldn't work! Julie is already being punished by the situation so adding another punishment could make her behavior worse.

Perhaps other parents would try to reward her for behaving better. This would have a better chance of success but the reward would have to be a very good one to counteract all the factors contributing to Julie's behavior.

In this family dinner, each person present – through behavior and words – contributed to the older girl's hitting her sister. Several different triggers combined to make it very difficult for Julie not to hit her sister.

We shall look in later chapters and in our other book – *The Parent-Child Connection* – at how to deal with sibling conflict and other distressing family interactions. At this point we just need to recognize that behavior is often triggered by other people's behavior.

Apply Your Knowledge

- Often sibling rivalry happens because kids don't have their own space or their sibling takes their things. What do you notice triggering fights among brothers and sisters in your family?

Having a Bad Day?

Why do you always choose to be obnoxious when I'm having a bad day?

Do you ever notice that when you are having a bad day, your kids just can't leave you alone? You may think or even say to your child, "Why can't you behave yourself when I'm having a hard day?"

An important way of changing the antecedents of a child's misbehavior is to change our own "triggering" behavior. A child's noncompliance may be triggered by the parent making a demand which the child finds unreasonable – for example, insisting that the child take out the garbage RIGHT NOW, five minutes before the child's hour-long television program ends. An older child may pick a fight with a younger child if a parent has picked on him. We tend to be very aware of the effects of children's behavior on us, but unfortunately much less aware of the effects of our own behavior on our children.

Often we treat them with much less courtesy than we expect of them. If your child's negative behavior is occurring regularly in response to a behavior of your own, it makes sense to help him change his behavior by changing your own behavior.

Parents often punish a child's misbehavior without recognizing all the important antecedents that led to that behavior. Then they are surprised when the discipline attempt doesn't work. It is most important to understand a behavior thoroughly before you attempt to correct it, or you may do harm to the child even when you successfully get him to change his behavior. For example, a child's misbehavior may be a result of his being abused outside the home, and if he's punished for the behavior he won't disclose the abuse. Or a child may be having legitimate strong feelings about a situation and feel rejected when the parent won't listen, as in the following story.

A Temper Problem?

Ross, a 10-year-old client of mine, was described by his mother, Linda, as having "a problem with his temper". One day Linda came to see me and reported that she and her new boyfriend had successfully cured Ross of his temper outbursts. They were using the consequence of walking out and leaving him alone when he had a tantrum. This sounded just fine until I talked with Ross. Crying bitterly, he told me that he had been angry about all kinds of unreasonable demands by Linda's new boyfriend. He had been expressing justified feelings, which had been interpreted as "bad" behavior. Linda and her boyfriend had triggered Ross' angry behavior by their unreasonable treatment of him, then interpreted his protests as misbehavior. Ross just couldn't win! His temper outbursts had stopped, since he was afraid of severe reprisals, but he was building up a level of internal anger and unhappiness which would create more serious problems for the whole family. *-- Alison Miller*

Apply Your Knowledge

- Is your child overly sensitive to your stress?
- When your child yells at you, or is rude to you, observe how you have just behaved. Did you yell or act rudely first?
- How could you deal with your own stress and frustration without treating your child in ways which cause him to act out?

Repetitive Family Patterns and Cycles

Interactions in distressed families tend to become repetitive, as each family member tries to find balance in his or her own way. Those who have studied distressed marriages find that there is always a cycle of behavior to which both spouses contribute, usually with one angrily pursuing and the other withdrawing. Emotionally-focused couple therapy works on changing this pattern and getting each partner to express his or her underlying feelings and needs directly.

Patterns become established in entire families, not just in couples. For example, fights between siblings often follow a predictable course, and seem impossible to stop once they are started. Even though each family member knows exactly what will happen, because it has happened many times, it still goes on. To change these patterns it is necessary to recognize them and consciously step out of them.   Unhappy patterns result from people feeling unheard and rejected, and communicating their needs indirectly. Couple and family therapy both work at replacing these dysfunctional patterns with direct non-blaming communication and empathic listening.

Need for Parental Attention

As a parent I (Allison Rees) have noticed times when my children's behavior is problematic. My daughter may be disagreeable, misbehaving, or withdrawn. Then I ask myself, "How much time have she and I had together lately?" Being an extrovert, she generally likes to be with someone doing something, especially with me. She wakes up in the morning and says, "I missed you last night. I never get to spend time with you." I think, "How could you? You were sleeping!"

Before I react, I have to ask myself what she is talking about. My perception is that I am already feeling spread too thin. I volunteered in her class yesterday, and I took her and the gang out Saturday. How much of me does she need? Then I realize she didn't really have me to herself during those activities. If my objective is to spend time sharing and communicating with her I need to think about what kinds of activities might facilitate this. Thank goodness she is past the playground stage! Heaven knows I could never climb through those brightly colored plastic tubes again with any real dignity!

What she needs is the experience of being alone with me in the moment, together. It isn't always planned. It might happen when she is helping me make dinner and chatting about how much her friends bug her at school. It might be having me in her room with the door closed while she dances for me and sings a (way too grown up) song to her latest CD. Sometimes it's having me in the room working on my computer while she watches a show, just being together. If we don't have these kinds of exchanges, her behavior lets me know.

My son becomes reactive and more sensitive when we don't get our time together. We have a mother/son book that we read a few nights a week. We play squash together and share music as well. What really counts for him is the time we spend talking. He needs to process his thoughts and experiences with me in order to keep them from building up.

In this busy world time passes by much too quickly. If we were to sort out our priorities we would all probably say the most valuable way we can spend time is to be with our loved ones.

What is Quality Time?

I (Allison Rees) have come to dislike the phrase 'quality time'. Too often when life was busy, I found myself being overindulgent with my children, splurging on lunch and a movie and whatever else we could find to spend money on, thinking that this would be quality time. Often we would go out and the kids would end up fighting: one would throw up from too much pop and the other one wouldn't like the movie or would fall asleep before the second act of a play. One look at my empty wallet would start me down the slide into a puddle of resentment. When I explored this, I realized that having a genuine encounter would be much more valuable to my children and me.

Presence Not Presents

It is important to spend time with your child doing something that you both enjoy. It's hard for some parents to sit down with Barbie dolls and have a genuine encounter with their child. But you can still go for walks to the park, play video games, or share novels and board games which are fun for you as well as your child. Your child will feel the difference and so will you.

Schedule time to be with your kids and stick to it. Nightly routines with each child, even 15 minutes of focused time, are a great way to stay connected. When your children are older you may need to make dates. Make this time a priority. Let your child take the lead and come up with ideas. Make this a time free of criticism or demands. Be available just to listen, and have things to do – playing cards or a board game – in case they feel put 'on the spot' and don't want to talk.

If you have more than one child, make sure you have one-on-one time with each child, rather than just time with all the children together. One of the advantages of co-parenting with an ex is that you can have one child while your ex has the other(s). Of course, married people can do this too – if they think of it.

Time with Them Matters

Spending time with our children tells them they matter. Last night at bedtime I (Allison Rees) was sitting on the floor with my daughter while she was doing her math. My mind started to wander off to my work when suddenly I realized how precious this time was. In looking at her profile, I could see every little hair on her face as the light shone from behind her. I was struck with the awareness that one day I would look back and miss these years.

It is so important to make the most of our time in the here and now. I felt so grateful to be her Mom and realized that all those other things on my mind could be pushed aside because nothing about work comes close to how important my kids are to me. Surely, I could give her all of me for that short time. Some parents don't know how to be with their children and just play with them or 'hang out'. If your own parents didn't do this with you, but worked and ignored you, or made you work too, you probably will have difficulty playing with your children.

The key is to let the children themselves take the lead. Don't try to direct their play, just be with them and let them involve you in playing or listening or watching, as they choose. Be *available* to them.

If you give your children lots of attention and show them that you enjoy their company, they won't need to engage in negative attention-getting.

Apply Your Knowledge

- Do you have regular times that you spend connecting with your child?
- If you have more than one child how do you juggle the demands for your time?
- Spending time with your child can often mean letting your child take the lead, whether playing, hiking or making decisions about what to do. Is there something that you both enjoy doing and that your child can take the lead in?
- Older kids may not want to spend as much time with you. How can you still have a genuine encounter?

Negative Attention-Getting Behavior

Because all human beings need attention, our children will seek attention from us and will relish whatever they can get, even if it is negative. Children are quick to figure this out. Behaviors such as sibling rivalry, whining, swearing, or bugging are often (though not always) designed for our attention. It makes sense to recognize which behaviors are designed to get negative attention, and remove that attention as much as we can.

The dinner table is the classic scene where parents fret about how much food the child eats and the child tends to refuse food to get attention if his parents respond to this. Many food problems are eliminated when the parents remove the attention and allow the child to take control of his own body.

We have had parents report that their children go into shock when they hand the food responsibility over to them. Parents simply provide healthy food and a pleasant atmosphere in which to eat. It is the child's responsibility to decide how much she wants to eat.

Whining is another example of behavior designed to get attention. The high pitch makes it nearly impossible to ignore. Whining seems to have developed for children's survival. If they didn't cry loudly or whine how much attention would we actually give them? Babies, of course, can't use words to communicate so they let you know they are distressed or have needs by crying. Some children continue to use this when they are older and quite capable of using clear words and making requests. But if they know the whining grates on us and gets immediate attention, they may continue it for years.

You can tell your child that this kind of voice is 'whining' and teach her that she will get better results if she asks for things with a 'big voice'. When your child uses the big voice you praise her and give her attention. When she whines you can turn your back and get busy doing something else so as not to reward the whining. Ignoring negative attention-getting behavior is technically called 'extinction' by behavioral psychologists (not to be confused with what happened to the dinosaurs).

Remember however that your child can experience your turning your back as a punishment rather than just neutral behavior. You need to make sure she knows that she will get results by asking directly rather than whining, so that she doesn't feel punished or abandoned.

Some temper tantrums are designed to get attention and are not just expressions of emotional overload. The cartoon on the next page shows me (Alison Miller) when my son Justin was having a temper tantrum in the park. I suspected it was for attention, and this was confirmed when an old friend came up and talked to me. I took my attention away from Justin's tantrum to talk with the friend, and the tantrum stopped.

Above all we have to remember that receiving attention is a basic human need, and ignoring children is abusive if it isn't counter-balanced with love, praise, affection and attention. We can ignore the behavior of a child yet respond to the needs of the child by asking ourselves about the need behind the behavior.

When you remove your attention, prepare to be tested! The behavior will get worse before it gets better. Don't give up – it just takes time.

Hook, Line and Sinker

One night at dinner my daughter really got my attention. She was doing the "I'm stupid, you don't care about me, nobody loves me" song with the most incredible whine in her voice. And because I was teaching a lot of classes and I was feeling guilty for being absent for three evenings that week, I bought into it hook, line, and sinker.

My son pointed out her negative attention-getting behavior (which made me feel even more vulnerable). When we discussed it, he was right. Our kids don't miss much, do they? She was using this negative behavior for attention and I was giving it to her. He offered to signal me the next time he saw me get hooked, before she could reel me in!

I had to decline his offer as this would be playing favorites. After all, I am the parent, aren't I? It really is tough being a parent, especially when your kids have read the parenting books too!

This is a good example because it is very clear that underneath my daughter's behavior was a strong feeling and need. Not all negative attention-getting behaviors point to such an obvious need but this one certainly did.

She wasn't yet old enough to identify her feelings and say, "Hey Mom, I'm acting out because I need more of your time. You haven't been very present this week." -- *Allison Rees*

You can ignore negative behavior passively or actively. Passive ignoring is when you do nothing. As far as you are concerned it didn't happen. Your child may swear to get a reaction and you simply pretend you didn't hear it. Without its expected impact, it will not be rewarded, so it may not be repeated (though swearing is complicated because other people reward it with attention even if you don't).

Active ignoring is actually turning your body away and looking in another direction. In some cases you need to be even more active and leave the room. Sometimes focusing on another activity or allowing yourself to be distracted helps you to ignore the behavior.

Ignoring negative behavior works well only if you make sure to give attention for positive behavior, especially when the positive behavior is an alternative to the negative behavior you are trying to ignore. For example, you might ignore a child if she is whining but praise her and give her attention when she speaks assertively. This can turn behavior around but again, it almost always gets worse before it gets better.

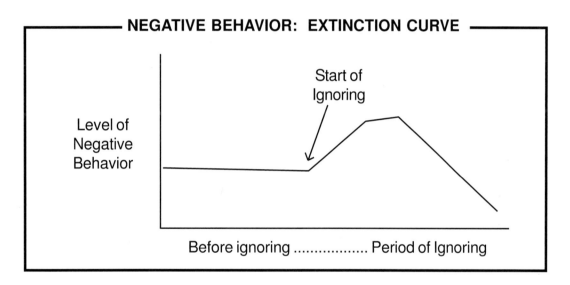

NEGATIVE BEHAVIOR: EXTINCTION CURVE

Start of Ignoring

Level of Negative Behavior

Before ignoring .... Period of Ignoring

The above diagram shows the 'Extinction Curve' – when ignored, negative behavior (whining or swearing or fighting) gets worse before it gets better. But if you continue to ignore the behavior long enough, it decreases in frequency and even stops. It's important to remember this and not give up. We don't for a moment suggest you apply this technique to your child's genuine needs. Babies whose parents don't respond when they cry eventually learn not to cry. But they also learn that no one will come when they let their needs be known, and this is not a lesson we want our children to learn.

Start paying attention to where you are putting your energy. Is it toward positive or negative behaviors? Can you ignore negative attention-getting behaviors and turn your focus toward the positive?

Parenting Pointers

We can put the brakes on negative attention-getting behavior by:
- ♦ validating our children's feelings and encouraging them to speak assertively
- ♦ meeting the needs of the child
- ♦ ignoring negative behavior rather than giving it negative attention.

Apply Your Knowledge

- Do you tend to focus on the negative behavior of your child?
- Which behavior can you ignore?
- What does it teach your child if you don't ignore attention-getting behavior?
- Parents often have a sense of whether the tantrum their child is having is designed for attention or comes from frustrated needs. If your child has temper tantrums, do you understand the reason for them? How could you figure this out?
- How would you deal with a tantrum that comes from frustration and a need for the child to have her needs heard?
- How would you deal with a tantrum that comes from attention-getting or trying to get you to give in to an unreasonable demand?

Catch Your Kids Doing Something Right

We all like to be acknowledged for what we do, and especially for what we do well. Why don't our family members say to us, "I notice you turned out the bathroom light" instead of "You left the light on again." Okay, that might be a bit much, but when your child or spouse does something positive, he'd appreciate your noticing it. Be careful, however, that you aren't being manipulative or insincere, or it will backfire.

We don't suggest that you go into your children's room when they are playing happily together and say, "Hey guys, you sure are getting along right now." That could backfire because they might act out just to prove you wrong. It would be better to wait until you have a quiet time and tell your child that you appreciate the positive atmosphere that he has brought into the house through his consideration of his siblings.

Apply Your Knowledge

- Think of a negative behavior of your child. What is the positive behavior that you want him to produce instead? If he whines, you want him to speak clearly and assertively. If she shouts, you want her to speak quietly. Define the behavior you want.
- Now, make a plan to focus on the positive. What will you say or do when your child produces the positive behavior?

"Okay" is Cooperation

During one difficult stage when my determined daughter was four, I was so desperate for something positive to recognize that I would even acknowledge her cooperation when she said "Okay." She didn't say this very often and nothing else seemed positive during this difficult time.

Was I sincere? Yes! I really did appreciate those "Okays" and I would have loved to have heard more of them! She got to the point where she would say, "Hey Mom, I said Okay!"
-- Allison Rees

It is so important to stop and appreciate the people in your life. Having them is a gift. We watch our kids swell with pride when we just stop and acknowledge them.

Children need positive attention because they need to be affirmed. (See Chapter 1 in *The Parent-Child Connection*).

The more attention and appreciation you give your children, the more they will learn to appreciate positive comments (versus settling for negative attention). Remember that negative comments are very powerful. Set a goal of giving them 10 positives for any one negative.

6 - How to Remove Triggers

Sometimes it is difficult to see past the details, but understanding triggers helps us see the bigger picture. Look beyond the behavior and remember that addressing a trigger is much more effective than implementing a consequence. *This isn't giving in to the child.*

Parents with a toddler often think they need to keep lots of 'no's' around so the child learns the meaning of the word. They keep the plants and fine china out and continue to scold the child. Children are curious about everything and can't resist such temptations. Avoiding these situations isn't spoiling the child in any way. It's recognizing and accepting the child's need to explore and removing powerful temptations. We need to appreciate our children's curiosity rather than curbing it by constantly controlling them.

In this chapter we have discussed many different antecedents or 'triggers' to children's misbehavior. If we can recognize what triggers our children's upsetting behavior (other than behavior which is just plain normal for their age), we can change the behavior by changing the antecedents. This allows us to get out of the cycle of rewarding and punishing behavior; this also helps us to develop empathy for what our children are going through.

Use the following worksheet to develop your awareness of triggers and the circumstances that surround and contribute to your child's behavior. This process isn't meant to find excuses for behavior, but to develop understanding. If our objective is to encourage positive behavior we need to facilitate an environment where this can happen.

Behavior Analysis

Here is a chart to work with. It will help you to understand the behavior of each of your children in specific circumstances.

Child's Name	Behavior Description

Physical Antecedents	Y/N	Solution
Is the child tired?		
Is the child hungry or thirsty?		
Temperamental Antecedents	**Y/N**	**Solution**
Is the child frustrated? Does she need help?		
Is a sensitive child being stressed by the environment? Lights? Noise? Sock seams?		
Has a slow-approach child been hurried into a new activity or place or meeting new people?		
Has a regular child's routine been disrupted?		
Has an active child had time to 'burn off steam'?		
Has a non-adaptable child been hurried through a transition or surprised?		
Is the behavior typical of an intense child?		
Other?		

Maturity & Expectations	Y/N	Solution
Is the child mature enough to resist temptation or is the temptation too strong?		
Are your expectations suitable for the age, temperament, and development of the child?		
Discipline	**Y/N**	**Solution**
Are limits concerning the behavior clear and consistent?		
Has the child participated in defining consequences?		
Is the child getting enough freedom? Is the behavior an attempt to increase his freedom?		
Parental Attention & Behavior	**Y/N**	**Solution**
Has the child spent enough time with you to satisfy his need for positive attention?		
Does the child need affection?		
Have you been too focused on negative behavior?		
Can you describe your child's positive traits and gifts? Have you told your child recently that you appreciate him?		
How is your own behavior affecting the situation? Have your needs for rest and relaxation been met?		

Triggers?	Y/N	Solution
Does the behavior happen at a particular time?		
Has an event (move, illness, loss, death, divorce, school change) happened that triggered the behavior?		
Does the behavior occur at a particular place? What can you do to prepare for places full of temptations or other triggers?		
Is the behavior of other family members contributing to the behavior?		
What can you do to plan ahead for the impact of triggers that cannot be avoided?		

Apply Your Knowledge

● Identify a behavior of your child that has remained difficult despite attempts to change it through consequences. _____

● How long has the behavior been present? Can you identify any possible antecedents?

_____

_____

● What possible changes in antecedents could be made to deal with the behavior? _____

_____

● Have you removed attention from your child's negative behavior this week? If so, how has it been replaced in a positive way? _____

_____

● What phrases can you use with your child to recognize positive behavior and express your unconditional love for him or her? _____

_____

Further Reading

Greene, Ross. *The Explosive Child.*
    Quill (2001)

Kersey, Katharine. *Helping Your Child Handle Stress.*
    New York: Berkley, 1986

Miller, Alice.

    The Drama of The Gifted Child.
    New York: Basic Books, 1983

    For Your Own Good.
    Farrar, Straus & Giroux, 1990

    Thou Shalt Not Be Aware: Society's betrayal of the child.
    Farrar, Straus & Giroux, 1998

    All of Miller's books are translated from German.

5

The Freedom of Responsibility:

Helping Children Develop Responsibility

Do we want our children to be blindly obedient, or do we want them to become mature, responsible human beings? Children don't develop responsibility through obedience; they develop it by learning to take responsibility for various aspects of their lives.

In this chapter we explain how to gradually turn over specific responsibilities to your children as they mature. We think it's important to distinguish between 'kid issues' (which should be a child's own responsibility) and 'family issues' (which affect other family members).

For kid issues we recommend that you allow your child to experience the natural consequences of his decisions. For example, if your child (who is older than nine) forgets to take his lunch to school, he simply misses his lunch; you don't drive to the school and deliver it. If a teenager doesn't do his homework before bedtime he can choose between staying up late to do it or getting a bad grade; we don't suggest interfering by doing the work for him, punishing him, or making him go to bed.

In this chapter we explore household responsibilities for children of various ages; we cover such topics as self care, money management, and homework. These are areas in which a child learns to become increasingly responsible.

Responsibility is a word loaded with expectations and often included in long lectures about moral standards. All parents want their children to become responsible, but what does this mean and how do we hand over responsibility so that our children will accept it and become self-motivated?

We need to begin by understanding what we want for our children. Do we want them to be blindly obedient or do we want them to become mature, responsible human beings? The road to mature responsibility does not lead through obedience; it leads through being in touch with feelings, developing empathy, and learning to understand what other people feel and need, making one's own decisions and experiencing the results of those decisions.

1 - The Importance of Choice

The happiest people in the world are people who have choices in their lives. We all want to be in control of ourselves. It is for this reason that the ability to make their own choices is very important to our children.

The ability to make decisions comes gradually. Young children can make simple either/or choices, while hopefully adults are able to examine many alternatives and their consequences before deciding on a course of action. It will help our children grow if we allow them to make progressively complex choices as they move toward adulthood.

Choices Show Respect

No one likes to be controlled; it goes against the core of our being. We will resist and rebel and become angry when we are not allowed to decide things for ourselves. Why would we think children are any different from adults in their need to be self-directed?

Anyone will become unreasonable when they feel imposed upon.

If we let go of control we will be happier people ourselves. The load feels lighter when we stop carrying somebody else's responsibilities and stop worrying about what people will think.

Giving kids choices and respecting their needs and feelings pay big dividends: it helps them form an identity and figure out who they are. They may try out various identities over the years, all on the way to choosing who they want to be.

Kids whose choices are respected know they are loved as separate and unique individuals.

Apply Your Knowledge

● Reflect back to your own childhood. Can you think of a person who treated you with respect? Was there someone who asked for your ideas about things and regarded them as worth considering? Do you remember how it made you feel? Do you remember how you felt about that person?

Choices Give Control

Choices are very important for children because they:

♦ provide children an opportunity to exercise their judgement
♦ help children develop a sense of self
♦ enable children to learn about consequences
♦ allow children to have some control over themselves

When our children resist taking responsibility (e.g. for household chores), it often isn't because they want to resist doing chores, it's because of our approach. If we offer them choices as to when to do what, they will be far more likely to co-operate.

Avoid giving choices as manipulation or threats. For example, "Do your homework or go to bed!" is not an empowering choice! Instead ask, "Would you like to do your homework at 4:30 or after dinner at 6:30?"

Autonomy (self-determination) is developed through decision-making, says Bruno Bettelheim. Unfortunately, many parents do not permit their children enough participation in family decisions or important decisions about their own lives. As Bettelheim writes (*The Informed Heart,* p.72): "Whether in childhood or adulthood if one finds it impossible, first to influence one's social and physical environment, and later to make decisions on how and when to modify it, this is harmful if not devastating to the human personality." In short, Dr. Bettelheim says that our ability to make decisions wastes away when it isn't used. Drs. Jordan and Margaret Paul agree:

"Since emotional and spiritual growth is dependent on becoming more personally responsible, anything that promotes a child taking personal responsibility is loving. (...) Allowing children to handle their problems, with guidance when asked for, conveys the message that you have faith in them. That's the loving way to help them grow into self-respecting, personally responsible adults."

Realizing we are contributing to our children's spiritual growth when we stop doing their laundry for them makes it a little easier to shed the old stereotypes of how loving mothers act. We guess this also means that dad has to put his shotgun away when his daughter starts to date. But before we put the laundry basket and parental gun away, we need to acknowledge that there are many lessons which must be taught before we hand over total responsibility. Responsibility has to be taught in stages.

Think of all the different areas where children will have to learn to take responsibility: personal care (keeping clean, being physically active), money management, personal safety, social skills, expressing anger, meal preparation. Children need to be given opportunities to learn these skills and take responsibility for them. As we teach these skills we have to

The Twins

Years ago, I had a friend with identical twin boys. At the age of eight, their feet were huge, especially in high-top running shoes. Their legs were like beanpoles with large, knobby knees. Their bodies were long and lanky and they had long, thin faces. They wanted to get their hair cut and their mother had no problem letting them decide what style they wanted. I really admired this woman for her attitude.

The boys announced to the two stylists that they wanted a haircut just like their father's. A true compliment to Dad, whom they obviously admired. Their father, however, was in his mid-forties and was bald with a little hair around the side-- you know the look. The stylists checked with my friend and she quoted Barbara Coloroso: "It's not life threatening and it's not morally threatening and it will grow back."

Out came the razors and off came the hair, buzzed on top with a little left on the sides. Their heads looked more pointed and shinier than you can imagine. They looked at each other and, feeling very pleased with their choice, gave themselves a big high five. "Wow, you look great! Cool!" As they set foot onto Shelbourne (a very busy street), my friend swears she could hear the squeal of braking tires! Old ladies would go by and look at them sadly, assuming they had some strange disease; little kids would just point and say, "Look at the weird heads on those guys!"

I love this story because these kids tried something new and had a strong enough sense of self to go there. Pretty soon the novelty wore off and they got a little tired of the attention. By the time these guys are teenagers, they will be able to say, "Been there, done that." They have had practice at thinking and trying out different hats (so to speak) and isn't that great?

-- *Allison Rees*

keep in mind that our purpose is to help our children become young adults who can manage their own lives and treat others with care and respect.

Apply Your Knowledge

- What is your child presently responsible for?
- How do you include children in your daily tasks?
- Think of a time when you let a child take a new responsibility for the first time. How did it turn out?
- What new responsibility is your child ready to take on?
- What kind of instruction is needed for your child to be able to do this well?

---

2 - Teaching Responsibility

A method which we call **The Level System** will guide you as you teach responsible behavior to your children. Children start at Level 0 and progress through to Level 3. When you are aware of their level it enables you to guide your children more effectively.

Level 0: Watch and Learn

WHY DO YOU ALWAYS YELL WHEN YOU WANT SOMETHING? NOW I WANT YOU TO ASK NICELY FOR THINGS.

At the earliest level (level 0) the child may be too young to take the task on by himself, yet he may be interested in participating. Although the parent has full responsibility for the task, she allows her child the joy of being included. If Dad is working on the car, he can let his five-year-old watch and ask some questions, and maybe let her hold a tool or two.

While I (Allison Rees) was writing material for my parenting course my daughter (then 11 years old) commented on how much time I spend on the computer before I give a course. It wasn't a complaint; she was curious. I took about 10 minutes to show her how I scanned in cartoons and formatted text. She thought it was cool and got excited at the prospect of making extra money by doing some of this for me. While that day was a long way off, she developed a better understanding of my work and got to watch me exercise my responsibility.

Children learn from example, so watching parents is an important step to learning new behaviors and taking on responsibility. They learn to talk by listening to us. When I tried to figure out why so many kids talk baby talk, the answer surprised me: Children learn much of their baby talk from their parents! It's we who put the "ie" in "horsie" or "doggie."

Children do what they see us do, in just about every area of behavior. I guess that explains why my daughter started cursing when she had trouble with her computer game!

I'm afraid not, son, you're too little. Go and see what your mother's doing.

Daddy, can I help you?

So including children is important and children want to be part of our daily tasks. Young children will mimic us and play with pots and pans and use the vacuum cleaner. They want to learn to do what we do, and they naturally learn from our example.

Son, come here and I'll teach you about baseball.

I'm afraid not, Daddy. I'm too little and I have to go and see what Mommy's doing.

Of course, we can't allow a three-year-old to drive a car but we can allow him to help with cooking or putting the laundry away. Young children are very eager to help us with things. If we reject their interest in our daily tasks (which we tend to do because we are in a hurry), we make them feel rejected and we destroy their interest in the very tasks we will later want them to do!

The best time to teach a new task is when a child expresses an interest in it. Taking the time now is a huge investment for later. The fact that parents are too rushed and busy to do this is one of the reasons kids don't take on responsibility.

If the task you're doing is one that your child will soon be old enough to do, you can explain what you're doing as you do it, so your child can understand what's involved. Use language which is simple enough for your child to understand. Perhaps he can help you with a small part of the task you are doing – hold the dustpan while you sweep the dust into it, or stir the batter of the pancake mix, or fold the towels from the dryer.

146

Level 1: Practice with Help

At level one, the parent gradually hands over responsibility to the child for a specific task, giving explicit instructions. It is important to let the child know what your expectations are so she will have a clear understanding of what you are trying to teach her. Of course kids do not automatically know how to do things when they get to a certain age!

How often we ask a child something without giving him adequate instruction! This just sets him up for failure.

Doing dishes, for example, is a lot more complicated than it looks. (1) We need the right water temperature. (2) We wash the glasses first. (3) We rinse them. (4) The plates have to be washed, top and bottom. (5) It really helps if we soak the pots before we even start the dishes. Taking the time to explain this (at level 1) can save the child from criticism later. It may take a few lessons before he learns the skill but the first few times can be considered a practice run!

This way of teaching can be applied to any new responsibility: spending money, street safety, manners, social responsibility, or driving a car. Any new responsibility requires explicit teaching and practicing until the child feels confident.

Remember to be open to your children's ideas of how to do things and watch that the standards you are setting aren't too high. (If you are a perfectionist in certain areas, it isn't fair to expect the same of your children.)

In *The 7 Habits of Highly Effective People* (pp. 173, 179), Stephen Covey has this to say:

> "There are basically two kinds of delegation: 'gofer delegation' and 'stewardship delegation'. Stewardship delegation is based on a paradigm of appreciation of the self-awareness, the imagination, the conscience, and the free will of other people. (...) The steward becomes his own boss, governed by a conscience that contains the commitment to agreed upon desired results. (...) With immature people, you specify fewer desired results and more guidelines, identify more resources, conduct more frequent accountability interviews, and apply more immediate consequences."

It is important not to make evaluative comments when a child is performing a task — just give feedback. When a child feels judged, even if it's positively, he tends to become self-critical, as shown in the cartoon on the next page.

The father in the cartoon intends to praise the child, but the effect was to teach the child to evaluate himself as 'good' or 'bad' rather than enjoy accomplishing his tasks. Praise can backfire when it involves evaluation rather than just observation and appreciation.

Good boy!

Apply Your Knowledge

- How could you give helpful feedback without evaluating your child?

Good boy!

Acknowledge the feelings of your child whenever she is facing a new or difficult situation. Although learning how to wash the dishes might not generate much fear, learning to walk to school on her own can, even if she has been asking to do it for a while.

Good boy!

Part of having a secure identity is believing that we have the capacity to deal with everyday realities. Parents who overprotect their children don't give them this confidence.

We need to prepare our children to deal with such big issues as rejection, grief, loss, criticism and pain. Talking to our children about the realities of life and acknowledging their fears helps them develop the courage and confidence they need to take on new tasks.

Bad boy!

Take, for example, a visit to the dentist for a filling. The child may be afraid that it will hurt. Rather than assuring her that it won't, agree with her that it may hurt a bit, but it will prevent more pain in the future from a rotten tooth. Listen to her worries, and express your confidence in her bravery and her ability to stand a little pain when the treatment is for her own good.

Often our own fears get in the way and we model them to our children. Very fearful children usually learn fear from a parent who has been fearful or overprotective.

Level 2: Guidance and Feedback

Reminder:

Once your child has learned how to do the task, he may need some guidance until he is ready to take it on completely. This might mean reminding him of the task, especially if it is a "family issue" which affects everybody. As we said earlier, reminding is different from nagging. Reminding is non-judgmental and it gives the child a chance to think for himself first. You can ask your child whether he needs a reminder.

Review the Steps:

This is helpful in areas like baby-sitting. A child goes through a period of instruction before taking on the responsibility. At the end of the teaching, there is an opportunity to review what has been learned. Reviewing the steps helps both the child and the parent feel confident. With less important matters the child can simply practice on her own until she feels she has mastered the skill. Some things just take time and hands-on experience.

Don't take over:

Taking over for a child can discourage her. If we respect the child's struggle and wait patiently rather than hurrying her up or taking over, she will gather the courage to see the job through on her own. If she becomes discouraged while trying, offer help rather than taking over.

Level 3: Letting Go

When the child can take the responsibility on without any supervision or reminders, he is at level 3. It is important to identify this stage because it keeps us, the parents, from nagging and taking over a child's responsibility. In the cartoon on the next page, the mother is refusing to respond to the grandmother's hints that she should be taking over for the child.

Parents can give their children two very important things at this stage: 1) room to make choices; and 2) trust in their abilities. Let them exercise their thinking power and be careful not to over-protect and coerce. If they are at this stage and you have gone through the appropriate levels of teaching and support – let go.

Accept a child's unique way of doing things as well as her own unique sense of time. When you let go, you are appreciating that people do things differently than you do.

Apply Your Knowledge

- What responsibilities did you take on when you were growing up?
- Considering the ages of your children, what responsibilities do you think they need to start owning?
- What gets in the way of your children assuming responsibilities?
- How do you teach your children to take on tasks? Does the level system work for you?

Trusting My Kids

My son (then 13) went downtown with a friend. We had gone together many times and I had talked to him over the years about various things to watch out for. He had made independent trips before so it would have been insulting to go through 'the rules'. He was a level 3. My daughter (then 11) left five minutes later to go to the mall (down the street) with her (12-year-old) friend. She was at a level 2. We talked about some 'what if's' and I asked the girls questions about how they would handle certain situations. Both felt confident and excited about their new experience (she had my cell phone!). She accepted the questions and the pep talk because it made her feel safe and cared for. Most of all, she felt trustworthy. My last question was: "Why am I letting you go by yourself?" Her reply was with a questioning tone: "Because I am responsible?" "Yes, you deserve to have this freedom." The situation can always be examined again if things don't go according to plan.

One more thing I found interesting: my daughter and her friend decided to tidy up the house that morning without my asking. She knew I was busy writing and she wanted to contribute. When I got home from work the house was very orderly. I was enthusiastic without gushing (I think) – "Look at this house! The furniture is shining, the dishes are put away, there is no clutter. It feels so organized in our house now. Thank you so much!"

I really believe that if I had been in the habit of giving rewards or punishments for housework done or not done, my daughter would never have taken such initiative. At least, not for the same reasons. It was an inside job! I didn't have to pay her or nag her.

-- Allison Rees

Bag those lunches!

Our day got off to an ugly start. The kids were complaining about their lunches and didn't let us know what they would or wouldn't eat. It was so frustrating. It felt so unpleasant to drop my kids off at school on a sour note.

When I picked them up after school we headed for the park with some snacks and began the process of negotiating the lunch issue. We did some brainstorming and came up with a great idea. They wanted total responsibility for their lunches. They wanted to shop for them and make them. Could I live with that? YES!!!

Off we went to the grocery store. They each got their own little basket and went their own way (ages eight and 10). I had my shopping cart and no kids, which was kind of fun. I spied on my daughter as she stood at the deli counter asking for 100 grams of "have-farti" cheese and passed my son in the juice aisle with a wink. Every now and then, they would chase me down asking if an item was okay.

Going through the check-out, we made the teller's day. Both the kids unloaded their own basket and put dividers between their loads and between their loads and mine. I arranged it so that each child had their own food bag and their own shelf at home. They each got a little basket in the fridge for their perishables.

[continued on next page]

[continued from previous page]

In the morning they were ecstatic. They worked like bees putting their lunches together. It was amazing for my husband and me to sit and read the paper on a school morning! My daughter even came to me once, kissed me on the cheek and said, "Thanks, Mom! I'm so proud!" Trying to look as if I was really worthy of that gratitude, I lowered my eyebrows and said, "No problem," hiding behind my paper with a grin from ear to ear.

I learned that it was important to keep my mouth shut. One morning I noticed my daughter putting very little in her lunch bag. I wanted to say something but I knew she would be sensitive to feedback because she felt so capable. Sure enough, the next day she said, "I have to put more in today – I was starving yesterday." Making lunches has been their job ever since. I help out occasionally by doing their shopping for them or helping them pour hot soup into a thermos.

I talked with the kids a few weeks after they assumed responsibility for their lunches because I wanted to put this level system into practice. I explained what each level represented and then asked the kids what level they were at with their lunches. My daughter immediately barked out "level 3!" My son, however, said, "I think I am still at a level 2. I get kind of distracted with other things sometimes when I am making my lunch." "What do you need?", I asked him. "Just a little help now and then."

-- *Allison Rees*

3 - Natural Consequences

Natural consequences are what will happen to the child if the parent doesn't interfere by nagging, lecturing or rescuing. If a child experiences the natural consequences of his actions, he learns that whatever happens to him is the result of his own decisions. This is an important lesson.

Logical consequences are actions taken by parents or teachers in response to a child's behavior. We will discuss them in detail in Chapter 7.

Natural consequences are the most powerful tool for promoting self-discipline and responsibility in our children. If we allow our child to experience the consequence of her own acts, we provide an honest and real learning situation. In this section we focus on how to allow a child to experience natural consequences; again, such experience is the most effective way for any child to learn and to develop self-discipline. Parents in courses often say, "You keep telling us what we can't do. What can we do?" Please note: not nagging, not rescuing, and not lecturing is doing something! When you try allowing natural consequences to occur, you'll understand why we say this is not a passive act!

Parents need to let go and yet support in such a way that the support doesn't prevent their child from experiencing. We need to look at responsibility and ownership in our relationships with everyone, not just our children. We must start to ask ourselves where our responsibility ends and our children's begins.

Age is the first consideration. Is your child old enough to understand her responsibilities? This is something that needs continual assessment and reassessment as our children grow.

> **Healthy parenting is as much about what you don't do, as about what you do! Doing nothing can be very difficult. It is not a passive act.**
>
>

Learning the Law of Cold...

I remember when my daughter Emily was about two. She was standing at the back door wearing only a diaper. It was a cold, wet November day. First, I gave her information by saying, "When it is cold outside, our bodies need clothing to stay warm." What does a two-year-old do when she wants something and she is persistent? You guessed it. "I WANNA GO OUTSIDE NOW, I WANNA GO OUTSIDE, WAAAAHHHH." At that point, I wanted her to go outside too! It was hard to let her go out because I was a little worried; no, not that she would catch a cold... that my neighbor would see what a horrible mother I was. And I really wasn't sure that Emily was old enough to understand about cold and clothing.

I shut the door and waited. Thirty seconds later I heard a little knock. When I opened the door, she had started to scream that she was cold and needed her "fweater". The experience of being cold had taught her far more than my words could.

How could I have taken this big "aha" away from her and claimed ownership of the solution? By lecturing with an "I told you so". Believe me, all this does is demean the child and stop her from learning. "I told you to wear clothes. You should listen to me more often. Now get in here and get some clothes on!"

So rather than lecturing with "I told you so" or turning it into a punishment I simply said, "What do you need?" If Emily was too young to understand this and stayed outside, naturally I would have gone out to get her, but at least she was given an opportunity to make a choice and experience a natural consequence. It doesn't mean that we didn't go through this again. Of course we did – it takes time to learn the natural laws of life.

-- Allison Rees

Don't Nag:

Nagging, which we have already discussed, is one way of preventing children from experiencing and learning from natural consequences. If a child is told 'what to do when' he doesn't experience what happens if he doesn't carry out his responsibilities.

Don't Rescue:

Rescuing is what we do when we don't allow children to experience the consequences of their poor decisions. In our parenting courses we have heard many stories and complaints about children not doing their homework, forgetting to bring it home or take it to school and leaving assignments too late. We all want to support our children, especially if they have learning disabilities, too much on their plate with extra activities, or too much homework. But a child's homework is his responsibility, and he won't learn that if you make it yours. If you are having lots of power struggles about homework and your child is resisting then you need to let go and allow it to be your child's responsibility.

> **We make the mistake of protecting our children from painful situations; yet we learn our greatest lessons from the painful, difficult times.**

When are Natural Consequences Appropriate?

To decide this in any given situation, we need to answer the following 7 questions:

Is my child old enough to manage this situation on his own?

Responsibility must be given slowly at an age-appropriate level. The message is not, *"Here, kid, you're on your own,"* rather it is, *"I trust you can do this. I have faith in you. I am here if you need support."* Children will vary in their readiness to take on different tasks. Age is often a good guideline yet some kids may be ahead or behind in certain areas. If you stay in tune with your child, you will get a sense of her readiness.

Will it pose a threat?

When it comes to safety, you must deal with the situation clearly, strongly and consistently. We shriek if our child runs toward the road and that is what makes him pay attention and learn very quickly about danger. When parents mean what they say, the children will know it.

Well, Bobby decapitated himself today. He wanted to help chop veggies with a cleaver and I decided to begin allowing him to learn through natural consequences.

154

So issues around safety are not negotiable. However, prevention is much better than consequences. We make the limits clear, while explaining why those limits are there. If the child violates the limits without getting hurt, we tell and show him what could have happened. As the child gets older, we hope we have provided him with enough education to make wise choices, since we can't watch him all his life.

Will the outcome be devastating in any way?

Give the kid a break! If your child spent half the night putting together a project for the next day and she forgot to take it to school are you going to make her suffer? This situation is different from that of a child who forgets her lunch or her gym strip on a regular basis. If you, the parent, are around to deliver the project to the school, and this is important and a rare event, your decision not to help your child would show a lack of empathy and support, and your child would feel uncared for and humiliated for having forgotten.

You need to know your child. If your child has been diligent in taking responsibility and slips up now and then, it isn't an issue. She is still seeing it as her responsibility. You only need to be concerned when a child hasn't got that sense of responsibility because you keep rescuing her from the natural consequences of her decisions. In this case, you must allow your child to experience natural consequences as soon as possible. In the following example, the consequences were unpleasant for the child but not devastating:

Hair Today – Gone Tomorrow

A few years ago my husband and I were invited to a gathering with other adults and their kids. These kids had formed close relationships over the years and are (as I write this) 12 to 15 years old. On my way to use the washroom, I walked past a hallway where my darling daughter of 12 was having her beautiful long, wavy hair ironed by one of the older, more experienced girls of 14. Steam was puffing out of the iron which was inches from my daughter's scalp. Stopping in my tracks I gasped – only to be met with rolling eyes and an explanation of, "I've done this before and it is fine!" from the person in charge of the iron. I looked at my daughter crouched in front of the ironing board and asked, "Is the iron Teflon?" "What is Teflon?" they replied. Yikes! So then with my best non-judgmental language in place I expressed my concerns that Emily's hair might be permanently scorched.

There was no stopping them and given her age I had to tell myself to let it go. Her hair looked great until she washed it (at which point every inch of her head was one massive tangle). It had damaged the hair just enough to make it impossible to wash without this happening. Devastated by this experience, the last thing my daughter needed to hear was "I told you so." I did what I could to help restore her hair but, as she said, "I learned a valuable lesson." Of course when I heard that I wanted to say, "Yeah, always listen to your mother, right?" But that would have spoiled the lesson.   -- *Allison Rees*

Will anyone else suffer a consequence?

We must not allow other people or pets to suffer the consequences of our children's actions.

Sometimes we end up being the ones to suffer. If your child constantly loses his coat and you keep replacing it, who is actually suffering? The child gets a new coat, and the parent continues to pay for its replacement. Since the child needs a coat, you can't just let him go cold, but remember that second-hand stores sell coats in all kid sizes.

Kids who have their bicycles stolen because they don't lock them can learn to walk or take the bus – at least for a while. We don't owe them a new bike when they've been careless, though perhaps we do if some thief cut through the lock.

It goes without saying that if your child forgets to feed the dog or clean the kitty litter, the animal should not be allowed to starve or to live in filth. This is a situation when natural consequences are **not** appropriate.

Stealing is another situation in which someone else suffers, whether directly or indirectly. Therefore we need to step in.

How do we step in effectively in a moral dilemma? By helping the child think through the consequences of his behavior on other people. If the child is hitting, ask him to imagine being hit. If he's stealing from the corner store, explain that it's coming out of the owner's pocket. Prevent him from stealing from you by making sure he has enough money for his needs. (See the section on stealing in Chapter 6.)

Will a negative behavior have a positive natural consequence?

Sometimes the positive natural consequence of a negative behavior is parental attention! Watch for negative attention-getting: "If I act out, my parent stays around me and gives me lots of attention!" Most temper tantrums, especially in preschoolers, result from frustrated needs and an inability to express these in words. But some tantrums are performed to get the attention of a busy parent.

Do you notice how often your children whine, fight with one another, or get 'up to' things when you're on the phone? Such things are often done for attention. If you reward these behaviors with your attention, they will increase. This is a situation in which you need to interrupt the natural cycle of events by either ignoring the behavior or imposing a consequence such as a time out. (See the section on negative attention-getting in Chapter 4.)

Stealing often has a positive natural consequence – the child gets to keep what he's stolen. So this is another reason why natural consequences are insufficient for dealing with stealing. Lying also has a positive natural consequence in the short term but has a negative natural consequence in the long run: a child who lies won't be believed when she is telling the truth. Therefore rather than punishing a child for lying, we need to teach her what will happen if she continues to lie.

Will a positive behavior have a positive natural consequence?

Kids can learn from positive consequences too:

♦   When a child cleans his room he can find things!

♦   When he is nice to people they are nice back.

♦   When he hands in assignments on time he feels good about himself and his accomplishment.

Having positive experiences and taking on responsibility feels good. When children don't have to rebel they make great choices. When they admire you and enjoy their relationship with you, they will emulate your highest qualities.

Is the consequence too far away?

Brushing teeth is a good example. Parent to adult child: *"Oh gee, honey, I know you have to have all your teeth pulled. I just didn't want to nag you about brushing."* Mom may not have wanted to tell the child to brush, and the child wouldn't have understood the importance of brushing teeth until it was too late. In such cases natural consequences do not fit. With young children you might use "when/then". "When we brush your teeth then we can read your story." Ages may vary but there will come a point when not brushing becomes his problem.

Is he old enough to understand the long-term consequence? For example, a parent is not willing to continue to pay for braces if the child doesn't clean his teeth. The child understands that he either brushes or the braces are removed until he is older and can pay for them himself.

Apply Your Knowledge

- Think of a situation in which you want to hand a responsibility over to your child.
- Are the natural consequences for not taking responsibility rewarding, like those for stealing?
- Will the natural consequence of your child's failure to meet this responsibility threaten your child's or anyone else's safety?
- Will the natural consequence affect anyone else in a negative way?
- Will the consequence devastate your child?
- Is the consequence too far in the future, like the consequences of not brushing teeth?

---

4 - Kid Issues and Family Issues

In order to know which responsibilities should be handed over to our children, along with their natural consequences, it is helpful to distinguish between 'kid issues' and 'family issues'. A lot of conflict between parents and kids could be avoided if parents made it clear which areas are completely up to the kids, and which are considered 'family issues' for which the parents will impose consequences if responsibilities are not carried out. Such a clear understanding not only gives children more freedom and responsibility, it also relieves parents of trying to enforce order and discipline in areas which the child should control.

'Family Issues' involve such things as safety, the feelings or rights of another person, the neutral area of the house (bedrooms slowly become kid issues), and protecting children from danger. Every household has different rules and what might be intolerable for one family is often okay for another. Some families can handle more noise than others; some parents don't mind shoes being worn inside but others do. Some eight-year-olds are allowed to walk to a store alone; others aren't. The child's right to do as he wants without considering others ends where family issues begin.

Common Family Issues

Here are some common examples of family issues:

- ☐ taking off shoes when entering the house
- ☐ contributing to family chores
- ☐ keeping noises at a comfortable level for everyone
- ☐ limiting phone use so others can receive calls
- ☐ privacy issues
- ☐ running, ball playing or rowdy horseplay inside
- ☐ locking up at night
- ☐ kids coming home later than expected or not coming home
- ☐ safety issues
- ☐ care of the family car
- ☐ illegal drugs or smoking in the house
- ☐ leaving a mess or dirty dishes around the house

Family issues require limits and sometimes rules, so that one family member's behavior won't violate other members' boundaries.

Common Kid Issues

Here are some common 'kid issues' – areas in which kids should be allowed to handle things on their own without our trying to control things by imposing rules or getting angry:

- ☐ toileting
- ☐ how much food they eat (within reasonable limits)
- ☐ clothing and fashion choices
- ☐ their bedrooms
- ☐ their homework
- ☐ their choice of friends
- ☐ how they spend their money

Be available to your kid if he wants to discuss any of these kid issues. But don't take over and tell him what to do. Being a consultant keeps the communication lines open as he struggles with decisions about the things he's responsible for.

Children May Want You to Remain Responsible

When parents start to let go and realize that they can detach from a lot of their children's behavior, life just feels easier. It takes time for kids to take ownership of their own responsibilities. They will also find interesting ways to keep you involved. They will complain to you about their laundry not being done even though it has been their responsibility for some time. "Mom, I have no clean clothes to wear!" Don't bite the bait. Just say, "Yeah, I know what you mean. I'm all out of socks today too." When new limits are established we need to maintain them by staying firm until responsibility settles into place.

If you're a kid, there are a lot of payoffs to having your parents nag and rescue – you don't have to suffer from the results of your mistakes. It takes some time for an over-involved parent to show her kids that she really is going to butt out of their affairs, and they may not like it.

At this point in time, it would be lovely if your child said: *"Thanks so much. I see the light. I am going to study right now. I love you."* Don't hold your breath! Expect the behavior to get worse before it gets better. He will resist, testing to see if you mean what you say. If you continue to stay out of his business, he will eventually take responsibility.

Einstein said, "The only good mathematician is a lazy mathematician." That's because lazy mathematicians figure out time-saving ways of solving problems. This could be said about parents too. In many, many situations a 'lazy' parent can allow a child to solve his own problems and the child will come through with flying colors. Not that we should be lazy in our parenting – just that sometimes it's much more efficient to allow kids to experience their own consequences than it is to intervene.

Your toddler won't wear a coat. Why argue with her? Just throw it in a bag and take it along. Maybe she will complain about being cold. If she does get cold, you don't have to make her freeze for an hour. Ask her what she needs, then pull out the coat without a lecture or making it a big deal. Some kids are just hot, and it is amazing how many people can't understand that. A child who's feeling nagged and coerced isn't given a chance to figure things out on her own. Her need is to make choices based on her own knowledge.

> ### Learning the Alphabet Late
>
> In ninth grade, my daughter transferred to a new school with a more challenging curriculum. When she got her first report card, she learned some new letters of the alphabet (previously she'd only known A and B). I could have rushed in to reprimand her, restrict her social activities, and set up a study schedule for her. But I followed the example of my own parents and just said, "Wow, I guess school is harder this year, isn't it?" That was the last time she got any bad grades. She figured out what she needed to do. -- *Alison Miller*

Family Issues or Kid Issues?

1. List some responsibilities of your child which affect the family if the child doesn't follow through. These are family issues.

_____   _____
_____   _____
_____   _____
_____   _____
_____   _____

2. List some responsibilities which affect just the child. These are kid issues.

_____   _____
_____   _____
_____   _____
_____   _____
_____   _____

3. Choose one kid issue for which you have taken responsibility. What would you need to do to hand over this responsibility completely to your child?

_____
_____
_____

> ### *Apply Your Knowledge*
>
> - What are the benefits for a child when the parent continues to take responsibility for kid issues?
> - What are the negative effects on a child when the parent continues to take responsibility for kid issues?

Whose Lunch?

My son started to forget his lunch in the middle of the sixth grade (age 11). The first time he called home from school at recess announcing that he forgot his lunch I didn't mind running it over.

The second episode came only a few days later. I felt a bit annoyed because I was busy and it was an inconvenience. So I reluctantly delivered lunch but stated my position: "This is your responsibility and the next time you forget your lunch you will have to go hungry or beg your friends for food. Got that?" "No problem, Mom, I won't forget my lunch again." Within a few days my husband pointed to the counter and there was my son's lunch. I was prepared for the 10:30 a.m. phone call.

Sure enough the phone rang: "Mom, I forgot my lunch again." My reply was "Yes, Peter, I know, and it was delicious." He actually hung up on me. This was clearly a kid issue, however, and my refusal to take it on helped him take responsibility. *-- Allison Rees*

In their book *Do I Have To Give Up Me To Be Loved By My Kids?*, Jordan and Margaret Paul say:

"Natural consequences are the most important form of discipline a parent can use. Children learn to be responsible from the consequences of their actions when allowed to experience them. Children are not fools. They know or can quickly learn how much sleep they need and when their stomachs are full. Imposing consequences is not the same as natural consequences.

Restricting television when your children don't do their homework is not the same as letting them deal with the consequences of not doing their homework. When you impose consequences, you are the controller and sentencer. Your children may learn only to be angry and blame you rather than take responsibility for their lives."

You are not giving up, you are giving over.

Apply Your Knowledge

- Think about all the different areas of your child's life that are her responsibility. Once you have identified kid issues what might stop you from letting go?
- Can you remember experiencing natural consequences growing up?
- How does this kind of experience help a child?
- Will you be able to let go yet continue to offer support?
  If so, how will you do that?

Steps in Passing Responsibility Over to your Child

1. **State your feelings and thoughts.**
   "I hate how I sound when I nag you to clean your room. I feel exhausted and grumpy about the whole issue. I realize my anger can't make you clean up."

2. **Give the responsibility over.**
   "From now on, I am going to shut the door."

3. **Show faith in the child.**
   "I know you are capable and I know you'll do what feels right to you."

It takes strength and faith to use natural consequences. It takes a big effort to let go of control and it takes faith in our kids to be able to let them think for themselves and do things on their own, in their own unique and wonderful way.

> **Children should struggle with their own kid-related issues rather than struggle with their parents' issues.**
>
>
>
> **When parents let go of a kid issue, they let go of a power struggle.**

5 - Household Responsibilities

There is so much controversy about chores that we decided to break some of them down for a closer look. Often people are confused as to when children should take chores on. The answer depends on a number of things: their age, their level of maturity, their ability to focus and stick to things, and their temperament.

The important thing is that tasks develop confidence. Tasks are also good for the soul. It's more than just learning housework skills, it's about developing a responsible attitude and there is something deeply satisfying about that.

Too often we parents don't allow our children to take on tasks because we feel guilty when we don't do these things ourselves. This sometimes makes us over-indulge and 'spoil' our children by taking on their responsibilities. Unfortunately, when one person does more than her share she can develop resentment. At our workshops we often hear comments like:

- Why does my family wait until I ask them to do something? It makes me feel like a nag.
- Whenever they do something, it is as if they have done me a favor.

- When they do something, they do a half-baked job and say, "At least I did it!"
- People just throw things everywhere, expecting me to pick them up.
- I get so angry every time I clean the house that my family runs!

Yuck, the voice of "Martyr Mary"! She isn't fun, and people run from her for a good reason. We can keep ourselves stuck in this rut by doing too much for those around us. Having standards which are too high, nagging, feeling guilty and making others feel guilty, not asking for help – all of these approaches keep us stuck.

Contributing Feels Good

Even if children complain and resist, by doing chores they will get to enjoy the good feeling which comes from contributing. Giving of their time to the family increases their sense of belonging and boosts their self-esteem. It also helps them to appreciate the tidiness if they have been personally involved in bringing it about.

> **It is loving behavior to assign chores and take the time to teach children how to master them.**

Consider Age and Workload

We all have different expectations about how much work our children should do. Going to school, doing homework, taking a music lesson, playing sports: these can take up an entire day. Sit down with your child and help him schedule things so he isn't overloaded.

Tasks which children should learn first are those concerning self-care. This means doing things for themselves which directly concern them. This is also where natural consequences will speak volumes because the child will feel the effect of the consequences directly.

Preschoolers - Age 3 to 5:

Preschoolers can help you put their toys away. Their centered thinking means they can only focus their attention on one part of a scene at a time so they often can't see a messy room in its entirety. They may clean part of it and not even see the corner with the crayons or books lying all over the floor. It is best not to expect too much of them.

Make Cleanup Fun.   At this age, they can help with chores in a playful way. Having big bins they can throw toys into will be helpful, as sorting and organizing is difficult for them. The Rees family made up our own version of Barney's clean up song: "Clean up, clean up, everybody do your share. Clean up, clean up, even in your underwear." (Thank goodness we've outgrown that!)

"Beat the clock" is another fun way to get things done. Whoopie! Really, it does make things a little easier. There is nothing wrong with using distraction or making something a game with young kids. They enjoy games and challenges and their main goal is to have fun. They don't care about a tidy house.

Playing Rules!   What can preschoolers do? They can bring their plates to the sink and they can help clean up messes that they make.

But a young child's main responsibility is to play, and *the importance of play cannot be overestimated.* Play is how children develop their imagination, work out their problems, and rehearse for life situations. Many preschool teachers tell us about anxious parents who want their children to start learning to read and write before age five. We need to watch our expectations. If children start in the school system already knowing the curriculum, those first couple of years can be pretty boring. Remember that for this age group, what they learn from play is much more important than learning to read and write. And if they are registered in music lessons or sports activities, it must be conducted in a playful manner, letting them explore their activities and interests.

The Mid-Years - Age 6 to 12:

At this age, kids can begin the process of taking responsibility *even though they haven't mastered the tasks*. We have broken down some of the jobs that they will probably be learning during these years.

Homework.   In most cases, at least in Canada, first and second grade assign-ments require Mom or Dad to read to the child. Somewhere in third and fourth grade kids begin taking responsibility for their homework, and you can assist them where needed and if requested. By taking responsibility we mean bringing the work home, doing it at a certain time, and getting it ready to take to school the next day.

Lunches.   Most eight-year-olds can make their own lunches. The biggest benefit of giving them this responsibility is that if they make it, they might actually eat it! They can also prepare a grocery list of things they need for their lunches. You may be thinking, "Yeah, chocolate bars and junk!" Choices within limits will work here.

Laundry. We may tell children in the mid-years that if it isn't in the hamper it doesn't get washed. Unfortunately, some kids will put clean clothes in the hamper to avoid folding them and putting them away. You may need to sort the piles for them and even go to the trouble of sticking pictures on the drawers to show them where everything goes. Sorting things can be tough for kids so this will make the task easier. But not all kids care about how tidy their drawers are; as long as they can find things, does it really matter? They'll get better at it when they get older. All our (Miller and Rees) children have improved in tidiness with age.

Cleaning Their Rooms. It goes without saying that children should learn to keep their own rooms clean. When they are little, we need to teach them how to clean up (Levels 0, 1 and 2). When they are older they should be responsible for keeping their rooms clean.

Many kids don't know how to clean their rooms because they have not been taught how. When they are little, they don't have the mental organization to put different things in different places; the most we can expect is that they throw everything into the toy box. As they become more mature, we need to coach them to organize their possessions.

What is clean? It usually means something different to kids than it does to parents. By the time a child is about eleven, she needs her room to be private, just her own. We parents need to back off and allow it to be only her responsibility, provided there are no dangerous things in there like decaying food and insects.

Some kids get overwhelmed with a messy room and need help from a parent who is willing to do a clean sweep every now and then. Helping a child get organized and doing a thorough cleaning with them can be really satisfying, even when they are older teens. The main point is to respect their privacy and not nag them every day about their space.

My (Allison Rees') kids really appreciate the days when I put a few hours aside, grab the big garbage bags and a sponge mop and help them attack their rooms. Now that they are teens, issues concerning a messy room are over. They want an organized space and enjoy their rooms. Getting rid of the clutter and sometimes redecorating can help them enjoy their rooms. Sometimes they might ask for help if the mess gets beyond them and I'm happy to contribute because they do the same for me when I ask for help with things. When boundaries regarding responsibilities are clear it is wonderful to be flexible. It is good role modeling to generously take time to help our children with a task.

Making Beds. Why do we make our beds? We just crawl back into them and mess those sheets up again anyway. We have much more important things to worry about when we leave the house in the morning than whether or not our children have made their beds.

If your kids don't mind making their beds, great! But if it's causing morning battles and difficulties, shut the door to your child's room. Incidentally, recent research shows that dust mites thrive in made beds and don't like to live in unmade beds; they like to be undercover!

Family Clean-Up Day. Again, in a loving family there is no way that one person should be doing all the chores. No matter how many people live in the house, you are a family and everyone needs to contribute! The attitude is: we all want to go out to play, so the sooner we get this done, the sooner we can all get on with our respective lives.

Charts can be very useful: if dividing up chores becomes an issue, get out the felt pen and cardboard. This lets people see what needs to be done and it also creates some choices. Make sure the male family members take equal responsibility and that everyone shares the jobs which nobody likes.

Dish Duty. Loading and unloading the dishwasher is my (Allison Rees') least favorite job and I love it when my kids take it on. After dinner there is no reason why kids can't rinse their plates and put them in the dishwasher. If you don't have a dishwasher, they can take turns doing those dishes. Try not to make it one person's job; it is much too boring. Many parents expect their kids to do the dishes every day.

Setting the Table & Preparing Meals. Everyone in the family can help put dinner on the table. They can prepare vegetables, set the table, and help with cooking. This can eliminate so many dinner-time struggles. It brings about a sense of togetherness and pride. Sadly, the process of preparing a meal together has been replaced with fast food. "Come on kids, it is breakfast time, jump in the car!"

Most kids like cooking, especially because it's a task that's usually reserved for adults. Some meals are easy enough for a 10-year-old to prepare. Why not have each child over age 10 make one dinner a week? They'll enjoy it and you'll get some time off.

Kids Need Variety. Sometimes a child is tired of his job, and needs to try something new. Kids always want to learn, and if their chores are monotonous, they are not learning so they become bored. If this happens, make a deal with the child to change his responsibilities every so often.

Helping, not Helping, and Making Deals

At the age of seven, my (Allison Rees's) daughter became so overwhelmed by the mess in her room that she couldn't possibly clean it herself. Even though she made a huge mess when she played she enjoyed a tidy room. We avoided the room cleaning power struggle by making a deal: I helped her with her room and she did one of my jobs, which just happened to be the bathroom ☺. She liked it and I was happy too.

About a year after our deal, my daughter and I had a disagreement about the mess in her room. I had been trying to hand it over to her gradually, yet she still saw it as my responsibility and in fact, it was. I found myself nagging her and getting angry when her room got messy and I cleaned it up.

Realizing that it was interfering with our relationship, I completely handed it over to her and promised that I would say nothing more about her room. I also wouldn't clean it any more. I wasn't angry when I talked to her about this – it was days after our disagreement. I recognized she mattered more to me than a clean room.

After four days she came to me asking for help. I explained that I was too busy just then but I would find an hour (ha ha) on the weekend. So the day came and we got started. Whenever she got distracted and started playing, I would stop working. She was still trying (hoping?) to keep me responsible.

Eight hours later, every corner and cupboard of that room had been cleaned. We got rid of lots of clutter and junk and she loved it. But parenting is a humbling job! A few years later when Emily was 11, her room had been messy for a couple of months. Back to square one? What happened? Her interests were in outside activities and her life became fairly busy. Horseback riding, soccer, school, friends – she just didn't spend as much time in her room any more. The messy room was a stop-and-drop spot. She hinted that she wouldn't mind if I went into her room to clean, and I must admit it was tempting but I didn't want to resort to that awful nagging. Sometimes I stepped in and gave her a hand and we did it together, or she would attack it when she couldn't stand it anymore. It was okay and it wasn't a reflection of me or of her future. She was a kid and her room was a 'kid issue'. *-- Allison Rees*

Putting it Together. Of course these are only a few examples of the chores and responsibilities children can take on in the mid-years. Individual readiness will differ with each child. Stay in tune with your child and he will show you what he's ready for. These years are a time of teaching, practicing and mastering tasks.

6 - Responsibility Equals Freedom

Make sure your mid-year children have lots of free time to rest and be kids. Sometimes the load of homework, activities, and chores becomes overwhelming. Just because they can do all these things doesn't mean they need to do all of them all the time. Be an advocate for your child. Teach her self-care and the importance of learning to rest as well. Many kids today take on too much and don't have enough down time. This is not a good thing.

Putting a job list together is a great way for the family to identify what has to be done around the house and make some decisions as to what each member will contribute.

Feelings and Needs

If you as the parent are doing more than your share of the household chores, you may feel resentful, frustrated, angry, even overwhelmed. These feelings can point to needs such as support, equality, rest and recreation. To meet these needs, you might try to work out with your family ways in which they can carry their share of responsibilities.

Apply Your Knowledge

- Am I a perfectionist, who expects my family to keep up with my impossible standards?
- Do I feel guilty if my children take on responsibility?
- Do I support my child enough with teaching and positive feedback?
- Am I organized myself?
- Do I nag and take over responsibility?
- Have I been over-indulgent, doing too much for my child so that his responsibilities have become mine?
- What tasks can I let go of?
- Do I offer my children choices as to what tasks they choose and when they are willing to do them?
- What gets in the way of my children assuming responsibilities?

---

7 - Allowance

Reward, Right or Privilege?

Many families go to bed hungry. Instead of attending school, their children work to contribute to the family income so they can have a roof over their heads and enough food. In more affluent families, however, children don't learn this because everything is provided for them. The privilege of an allowance is a very helpful way for children to learn how to manage money.

In our view, if parents can afford it, every child should be given an allowance. An allowance is the money the child gets to be in charge of so that he learns how to save and spend money wisely.

How old should a child be when he first receives an allowance? Old enough not to eat it! At first, he won't have a clue what it represents, but eventually he will catch on. An allowance should be in place by the time a child is about four or five, and should last until the child is able to earn her own income from babysitting or a paper route. It should be given simply because the child is a member of the family, and because you want her to learn the value of money, and learn how to manage it by buying the small things she needs. Kids who have to ask when they want small things have no idea of the value of money.

Ask other parents how much is appropriate. What we have found workable for many families is giving their children their age in dollars every two weeks. A four-year-old would get $4; a 10-year-old would get $10. This might not work as inflation kicks in but presently this amount seems to keep things clear and reasonable. A younger child should receive his allowance more frequently, as two weeks seems an eternity to him.

Maybe we've been too generous with his allowance ...

It would be wise to stress that this money is for buying whatever your child wants, and this should include toys. What if your child spends all her allowance on candy? Well, she won't have any money left to buy anything else, and when she wants something else you can point out that unfortunately her money has all been eaten! She will learn from that. Don't bail her out!

Children need to make some of their own choices about what they own. Take your child shopping to spend his or her allowance – to a toy store, a bead store, a store which sells shiny rocks – places where he can find things he likes and will be able to afford to pay for them. Let him count out the money himself, help him figure out what he can afford, and let him give the money to the sales clerk. He will come to understand that possessions cost money, and that money is limited. If something costs more than his allowance, help him figure out how to save up the money.

We don't agree with telling children what to do with their allowance. Better that they make some mistakes with their money now, rather than later when they are dealing with cars and a mortgage. Children really appreciate something when they buy it for themselves. It gives them a sense of ownership and pride. Kids really do think twice when the money is coming out of their own wallets.

Marketers are encouraging everyone – including children – to buy on credit, and kids have a lot of stuff today. If they aren't buying it with their own money, you must be footing the bill. An allowance helps kids accept delayed gratification. Sure, you can pay half for those bigger items but kids can also save part of their allowance until they have enough for a bigger item. If we're wise with our money, we save rather than ending up owing thousands to the credit card companies. We can teach our kids to do the same.

Buying a child something when you can't afford it and resenting it later will have negative effects. Overindulgence is a sure-fire way to set your child up for financial disaster. Many parents of adult children have regrets for having over-indulged their children. One father commented that even though his daughter (age 27) worked hard at two jobs she would spend her money on elaborate things and beg her dad to bail her out when she couldn't pay her rent. He confessed that as a divorced dad he raised her with a large dose of parental guilt so he didn't require her to be financially responsible.

Both of my (Allison Rees') teenage kids have their own bank cards. They understand that they are entitled to this privilege because they accepted responsibility for it. Proud and responsible, they handle that responsibility better than I can. They wait for their bank statements every month like I used to wait for the ice-cream truck. They don't buy silly things with their bank cards and they leave them at home when we go out so they won't buy on impulse. They use their cash for gum and all the little goodies. This is how the world works so why not teach it to them?

Don't Tie Allowance to Chores!

Have you ever had a job where your paycheck was the only motivation? I'll bet you didn't stay with it any longer than necessary. Satisfying work is as much about companionship, recognition, challenge, teamwork, encouragement, the physical environment, and helping others as it is about money. When a child does chores only for her allowance, as opposed to the feeling of contributing and belonging to the family team, she is not learning responsibility, she is being bribed.

If you dangle a reward at the end of chores, kids miss out on the process of taking responsibility. We give them privileges because we love them and they are part of the family. They contribute because they love us and they are part of the family. The family is a home and a community, not a workplace.

I don't care if you never give me an allowance again!

When allowance is tied to chores, outside income (e.g. from baby-sitting, lawn mowing etc.) undermines kids' motivation to do chores! When they hit the teen years, they will not have mastered responsibility because they were simply being bribed into doing a task for money. You also don't want to discourage earning outside income simply because they already have a job at home!

Do you get paid for washing your own clothes? I don't think so. You do it because it needs to be done.

We can provide opportunities for children to make some extra money. Having my (Allison Rees') own business provides plenty of opportunity for my children to make extra money photocopying, stapling and sorting. And I (Alison Miller) pay my kids for heavy yard work or house painting.

It is important not to take an allowance away or deduct money from it as a punishment or consequence for misbehavior. The purpose of an allowance is for the child to learn money management, and this will not happen if it is taken away. Also, if a child does not have enough spending money, it provides a temptation to get things by stealing.

Allowance and Teens

Teens feel they need money and lots of it! Parents need to have a bottom line in place if arguments about money are going to be avoided. Every child up to age 12 should receive a basic allowance. As they move up into the teen years they want more independence and more money.

Decide which financial responsibilities you can (slowly) turn over to your teen. She may need an entertainment budget, a clothing budget, and a bit of a cushion for snacks, makeup, bicycle gear, or whatever else is basic to her life. This means that if it is up to her to buy these things, it is up to you to see that she has enough money to buy them without always getting the most expensive item.

Sit down with your teen and find out what is reasonable. You will find that you spend less if you come up with a budget because you won't be bailing kids out if they blow their money on dumb things.

The chart below shows how one family divides up financial responsibility:

Parents' Responsibility:

Food
School clothes in September
School supplies
Books (2 per month)
Friends' birthday gifts

Teen's Responsibility:

Movies and entertainment
Clothes throughout the year
Fun stuff (e.g. makeup, CDs)
More books
Family gifts

What do you want your teen to take financial responsibility for?

Parents' Responsibility:

Teen's Responsibility:

_____   _____
_____   _____
_____   _____
_____   _____
_____   _____

Childhood is a time when children are protected to some extent by their parents from the harsh realities of adult life. One of these realities is that money has to be earned. As children move towards adulthood, they need to learn this.

If a teen is working hard in school, contributes chores to the family, and has to spend a lot of time on his schoolwork, it is reasonable not to require him to earn his money either inside or outside the home. However, if he is over 16, not in school, and is living at home, it is reasonable to expect him to earn more of his living expenses, either through a job outside the home or through extra work around the home for which he receives remuneration. This teaches him the reality that life does not pamper you forever and that you have to earn what you live on. This lesson, although hard for some parents to give, does the child a favor in the long run. If the child has finished or quit school, it is reasonable to expect him to get a job and pay you some rent. I (Alison Miller) had my grown son pay me rent for my basement suite when he got his first real job. He was proud to do it! I gave it back to him as a wedding gift.

Parents of teens need to set clear boundaries about their bottom line for extras and stick to them. No matter how rich they are, they should not buy things for their kids whenever the kids ask. Kids will not learn how to manage money if their parent is a bottomless money pit. If parents can discuss this bottom line with their teens (at a good time) then all they have to do is stand strong and resist the urge to rescue if their kids spend too much and want more. The less responsibility kids take, the firmer a parent will have to be. This is important.

Kids need to learn to budget and to experience the consequences of poor financial decisions before they are out there in the real world where they have to pay rent. Also, kids whose parents give them a lot may begin to feel entitled: this can lead to serious demanding behavior. And look out when they are given a credit card!

The Ugly Black Skirt

When my daughter was 14, we agreed that she would receive a clothing allowance and would buy her own clothes. She promptly bought an ugly, expensive little black skirt which was in fashion at the time, using up all of a month's allowance. She wore it perhaps once! It sat in her closet as a reminder for her to use her money wisely. It was much more effective than anything I could have said. *-- Alison Miller*

If your teen is engaging in risky behavior, he may not be ready for budgeting. A living allowance is earned by displaying accountability, readiness and an ability to make decent choices. This doesn't mean that you don't make allowances for mistakes; it just means that your child has an overall sense of responsibility. You don't want him spending the money you provide for him on drugs or cigarettes, for example.

But it's important not to take away the basic agreed-upon allowance, regardless of your kids' behavior and attitude. Teenagers need clothing and enough money to spend time socializing with their friends. Withholding the money for these things tempts them to find illegal ways to get money. If a teen has a bad attitude, you can refuse to grant favors like giving her a ride. It's not a good idea to remove her allowance.

Apply Your Knowledge

- Were you given an allowance when you were growing up and do you give one to your children?
- Is your child's allowance tied to chores? How could you change this?
- What financial responsibilities should you turn over to your teen?

---

8 - School Work and Homework

School Work

Not Working Up to Her Potential

One of the things I am very thankful for in my own parents is their relative lack of emphasis on schoolwork and especially on grades. They didn't interfere with our developing a natural life-long love of learning. Mark Twain wrote, "I never let my schooling interfere with my education" and this has been my motto. My parents let us know that they had confidence in our ability to succeed academically, and that grades weren't nearly as important as our finding life paths which would be suited to us and would enable us to exercise our creativity and make a contribution to the world.

I remember countless instances of coming home with report cards which said, "She isn't working up to her potential. She should be getting A's." But I wasn't worried, because I knew my parents understood that learning was more important than letter grades. They never pressured me about schoolwork until my final year in high school. Then they said to me, "You have four younger siblings and we can't afford to pay a lot for university. Would you please do some school work this year so you can get scholarships?" I felt this was reasonable, so I did.

Despite (or perhaps because of) the fact that no one stood over us to make us do our schoolwork, all five of us children ended up in careers requiring lots of university education. And all five of us still read for pleasure. I raised my own three children this way, and all three of them continue as adults to love to learn. -- *Alison Miller*

It's very important to make sure our children grow up loving to learn rather than being anxious about performance or hooked on doing everything perfectly. Studies have been done to see what effect extrinsic motivation (rewards such as grades or money) has on intrinsic motivation (enjoying a task because it's interesting). It appears that extrinsic motivation has the capacity to destroy intrinsic motivation. Little kids love to learn new things and attempt new tasks, whether it's talking, sounding out words, walking, climbing, or helping wash the dishes. But as they become older they frequently lose their love of learning. If you make learning a duty, and attach rewards and punishments to it, you take away the natural excitement of learning. Love of learning is a lifelong thing; love of grades sometimes interferes with it.

It appears that for many children school learning has now become a source of anxiety and overwhelming obligation rather than fun and accomplishment. If this is the case with your child, it's important to turn this around as soon as possible. Let him know you have confidence in his ability to learn and to do the work, and that you believe it's important that he have a personal and social life as well as do schoolwork. Let him know that you believe his grades aren't as important as enjoying his work and feeling he's accomplished something. Do not offer rewards for A's or B's, as these only encourage him to focus on the grades rather than on the learning. Express confidence that he will be able to handle the challenges before him, and offer help to make the load manageable.

Demystify for your children the requirements of higher levels of schooling if they are becoming anxious about doing well enough. At the higher levels the main differences are that children have to spend somewhat longer completing their work, more research is sometimes required, and they have to organize their work over a longer period of time. That's all. It isn't insurmountable.

Help your children organize their study habits to cope with the new challenges. Give them a regular time and place to do their work, and teach them (if the school hasn't done so) to make a list of assignments and their due dates. Help them figure out how long each assignment will take, and which tasks they need to do first. It's best to avoid monitoring them constantly, lecturing them or, of course, doing their work for them.

Let them organize their schoolwork so that they feel comfortable with it. Different children study in different ways. Remember the differences in temperament discussed in Chapter 1. Some need silence; some need music. Some need regular short breaks, others work for a long time and don't like interruptions. Allow your children to study in the way which works best for them. But don't let them stay up past their bedtime doing schoolwork (unless they are at least in their teens).

Make sure they start their homework early enough to get it done and have some relaxation time. If there's too much work for the time available, you may need to intervene with the teacher, as she may not be aware of the problem unless an adult lets her know. Your child probably isn't the only one with the problem.

Meaningless Homework

When my son Justin was 10, he came home with pages and pages of boring arithmetic problems, all of which he already knew how to do. I didn't want him to start to hate school-work, so I wrote on the assignment sheet "I refuse to permit my son to do this meaningless work. Please assign him something more suitable to his abilities." Justin was shocked, but the teacher did as I asked and my son's interest in math revived. (He followed his math skills and is now a computer programmer.) *-- Alison Miller*

I (Alison Miller) feel that we as parents have a responsibility to see that what our children are being taught challenges them just enough to keep them interested. If there is too much work – or it's too monotonous, too easy, or too difficult – talk to the teacher. Chances are other children are having the same difficulty as your child.

Apply Your Knowledge

- What are your children's feelings about school and homework? Are they anxious about grades and performance, bored, or interested in learning?
- What do you need to do to make sure they keep or regain a love of learning?

Helping with Homework

There are times when homework makes our home grind to a halt. What's a parent to do? Sometimes I'm the one who feels like quitting school. The demands of homework can be overwhelming. All parents want their children to get good grades because as adults we understand their long-term importance: our child is part of an educational system in which high grades are required for success.

Our high expectations make it very difficult to watch our children struggle, sometimes unsuccessfully, with schoolwork. *It's vital to remember that grades are never as important as our relationship with our child.* They also aren't as important as our child's love of learning.

When it's homework time, no one in the room watches TV or makes noise of any kind, although it is true that some people work better with music in the background (maybe they can use headphones).

Here are some guidelines for helping with homework. Start by designating a *Daily Study Time* (at least 30-60 minutes every day, depending on the child's age). Some children don't need help with homework; the following guidelines from the Learning Disabilities Association are for parents whose kids do need help.

Managing Your Emotions

Stay positive to keep your child positive. Your child is already aware of what she can't do and is reminded of this often enough by her peers. Praise and acknowledge what she can do. Your positive attitude will be passed on to your child.

Quietly observe and support, but don't smother. Children can interpret too much attention as a lack of confidence. Standing over her reinforces her belief that she is not capable. To give her approval and encouragement remind her of what she does well, and tell her that your love isn't conditional on her grades, that she will overcome this difficulty, and that you are always there to help.

Avoid letting yourself get impatient and angry. When you feel your patience wane and your frustration escalate, step away, breathe deeply, and remind yourself that this is your beloved child. Many parents find tutoring their own children to be extremely difficult, because they are just too close. Also let go of any guilt about being upset in the past – this is a new day, and all any of us can do at any given time is our best. Sometimes older siblings can be very effective tutors when parents can't manage it.

Watch your expectations. Do you perform your daily tasks consistently from day to day? Children are as susceptible to exhaustion from the daily grind as we are. Watch for signs of being tired, over-excited, recovering from illness, allergies, etc. and make allowances. The pressure of working for someone who expects optimum performance at all times is unbearable!

Helping Your Child Succeed

Confidence comes from success. Encourage your child to complete assigned tasks. This leads to success. As adults, we know how to learn from our mistakes but children sometimes repeat errors endlessly, which only reinforces them.

They develop habits that do not result in success. When you hear "I don't like to . . ." or "I hate that," it often means "I don't think I can." If you think that the issue is confidence, not ability, bring the child back to the task and help him complete it.

When a task is too difficult – adapt it for success. When you see that a task is too difficult, and success is not likely, change it a little. Talk to your child's teacher about adapting tasks for your child. The same thing applies when the task is too easy and the child is bored.

Help your child eliminate distractions. Children who struggle with schoolwork are often easily distracted and learn to use their distractibility to become skillful procrastinators (chattering incessantly, sharpening pencils, getting a drink, going to the bathroom, etc). Let them know that there will be time for fun when the work gets done. Some children need short breaks every 15 or 30 minutes. Determine how long your child can concentrate for, and allow her regular breaks.

When and How to Give Corrections

Offer help when it seems necessary, but give it only when accepted.
Don't insult your child by taking work out of her hands. Don't force her to make corrections according to your standards. Teachers don't expect work to be perfect; you shouldn't either.

Corrections – When and How. Always give your child the opportunity to find his errors first. It is important that he learn to judge his own work. Avoid making critical comments. Suggest respectfully that something may be amiss: "Hmm, do you think these two questions are exactly alike?" or "You might want to have a look at the third one again." Remember – say it the way you would like to hear it.

Humor is often a great relief. Try comments like: "Hah! Caught you at last!" or "Hey, I've been looking everywhere for a mistake, I think I've found one at last!" Be prepared for them to say, "It's good enough. I just want to get finished!"

Give honest and effective praise, but don't judge. Always make sure that praise is warranted – children know if their work is well done without your judgment. To make praise effective, focus on the specifics of the task, never on the child. Comments like "good boy," "good job," or even "good work," are subjective and judgmental and the child might secretly reject them.

Instead, make objective comments that describe the child's effort, "You got that many done in such a short time? You really kept focused!" "Your numbers are very neatly written." "I understand that creative writing is hard for you. Two paragraphs are more than you've ever written before. I can see that you tried really hard."

Effective praise recognizes the child's effort. The result is secondary. Avoid demanding perfection: "It's great that you got through all the questions. Everyone makes mistakes when they are learning. You can do any corrections tomorrow."

Keep a close eye on your child's emotions. Watch for and try to prevent catastrophic reactions, like going to pieces and floods of tears. This kind of reaction indicates that the child has reached her limit of frustration and pressure. She is afraid of her behavior and her inability to control it. If this happens, hold her gently and provide reassurance and understanding. Now is not the time to reason or continue with the task. It is seldom an issue of discipline – the child doesn't react this way on purpose.

Try to anticipate these reactions and avoid them. Persistently avoiding a task may be a warning sign that the child can't cope with it right now or today. Be flexible, and suggest an alternate activity.

Your relationship comes first. The way you communicate (your tone, your attitude) is far more important than the details of what you say. Your job as a parent is to see that your child has: challenging tasks that he is capable of doing; support as he needs it; praise as he earns it; and above all a healthy parent-child relationship! The love and security of your relationship will help him to enjoy himself and gain satisfaction from what he is doing. Don't lose sight of the fact that school performance is never as important as your relationship with your child.

Apply Your Knowledge

- How do I feel about my child's homework? Am I anxious, impatient or angry? Can my child see this?
- Am I able to stay positive and encouraging when helping my child with homework?
- Am I able to stay out of the way when my child wants to do it herself?
- Have I made it easy for my child to concentrate on homework?

This chapter has considered the complexity of the issues involved in helping our children take responsibility. By the time they are about 19 they need to be able to manage their lives as adults, so it is entirely appropriate that we hand that responsibility over to them gradually rather than suddenly.

Remember to distinguish between 'kid issues' and 'family issues', and to allow natural consequences for kid issues, so that your children feel that they are in charge of these aspects of their lives.

Further Reading

Bettelheim, Bruno. *The Informed Heart: Autonomy in a Mass Age.*
New York Free Press, 1969.

Coloroso, Barbara. *Kids Are Worth It.*
Toronto: Somerville, 1994.

Crary, Elizabeth. *Pick Up Your Socks and Other Skills Growing Children Need.*
Seattle: Parenting Press, 1990.

Dreikurs, Rudolf. *Children: The Challenge.*
Fitzhenry and Whiteside, 1964.

Paul, Jordan and Margaret. *Do I Have to Give Up Me to be Loved By My Kids?*
New York: Berkley, 1987.

6

Developing
Caring People:

Helping Children Develop Values and Empathy

None of us want our children to become spoiled, out-of-control people who take what they want at the expense of others. Nor do we want to produce unthinking robots who obey us and 'the rules' without thinking for themselves.

What should be our highest goal for our children? Surely it is to produce responsible adults who care for others, themselves and the environment. All our discipline should be directed towards this end.

The heart of morality in all cultures is the *Golden Rule: Treat other people the way you would like them to treat you.* Healthy family values are applications of the Golden Rule in different areas of living, such as honesty, respect for people, and respect for property. We show you how to link your household rules to the Golden Rule with explanations that make sense to kids.

In this chapter we discuss how to guide and support your children in a world where peer influence, television and the Internet all too often exert morally negative pressure. Trying to keep kids away from 'bad influences' usually leads them to be deceptive; it's wiser to 'inoculate' them against these influences through open discussion.

We look at two specific problems – lying and stealing. We explore why kids lie and steal, how to prevent it from happening, and what to do when it does happen.

1 - Moral Development

Human beings go through stages in the development of their understanding of right and wrong. An individual's ethics, behavior and conscience will depend on the stage he has reached.

General Development and Moral Development

Children's ability to understand right and wrong depends very much on how they develop in the areas we discussed in Chapters 2 and 3. These areas are summarized below.

To develop mature moral values, a child needs to:

1) Know the realities of life, the meaning of truth and falsehood, and the results of deceptive behavior.
2) Be able to think maturely and flexibly, consider the long-term results of his actions, and look at all aspects of a situation.
3) Have a sense of himself as an independent human being rather than someone who blindly obeys rules or disobeys them.
4) Have the ability to recognize his own feelings, express them appropriately, refrain from hurtful actions which might result from those feelings, and meet his needs in ways which do not harm either himself or others.
5) Understand thoroughly that all other people are like him and that his actions can affect them either positively or negatively.

These five things come only with maturity; when our children are young it is important for us to see them as immature rather than 'selfish' or 'bad'.

Stages of Moral Thinking

Research by such psychologists as Jean Piaget, Lawrence Kohlberg and Carol Gilligan suggests that children go through three major stages in the development of their moral understanding. We have developed our own titles for these stages in the context of parenting and child development:

Stages of Moral Thinking

1. Reward-and-punishment morality.
2. Law-and-order morality.
3. Love-your-neighbour morality.

Stage 1:   Reward-and-Punishment Morality

Reward-and-punishment morality is the earliest stage of moral development and usually lasts up to about 10 years of age. In this phase a child responds to the rewards and punishments he experiences but has acquired no internal moral values as yet. He judges whether a behavior is wrong by whether or not it is punished. His judgment is based on obedience to whatever authority is present at the time. The child's aim is to protect himself, ensure his own happiness, and avoid being hurt.

There is little if any evidence of caring for other people, even though he might cry if someone else is hurt. He has no consideration of abstract ethical principles or values. A child at this level of development will judge the rightness or goodness of behavior by the outward consequences of the behavior, rather than by the intentions of the person who performs it. For a child at this stage, breaking 12 cups accidentally is worse than breaking one cup intentionally.

Didn't he do something wrong?

When my son Alex was eight he dropped a plate one evening when he was serving me dinner. The plate smashed and sent food and plate fragments all over the kitchen floor. Alex was terrified that I'd be angry with him. This situation gave me a great opportunity to explain the difference between accidents and things done on purpose.   *-- Alison Miller*

Some adults, unfortunately, don't make this distinction. They will punish a child just as severely for dropping a plate accidentally as they would if the child threw the plate at them with the intention of hurting them. We cannot assist our children to gain maturity in their values unless we look at our own values.

Whether a person develops beyond this level of moral understanding depends on the way his parents teach him morality. Prisons are full of people who were severely punished as children for wrongdoing, yet they continue to do wrong. Their morality is still based on reward and punishment — they will do what they can get away with. They lack understanding of any higher reason for obeying the law, doing the morally right thing, or caring for others. Theirs is survival level morality. Insisting on obedience and punishing disobedience keeps a person at the survival level of moral development.

Stage 2: Law-and-Order Morality

When a child's morality has progressed to the law-and-order stage (normally at about age10), the child has learned the lessons taught to him about good and bad behavior. He takes the laws and rules laid down by parents or society as absolute and right, rather than questioning these and judging them by a higher standard. His moral sense is still based on obedience rather than an inner sense of what is right or an awareness of the needs and feelings of himself and other people. This kind of morality is similar to the 'being good' morality which we discuss in the first chapter of *The Parent-Child Connection*. According to this morality, 'right' is externally defined by church, holy book, parents or society.

Research shows that many adults still have moral values at this level. If our understanding of right and wrong is based only on law and authority, we are unable to convey any higher understanding to our children. If a person learns his moral values with rewards for 'good' (obedient) behavior and punishment for 'wrong' (disobedient) behavior, he will develop to the law-and-order level of morality and see good behavior as obedience. The child (or adult) at the reward-and-punishment or the law-and-order stage does not necessarily know why certain behaviors are right or wrong, only that they must be right or wrong because the authorities say so. If he doesn't develop beyond this point he may become a parent who has rigid rules which he applies to his family without exploring them to see if the values underpinning these rules make sense to him and to his family.

What happens when a government imposes laws and behaviors that are morally wrong? Many fine, up-standing members of society upheld and obeyed the Nazi government in Germany, becoming soldiers, policemen and prison guards. They had learned that authorities were to be obeyed, and they had no higher inner law by which to judge the authorities of their land. A morality of obedience to law and authority breaks down in situations in which the law or authority is immoral. A famous experiment by psychologist Stanley Milgram in the 1960s shocked the world by showing that most ordinary people would obey a 'doctor' in a white coat when ordered to give other people painful electric shocks as punishment for making mistakes in remembering a list of words.

Obedience to authority is a good basis for morality only when the authority can be trusted to be wise and good. Most people do not question authority sufficiently. There is a documentary film, *The Corporation (2003)*, which offers pretty compelling evidence that in present-day society large corporations operate only by the law of profit, without regard for the rights and safety of their employees or the environment. Most people accept that this is the way things are and there's nothing wrong with it. But don't we need to adopt a higher level of morality and values and stop our environment from being destroyed? Don't we need to prevent those in the rich parts of the world from devastating the lives of those in the poorer parts of the world?

Stage 3: Love-Your-Neighbour Morality

As a child (or an adult) matures from a 'conventional' rule-based morality to a perspective of empathic caring for self and others, there is a shift in concern from obedience to truth, honesty and kindness. At this level, a person sees that morality is not simply a matter of obedience to rules, but is the basis for our living in harmony with others. At this level there is more flexibility, thoughtfulness, and struggle with moral dilemmas than when morality was a simple matter of externally defined 'right and wrong'. The simplest way to put this mature morality is, of course, the way it has been put by great moral thinkers in all major religions and cultures: The Golden Rule. This is the great universal truth in the realm of morality.

The Golden Rule

Love your neighbor as yourself.
or
Treat others as you would like them to treat you.

The Golden Rule is the highest moral standard, and other beliefs about right and wrong have to be judged by the standard which it sets. In a love-your-neighbor morality, all other laws should be just applications of this universal law to specific situations. Doing good is caring for both self and others, and 'others' may include other species and the environment, not just human beings.

"Getting" the Golden Rule

I remember the day when a 21-year-old university student I was counseling 'got' the Golden Rule. She came in from walking around town with a huge smile on her face. She'd been looking at all the people, so different from herself, and suddenly recognized they were all people just like her, worthy of respect and love, just as human as she was. We may give lip service to this idea, but how many of us really believe it?   -- *Alison Miller*

Every one of these people is a ME!

In its least demanding form, the Golden Rule defines boundaries: "Your freedom to swing your arm ends where my nose begins." We teach this to our children, and it is the basis for the rules of behavior in our homes and schools. The laws of society punish those who disrespect the boundaries of others in any way, whether it be physical violence, stealing, or even aggressive driving.

However, the Golden Rule goes beyond boundaries to include altruism:

  treating others with kindness and empathy. The entire purpose of morality is to ensure that everyone will receive kind and respectful treatment.
  the love and respect that everyone needs in order to flourish.

If we want our children to develop to the highest level of morality we need to teach them to have empathy for others. Caring or empathic behavior stems from understanding how other people feel. When a child comes home on time because he understands that his parent will be worried if he doesn't, he is beginning to understand the "love your neighbor" morality; he is motivated by empathy, not fear of punishment.

When a child is allowed to express his feelings and has them respected, he in turn will respect and learn to understand the feelings of others.

Conscience

If we believe something is wrong only if we get punished for doing it, our conscience will trouble us only when we are caught doing something which some authority considers wrong. If our moral values are based on keeping rules and laws, our conscience will trouble us only when we break a rule set down by some authority. On the other hand, if our moral values are based on the higher moral principle of the Golden Rule, our conscience will trouble us every time we harm another person or ourselves.

Apply Your Knowledge

- What level of moral development do you think each of your children has reached:

  ☐ Reward-and-punishment
  ☐ Law-and-order
  ☐ Love-your-neighbor

- What level do you usually function at? Do you think of morality or 'being good' in terms of:
  a) doing what you want without getting caught,
  b) obeying the rules and the law, or
  c) acting lovingly towards people?

- Do you expect your children to obey you without question or do you expect them to be caring people? Be honest!

Respect

Treating others with respect is an important part of the Golden Rule. In the interactions of daily life, respect becomes an issue when a person does not consider the needs and feelings of another person. As parents, we need to understand our children's development enough to know at what level to place our expectations. There are some behaviors that we should simply ignore and not take personally, for example: whining and toilet talk from preschoolers, or mouthiness and cursing (under their breath) from teens. But when a child's behavior crosses a boundary and hurts someone else, we need to state our disapproval. Some parents become upset by normal child behaviors; this is over-reacting and such parents need to examine why they react like this. Other parents don't react strongly enough when their child acts in a very rude and inconsiderate manner.

Even though a child may not be mature enough to understand the feelings and needs of others, limits and boundaries can teach him about such feelings and needs and why he should respect them. "Your freedom to swing your arm ends where my nose begins – because my nose can get hurt!"

Now you do as I say, young woman, OR ELSE!

Now you do as I say, old man, OR ELSE!

For a child too young to understand others' needs and feelings, this rule teaches the equality of human beings in a way which is easy to understand.

The essence of moral behavior is to treat others as we would like them to treat us. If we do not do this, sooner or later they will treat us as we have treated them. Many parents who have mistreated their young children find that their children start to abuse them upon entering their teens. Research now shows that a lot of 'elder abuse' involves abused children as adults getting their own back at their aged parents, as shown in the cartoon!

Likewise, if we respect our children (their space, privacy and need to make reasonable choices) we show them how we ourselves want to be treated. Being willing to listen to our children and respect their feelings is a big part of teaching them respect. If we listen well to our children and respect them we are likely to be treated the same way by them when they mature.

- How would you define respect?

- Describe any disrespectful behavior you have noticed in your child. What is your reaction to this behavior?

- How does this behavior affect you or other people?

- Is this behavior at all common at your child's age? If so, what would happen if you ignored it?

- Has your child learned this behavior from someone else's example? Whose?

Anger Management for Parents

Ten-year-old David became frustrated with his Dad (Ian) and called him an idiot. Ian reacted with anger, yelled back at David and lectured him on respect. Ian had quickly fallen into a self-protective state and wanted David to know just how wrong he was. He overpowered David with his temper and authority. Here's an example using the A-N-G-E-R of our chapter on Conflict Resolution in *The Parent-Child Connection*. Here's how Ian used these ideas to work things out.

A – Attention:
Ian caught himself yelling at his son and realized he wasn't teaching him anything. David became upset and started to cry. Ian could feel his heart pounding and his fists clenched tightly. He could feel the adrenaline. Ian knew he only had one choice: Get out before he 'lost it'.

N – Negotiate:
Ian stopped lecturing, left the room and went outside. As he left, he said, "I can't talk right now; I'm too upset."

G – Gearing Down:
Ian started working in the yard to release some of his anger. As he worked in the yard he started thinking about how explosive he felt when he was called a name. It hurt a lot. He wondered why he reacted like this.

E – Exploration and Expressing: Ian thought that he never would have talked to his own Dad like that (but mind you, his Dad had no qualms about using a belt). He came to realize that it was hard not to take it personally because his own father had been punitive and often had called him names simply because he was in a bad mood. He thought again about David, and recognized that David was intense and that he was still young. David had hormones at work too and probably needed some support. Ian thought about his belief system regarding obedience and knew that fear was not the same as discipline. He knew that David's words were a trigger for him and that some of his anger at David actually should have been directed at his own Dad. He came up with some coping thoughts to help him stay grounded. "David is a kind kid who gets mad just like everybody else. He has feelings too. He's young." Ian went back to David and made the following I-statement: "When you call me an idiot, I feel angry and hurt. Please try telling me how you feel again without calling me a name."

We can set limits simply by giving an 'I-message'. There may not be any consequence attached to it or any need to sit down and discuss it. Now remember body language here. Once he has taken the time to cool down, Dad can fully express his anger within the safety of an 'I-message'.

If Ian expresses himself this way, he is teaching David that everybody has feelings. He is also showing David how to deal with his own frustrations. How else can David learn how to make an 'I-message' himself? David will understand why calling someone names isn't okay; he will not be acting simply out of fear.

R – Resolution:
If David continues with this behavior, Ian will need to address the situation through conflict resolution: exploring feelings and needs, and perhaps establishing a suitable consequence for everybody if name-calling is involved. The beauty of conflict resolution is that we can engage in it when both people are calm, relaxed, rested and well fed. Ian and David can decide on things together and David will feel respected even though Ian is setting a limit. Consequences can be discussed and decided upon by both David and his Dad. If David slips and breaks the limit, Dad can simply remind him of the consequence without a lecture, shaming comments or threats. Likewise, if Ian slips he may be the one throwing coins in the jar!

When feelings are hurt and someone experiences sadness or anger, it is often an indication that a respect boundary has been crossed. Basic human needs around this boundary include: emotional safety, consideration, empathy, support, peace, autonomy, love and reassurance.

Manners

Manners are ways we have developed in society to show respect and caring for other people. Children, who are by their very nature egocentric, often don't understand manners and need to have the reasons for them explained. This is especially true as they get older and develop values which are internal rather than centered on obedience and social acceptability. Some accepted manners don't make much sense now. For example, hand-shaking was developed as a way of indicating you weren't holding a weapon. But the most important manners, like saying "thank you", show respect and kindness.

Why Teens Lose Their Manners

There is a stage in or just before the teen years in which kids abandon manners. It can be a little shocking to see your 14-year-old act in a way that she wouldn't at six. It is as if kids at this stage have to abandon all the values and manners that they learned before the teens. The reason for this is that they are moving from an obedience-based morality to one based on caring for other people from the heart.

That's one reason teens are so oriented to their peers: they spend a lot of time supporting one another, learning through interaction with their friends to "love their neighbor". Instead of obeying and following rules, they develop values from their own inner experience. Take heart, they will develop deeper values, and all the good stuff you have shown them through the earlier years will resurface!

I'd rather be rude than phony.

At the age of about ten I refused to say "please" or "thank you" or smile for photographs, because these things seemed phony to me. I didn't want to say "thank you" for gifts I didn't appreciate; that would be lying! I didn't want to apologize when I wasn't sorry. I didn't want to say "please" (which is short for "if it pleases you") if I wasn't giving the person a choice.

Believe it or not, this insisting on being genuine and not phony was a step towards developing values of genuine respect for people. To my amazement, my son Alex developed exactly the same behavior when he reached the same age! Now he's an adult and understands that the little acts of kindness that "oil the wheels" of society aren't all so bad. But for a while he needed to discard everything that seemed false from society's conventions in order to develop values of his own.   *-- Alison Miller*

Manners are like an exchange of energy. When someone does something for us, they are extending energy. We give energy back by showing appreciation and respect. We can do this even with strangers – with a smile or a few words. Children need this explained to them and then they can make their own choices about using manners.

How do you teach empathy? Well, you can say this: "People feel good about doing things for you when you use polite words and gestures." That helps, but it appeals to the child's self-interest. You want your child to understand how others feel. Try role-playing with her to show how it feels when someone is or isn't respectful to her.

There is a saying which goes something like this: "You don't have to like me, just be polite." Mutual respect can go such a long way and to me that is what manners represent. The forced "please" and "thank you" don't mean much. Children with a cautious approach often find a simple please and thank you very difficult. Don't judge them as rude because they feel this way.

Remember Eddie Haskell in the 1960s family sitcom *Leave It To Beaver*? He was polite and acted very nice in front of adults, yet he was full of mischief when no authority figure was present. This isn't what we are after. His morality was clearly at the reward-and-punishment stage.

What if your child is going through a 'rude stage'? Let go of your own embarrassment and allow your child to make his own choices. It is much better to just say it ("please" and "thank you") for the child than it is to humiliate him in front of others. If you are at the bank and the teller gives your child a sucker, you can say: "Johnny looks really happy with that sucker. Thank you." If the teller is wise, she will see by the look on Johnny's face that he appreciates it.

Apologies: Genuine and Forced

Well, are you ready to have a few feathers ruffled on this one? WE HATE FORCED APOLOGIES! They teach children to be insincere and give them the false idea that "sorry" fixes things. *When you force a child to apologize you are teaching him to lie!* Stephen Covey puts it well: "Sincere apologies make deposits in the Emotional Bank Account; repeated apologies interpreted as insincere make withdrawals." (*The 7 Habits of Highly Effective People,* p.199.)

If you witness conflict between two children, acknowledge the feelings of each child without playing judge. Most of the time we don't see the whole picture anyway. Saying, "I'm sorry you have been hurt" is a nice neutral way of addressing the children's feelings without assigning blame. In most cases you don't know what happened.

One mother of teens told me (Allison Rees) she wouldn't forgive her children until they apologized to her. I asked her what she thought such an apology would really mean if it was forced. Her only answer was that it was the right thing to do. Giving 'I-messages' about your feelings and needs is much more powerful. (See the discussion on Speaking without Regrets in *The Parent-Child Connection*.) It helps your child develop the empathy that will eventually teach him to apologize. But you must take ownership of your feelings and avoid manipulating and guilt-inducing statements. Just be clear, own your stuff and state it clearly. Even if the child doesn't apologize he will learn something valuable.

2 - Telling the Truth

Why Children Lie

If anything really pushes a parent's buttons it is dishonesty. We were taught when we were children that dishonesty is wrong, and many of us got punished for it even before we were old enough to understand why it was wrong.

Exaggeration and Story-Telling

Young children will often exaggerate because it captures your attention – it makes a better story. Sometimes they simply say what you want to hear. Don't invite a lie by asking, "Who spilled milk all over the floor?" If there are two of you home and it wasn't you, you already know who did it. "I see you spilled milk on the floor. Here is a rag."

Four-year-olds often tell tall tales. They tell you what you want to hear without grasping the concept of a lie. This can last for a few years or a few months. Don't overreact! You can say things like, "It sounds like you are telling me a story right now."

Lying to Avoid Consequences

Older children and teens often lie to avoid consequences. They do this because they just don't realize why it's wrong or because the discipline they face for minor misbehaviors such as not doing homework, is too harsh. In one family, natural consequences are used. If homework isn't finished, it's up to the child to choose between getting a bad mark, staying up late, or getting up early to finish the homework. This child has no reason to lie, and he will probably do his homework, because it's his homework, not his parents' responsibility.

In another family, the child is grounded from seeing his friends for a weekend if his homework isn't done. Seeing his friends is very important to him, so he'll lie about his homework, and he'll think it's up to his parents to see that he gets his homework done. By taking responsibility for something that is up to the child, and by imposing harsh consequences when natural consequences were already available, the parents have set the stage for the child to lie.

This child's parents need to: a) teach the child why lying isn't a good idea (see below), and b) help meet the needs which were being met by lying. This child's need is to be treated with respect and kindness, as someone who can make his own decisions and does not need to be punished severely for minor infractions.

It is important to remove the reasons which cause a child to lie. If you have too many power struggles over rules, your kids will just go ahead and 'do it anyway' when you aren't around. Keep the home atmosphere one in which children can continue to be honest. This means letting go of issues which you can't control and don't need to control. Passing moral judgment on kids and then laying down the law doesn't produce honesty or integrity. There comes a point when we need to realize that control doesn't work.

Lying and Trust

Children do not naturally know that there is anything wrong with lying. Why do we think it's wrong, anyway? Basically, because when a person sometimes lies, you don't know at any given time whether or not they're telling the truth, so you can't trust them. The story of "The Boy Who Cried Wolf" is a good story to help a young child get the idea. (For those who haven't heard it, a shepherd boy gets bored and lonely while he's looking after the sheep, so every so often he cries "wolf" so that people will come and pay attention to him. After a while they stop coming, and then the wolf really comes.) Tell your child this story, or borrow it from the library. Then ask her how she'd feel if you lied. For example, if you said she could have a treat, then didn't give it to her, again and again. Let her figure out that she'd learn not to believe you.

The Emotional Bank Account which Steven Covey teaches about is built on trust (see Chapter 8 of *The Parent-Child Connection*). The strongest and the best relationships have trust going both ways: kids trust parents to be both fair and kind; parents trust kids to be both honest and responsible. Teach your children the importance of trust with examples of how they trust you to do what you say you are going to do. Trust is present in everyday things like being on time to pick them up and reading to them at bedtime, no matter what kind of day you've had.

3 - The Power of Example

The most important and effective way to teach any kind of values is by example. If you want your children to learn manners, show them how it is done by modeling politeness to others, and especially by using manners with your children. It's that simple. But the power of example goes beyond manners and politeness.

Won't your Dad be mad when he finds out we've eaten his chocolate bars?

Yup. But he won't say anything. He was hiding them so he wouldn't have to share. Officially, these bars don't exist.

Anything to declare, sir?

Just four bottles of pop and a gallon of milk...

And don't forget the Scotch bottles, Daddy...

I knowed you just forgot, Daddy, and wouldn't tell a lie to that nice lady.

Research consistently shows that a child's moral development is a reflection of parental behavior rather than parental preaching. This cartoon about a family crossing the Canada-U.S. border, and the previous one about hidden candy bars illustrate typical parental hypocrisy about telling the truth. And then we wonder why our kids lie!

Some parents and teachers feel they have to dominate their children in order to feel they have authority. This kind of authority is not truly respected by the child. If you think back to high school, you may remember a teacher who did this and was either hated or ridiculed by students behind his back. Then again you can probably remember a teacher who treated kids with respect and took a personal interest in them as individuals. This teacher was given the same kind of respect in return.

Our communication, honesty and ability to show vulnerability all contribute to our children's developing moral judgment and self-esteem. They are watching us: the way we think, our integrity, our sincerity, our truthfulness, and our kindness and empathy.

Apply Your Knowledge

- Can you think of some areas in which you can set a good example for your children so that they will develop into mature, respectful, empathic human beings?

---

4 - Establishing Family Values

Family values are important moral values which you would like your children to believe in. Examples: honesty, respect for other people's property, respect for your own and other people's health, respect for privacy, respect for other people's feelings, and kindness to those who are weaker.

Parents often set down a lot of rules for children, and give a lot of orders, with consequences for disobedience. Children learn that being 'good' means obeying the rules and obeying orders. Obeying the order of the moment leads to children having a reward-and-punishment morality, thinking that 'right' is what gets a reward and 'wrong' is what gets a punishment. Living by rules leads to children having a law-and-order morality, believing that the rules are absolute: 'right' is obeying the rules and 'wrong' is disobeying them.

It is often unavoidable to have rules and give orders to children. But in order to help our children develop to higher levels of morality, all our rules and our requests need to derive from our family values, and our family values need to derive from the Golden Rule – treating other people the way we would like to be treated. The connection between our rules and requests and these underlying values needs to be taught to our children. In this way, they will learn to look beyond specific rules or requests and examine the reason behind them.

Applying Values

Golden Rule   Love your neighbor or brother
⇕
Family Values   Equality, cleanliness
⇕
Rules & Limits   Contribute to chores
⇕
Requests   Take out the garbage, etc.

The arrows in the above table show that specific requests come from general limits, which come from family values, which derive from the Golden Rule. The Golden Rule gets applied through different values, which are made practical by family rules and limits, which are made really specific by our requests.

If we consider our children's feelings, share our own feelings and help our children reflect on the feelings of others then we raise our children to a higher level of moral development. This teaches them why the rules are there – to state precisely what it means in practice to "treat other people the way you would like them to treat you".

Teaching Values

As a child listens to explanations of the rules, he learns the meaning of right and wrong. Explanations need to be brief and explained in terms which respect the child's age. Children need to see reasons for the rules and requests so that they will want to obey them.

Requests have to be within a child's grasp. A very young child is incapable of being in a room for 15 minutes without touching anything. A child who doesn't know the meaning of truth can't be expected to tell it. Expecting siblings to 'always be kind' stretches them beyond their ability. Children feel like failures when they are required to do things that they simply can't do.

It pays to be specific when you make a request rather than using generalities such as "be nice". Rather than saying "don't be mean!", you should say "don't call people names". Rather than saying "don't be lazy", you should say "put away your dishes when you've finished with them".

Kids can be very literal in how they interpret what you say, like the kids in the cartoon, who are making sure Mom doesn't hear them.

The Golden Explanation

Your explanation of rules and requests should refer back to the Golden Rule. This is a good reality check to ensure you are being reasonable; if you can't relate the limit to the Golden Rule, rethink its importance. It may be a silly rule that really doesn't matter, like the bed-making rule in the next cartoon.

Ensure that all limits are clear to your child. Give children the chance to ask "why?" Explain each limit to the point where you reach the Golden Rule and only to that point. Here's an example:

Exploring the Golden Rule - #1

	Parent Dialogue	**Child's Response**
What (request)	Give Amy back her doll, please.	Why?
We (rule)	Because you know the rule about no grabbing.	So?
We (family value)	We respect other people's property and don't use it without permission.	Why?
Do (relate limit to the Golden Rule)	Because people's things matter to them, and Amy's doll matters to her just like your video games matter to you. We treat others the way we'd like them to treat us (Golden Rule).	Fine. Dolls are stupid.

An explanation of a rule or request needs to include:
♦ **what** behavior is required
♦ why members of our family (**we**) are expected to do this
♦ how it ties in to the Golden Rule:
 ("**Do** unto others as you would have them do unto you.")

You can use the acronym "**what we do**" to remind you. It describes the limit in terms of the needs of others and supports one of the most important lessons of childhood: respect for others. As we said earlier, children are egocentric by nature and this lesson takes time to learn. *It is normal for them to think of themselves before others.*

Children need to develop empathy and understanding for others. When we teach our children these things, they learn that other people matter too. While moral development comes in various stages and much is learned from what our children see, we also need to teach it explicitly with words.

Here's another example:

Exploring the Golden Rule - #2

	Parent Dialogue	**Child's Response**
What (request)	Dad is lying down with a head-ache, so please keep your noise down.	I don't want to.
We (rule)	The noise will make it hard for him to rest.	Why should I care?
We (family value)	In this house we keep our noises down when others are sleeping.	That's a drag.
Do (relate limit to the Golden Rule)	If you were resting, you would want quiet too. Wouldn't you want Dad to be quiet for you?	I don't rest in the daytime.
Do (Golden Rule expanded)	Imagine you have an awful headache and are lying down in the dark to get rid of it. Then Dad and I start yelling at each other really loudly right outside your door. We don't do that, of course, because we're thinking of you. And we'd like you to think of us too.	Okay.

"Because I Said So!"

"What we do" expresses the importance of caring about other people and ourselves. It develops children's values to a higher level than the phrase "because I said so", which merely tells the child that the rule in your family is that big people have the right to order little people around whenever they please simply because they are bigger. It teaches immature morality based on unquestioning obedience rather than on understanding moral values and developing empathy for the other person. The next example applies the Golden Rule to chores:

Exploring the Golden Rule - #3

	Parent Dialogue	**Child's Response**
What (request)	Please take out the garbage.	Why?
We (family value)	Because we have agreed that everyone in the family will help with chores and that everyone will get a different chore each week to keep things fair.	Why?
Do (relate limit to the Golden Rule)	Because everyone in this family matters equally, and we must all learn to help each other. It wouldn't be fair if some people did all the work and others did none. So we help each other out.	That stinks!

Teaching Altruism

The highest form of morality is positive, helpful behavior towards other people. This is altruism and it means more than just refraining from harming other people; it means actively nurturing and helping them. We can't require a child to help others in the same way we can require him not to hurt others. But we can teach him by our words and our example to actively love and help others rather than just avoid mistreating them.

Stephen Covey says in *The 7 Habits of Highly Effective People* (p. 195):

> *"Integrity includes but goes beyond honesty. Honesty is telling the truth – in other words, conforming our words to reality. Integrity is conforming reality to our words – in other words, keeping promises and fulfilling expectations."*

Most of us want our children to have integrity and to be caring persons. The best way to convey these qualities is by example.

Empathy Training

Martin Hoffman and Herbert Saltzstein carried out an extensive study on seventh-graders in 1967. Their study measured relationships between types of parental discipline and moral development of the child.

Each child's moral development was measured by teachers, peers, and the child's own parents. The children and the parents then reported the kind of discipline they received at home. Discipline techniques were divided into three categories:

1.   power assertion, in which the parent asserted power and authority over the child;

2.   love withdrawal, which included forms of anger and disapproval, but no physical punishment; and

3.   'induction', in which the parent focused on the consequences of the child's action on others.

Induction was much more effective than power assertion and love withdrawal. This means that a child who is consistently told the effect his bad behavior has on others has a better chance of internalizing the lesson and not repeating the behavior. The child who is physically punished for his behavior, or who has love withdrawn, has less chance of incorporating the lesson. The father who explains why missing the curfew worries him has a better chance of getting the lesson of responsibility and truthfulness across than the father who 'blows up'.

Empathy training is useful whenever a child has inadvertently harmed someone else. If a child has come to truly understand how his behavior affected another person, he can make amends by apologizing. When a child imagines what it is like to be in the other person's shoes she might be able to imagine that person's experience. Without this kind of understanding an apology is inappropriate and is only teaching the child to lie and to feel humiliated. This could be especially upsetting if the other person started the fight and/or hurt the child as well.

Apply Your Knowledge

- What makes some children stay stuck at the level of moral development at which they believe something is wrong only because they are punished for it?
- Describe some effective parenting strategies for helping children develop a caring attitude for others and a more mature level of moral development?
- Children are egocentric, not selfish (see Chapter 3). Being egocentric helps the child develop a sense of self so that he can eventually understand that other people are persons with feelings and needs just like him. How can we help a child understand himself as one self among many?

Influences Outside the Home

Many parents complain that their children are exposed through friends to movies, video games, and Internet content that they would never permit in their own homes. Should we be locking our children up and preventing them from any such exposure or is there a more effective way to handle it?

This is a difficult question and one we've heard many times from idealistic parents who want to protect their children from frightening experiences and bad influences. We need to protect our children as much as we can while they're still young yet at the same time we have to build in them strength to resist some of the things which they will inevitably be exposed to sooner or later.

We regard the confused and unhealthy values expressed through these media as 'social germs' which can spread like contagious diseases to our children. How do we handle them?

If an epidemic strikes, the safest people are those who have been inoculated against the disease; most of those who have had no previous encounter with it die. Because of this, we make sure our children have their shots. What is the magic substance in the needle which prevents the child from getting the disease? Dead germs! The child's immune system forms antibodies so that when he encounters live germs the antibodies will attack and kill them. We believe we need to 'inoculate' our children against 'illnesses' of the value system by exposing them early in life to less harmful forms of the 'germs' of dangerous lifestyles.

Teaching children to deal with scary movies or morally degenerate television shows is actually no different from teaching them how to ride a bicycle or to manage their money. You don't let a child be exposed to what she isn't yet ready to handle. But as the child grows, you gradually teach her to deal with progressively more challenging situations. With bicycle riding, you begin with a tricycle in the back yard or on the sidewalk. Then you move up to training wheels with you walking beside her and eventually you remove the training wheels.

Throughout the whole process you teach your child the principles of safe riding. With money management you begin with a very small allowance just for treats, then gradually increase it and let it cover more areas of the child's life (bus fare, clothing, charity) while teaching principles of money management.

It's no different with a child who is learning to deal with what's on television or videos. Increase exposure gradually, while teaching and questioning, so that your child learns to discern for herself which shows are (or are not) worth watching, and which shows are (or are not) telling the truth. Refer to the Level System in Chapter 5.

When a child is very little, she can't tell the difference between reality and fiction. She thinks the lion will jump out of the television set and eat her. She thinks the ghosts and monsters are real. So you have to be very careful with 'horror' films and shows, including the news, so as not to traumatize your child. She also thinks the world is the way any adults portray it, and copies whatever she sees; if she sees adults on TV with shallow values, she will imitate what she sees. And if she sees a lot of violence without real consequences to the supposed 'good guys' she begins to believe that violence is the way of the world and that might makes right, especially if she sees herself as the 'good guy'.

When your child is very little (under about eight), it's possible to shelter her from this strange and dangerous fictional world. And you must do so as much as possible, which may mean phoning her friends' parents and asking them not to have such shows on TV when she's visiting.

But as she becomes older, preventing exposure becomes less and less possible and feels more and more like a violation of your child's freedom. Now it's time to 'inoculate' her against the influence of these shows by watching them with her. Turn on your television and look at the shows together. With regard to the scary stuff, show her how the 'monsters' are made. Give her information about what is real and what is fake so that she can tell the difference. If she's been exposed to a lot of frightening realistic violence, like action movies, let her know that most of the real world isn't like this, that most people don't carry a gun, and that she is safe at home.

If the news is bothering her, let her know that the frightening stuff is on the news because it is news, which means it is not a common occurrence.

Set limits on TV watching but don't forbid *all* low quality TV. Instead, watch some inferior TV shows *with* your child, and discuss with him why what they portray isn't good or isn't realistic – for example: "TV says it's okay to be violent if you're the good guy". Be prepared that some shows may not be as bad as you expect. I (Alison Miller) loved watching *The Simpsons* with my kids when they were younger because in my opinion it's great social satire. The same thing with video games – I found that they teach turn-taking and cooperation as well as visual-motor skills, and many of the quest-type games teach creative thinking and problem-solving. However, it's important to watch how many hours your child spends involved with the TV or game machine; some kids will completely neglect physical exercise and the outdoors in favor of these activities.

How do we handle the modeling of violence on television? Watch the cartoons with your child, see the characters dying and coming alive again, and tell her that this is unreal, that real dead creatures don't come alive again, and that it's okay to pretend as long as she knows it's just cartoons. If she's being exposed to violent action shows at other people's homes, watch some of this with her too, and inoculate her against its effect by discussing it. Point out that everyone thinks they're the 'good guys', and discuss whether it's really good to get revenge, as so many of these shows teach. As she becomes older, there will be lots of shows with questionable moral content, including sexual promiscuity, preoccupation with appearance, and materialism. Again, watch with her and question things. If she's moving into her teens, let her know that most people don't have sex on their first date, and that if they do they don't enjoy it, despite what the movies portray!

It's best not to lecture her, but rather ask her questions which make her think. You may find that your child becomes temporarily 'addicted' to shows which teach her about parts of life she's never seen at home. I know this feels awful, but perhaps it's better that she learn about these things from the movies than from real life experimentation. I know I learned a lot about what I *didn't* want to do from watching such things as a teenager. You'll find that the addiction wears off once she's acquired some understanding of what such shows portray – and you can speed up this process by watching with her and helping her ask useful questions which will lead her to thinking through the possible consequences of doing the things that the people on TV do.

Be wary of overprotecting your child. We have seen many children who were very carefully protected right up to high school or even college, and then went completely wild, trying out whatever had been forbidden, because they had developed no capacity to assess what was dangerous in their new lifestyles. Sometimes when well-meaning parents keep their children isolated from social dangers, they not only postpone the problem but make it worse when it does happen.

Watch TV commercials with your child and discuss what lies they may be telling. To demonstrate this, buy your child one of the toys the TV says is so great, and empathize how the advertisers lied when the toy falls apart after two days!

Don't let your child go to his friends' homes if there's no supervision. But don't necessarily ban these friends, because exposure to a variety of peers and adults can do wonders for him! Have your child's friends over to your house and supervise their play. Set some behavioral limits for all the children present, and discuss values with all of them. Teach and nurture the other children as well as your own when they're on your territory.

Recognize which social 'germs' or 'viruses' are so dangerous that they must be avoided completely. There may be times when you need to intervene to change your child's friendships. Don't let him be around adults (parents) who have serious behavioral problems such as yelling, hitting, stealing, or using drugs.

At age seven, children form friendships mainly on the basis of proximity. If necessary, ask the teacher to change the seating arrangement if you are convinced that it would be helpful for your child. Invite over peers from healthier families. If these measures don't work, consider moving your child to another class, or even a new neighborhood. A healthy neighborhood helps your child's exposure to dangerous lifestyles be more gradual – an inoculation rather than an infection. But many people can't afford to move, and many apparently 'good' neighborhoods have lots of drug problems and crime although they are sometimes well hidden under the surface.

You can't just move a teenager, however, and you really can't control her choice of friends. So by the time your child is in her teens you hope she's developed some internal values which will help her resist peer group temptations. At this stage you need to talk to her about what you're worried about rather than restricting her friendships. If you got into trouble in your own teens, be open about it with your teenager, and turn your own difficulties into a resource which can help your teenager understand what could happen.

The Internet has introduced much explicit sexual material into children's lives long before they are old enough to handle it. We recommend a 'Net Nanny' sort of software as well as having the computer in the living room where everyone can see what your child is looking at.

Many parents complain about their teenagers' use of the Internet, in particular MSN and chat lines. Many teens spend a lot of time on MSN and parents see them doing this at the expense of homework and chores. Computer communication feels alien to quite a few parents, and it's hard to understand that this is a way for teens to develop friendships and social skills without actually leaving home. Computer use can be relaxing and fun and we need to acknowledge that. Remember when we only had Etch A Sketch and paint-by-numbers. Just think of how much enjoyment we would have had with computers.

But just as with 'hanging out' at the park or the mall, there are dangers in 'hanging out' on MSN or other types of Internet communication forums. Some of these dangers can actually be devastating. Many young teens unwittingly expose themselves to predators as they post pictures of themselves that they easily snapped with their web cams or cell phones. They need to be educated about the kind of people that may look at these pictures and gain this information. Among teens, gossip and hurtful discussions can spread quickly and leave many kids faced with a sense of devastation that goes beyond schoolyard banter. News about parties also spreads quickly, and your teen can find herself at a party with hundreds of kids, most of whom she doesn't even know.

The Internet is a powerful medium which needs to be understood. Stay up to date on technology yourself so you know what you are talking about. Ask your kids to educate you about it if you don't understand it; kids love to be our teachers.

Kids' freedom in computer and Internet use should not be taken for granted, because there are real dangers. When your kids are young, limit their computer use and have the computer in the central area of your home rather than in their bedrooms. As they get older, teenagers need some privacy and won't want you behind their shoulder reading their messages. Kids have a code for this which is POS (i.e. parent over shoulder).

Apply Your Knowledge

- Does your child have any friends with questionable values? How do you plan to handle the situation?

- Do you watch TV with your child and discuss what the shows are teaching either directly or indirectly?

---

6 - Stealing and How to Handle It

Why Do Kids Steal?

Most children steal at some time in their lives. It is only abnormal if it continues or grows. A seven-year-old probably does not understand private property. Perhaps because you have always given him everything he needs, he doesn't understand that things belong to certain people, and that money has to be earned and spent from those earnings. It's normal for children of this age to steal. It does not mean that they will end up in jail. I remember the day when my (Alison Miller's) brother at age seven came home and shared his new fancy construction set with all the neighborhood kids. It didn't occur to him that there was anything wrong with helping himself from the store shelves, since my parents weren't about to buy it for him. He turned into a responsible adult. So did my son, who at five was found with about a hundred bubblegum packets under his pillow. Your job is to teach your child about private property, so that he will understand that some things belong to him and some belong to other people.

A 10-year-old may also be stealing because she has no clear sense of personal property. Do you allow her to have private possessions which she does not have to share with others? Do you respect the privacy of her room, her clothes, and her possessions? In our experience, older children who steal almost always have parents who don't respect their possessions. They don't know the meaning of private property because they haven't had it themselves. The first step in helping your child respect others' personal property is respecting hers.

Sometimes a child steals because she has no money or not enough toys. Do you give her an allowance or does she always have to ask if she wants something? Does she have toys that she has chosen to play with? Kids need toys – ideally things they can play with creatively rather than toys which have been designed with a purpose by someone else. Creative play does much more for a child's intellectual and personal development than the kind of learning which comes from many so-called educational games.

There are several reasons why kids steal. A child can be meeting an important need by taking things. He may need the sense that he can obtain what he wants without always being dependent on your "yes" or "no". A child may also steal because he compares himself to other kids his age and he doesn't have the kinds of things they have. This can both deprive him of fun and make him a social outcast. Kids whose parents choose all their possessions don't have a sense of making their own choices, and they feel they can't keep up with their classmates. Other kids may laugh at them.

Some teens steal for the thrill of it and the desire to have all the attractive items being sold for 'too much money' in their favorite stores. Many adults can remember getting caught and being scared straight.

How to Prevent Stealing

The first step is to make sure that your child has some personal property which no one else is allowed to touch without his permission. He keeps it in his room and he does not have to share it unless he chooses to. You ask his permission to use it. If he takes something from you, explain to him that the thing he has taken is your personal property, and that he has to ask when he wants something of yours, just as you have to ask if you want something of his. By having his own personal property, your child will learn why stealing is wrong – because everyone has a right to have things that are specially theirs, which were given to them or which they bought with their own money.

Back this up by giving your child an allowance to buy things of his own, so that he can learn what things cost and why someone's property is important to them. (See Chapter 5.) Also, give your child an opportunity to earn money in addition to the allowance which he gets every week. Find small jobs (above and beyond chores, which should be unpaid) which he can do for a dollar or so. This will teach him the connection between money and work. Now he will know that possessions cost money, and that people have to work to earn money. Explain to him that you have to work to earn the money you give him for an allowance, and that the sales clerk works to earn the money she is paid. You should also mention, of course, that stealing is against the law and is a crime.

How to Handle Stealing

Don't make a big deal about it if your child steals when he's under eight or so; just use it as an opportunity to teach. And don't focus on frightening your child about the consequences of stealing; just teach him about private property, money, and work, and the problem will disappear.

Stealing is more serious with an older child, who should know better. If you think she has stolen but can't prove it, don't make too much of it. Stealing isn't the only way kids get things; they may sell or trade their toys. Whatever you do, don't harass her until she 'admits the truth' when you suspect she has stolen. This will only cause her to cover up, and add a lying problem to the stealing problem she already has. Your anxiety can lead you to lecture interminably. When you've taught her why stealing is wrong, stop talking. She knows it's wrong; now it's up to her.

If you have clear evidence that she has stolen something, state that you know she has stolen. Talk with her about the possible effects of her stealing on others – the person she has stolen from will miss what she lost and won't trust your child, or the store will have to raise its prices to make up for theft, or an employee may have to pay for missing store inventory. You want her to learn, not to just feel she is 'bad'.

Together you and your child can work out what to do about the situation. Does she choose to apologize to the person or store? We don't believe in forced apologies, but if she genuinely sees the effects of her behavior she may want to do so. Can she give something back, or give something of her own to the person she has stolen from? If she has stolen money and it's gone, can she pay it back in installments? Kids often come up with stronger consequences than parents, when they are consulted.

If your child has stolen before, and you think she has stolen now but can't prove it, state that you are suspicious, but since you can't prove it, she will not be penalized. Don't get into an argument about whether she is innocent or guilty. State that since she has stolen before, you don't know whether or not to believe her when she says she didn't do it. If she says, "You don't trust me!" agree with her and say that you would like very much to be able to trust her. Explain that the problem with deception (stealing or lying) is that when a person deceives you once, from then on you don't know whether you can believe him, even when he is telling the truth. Tell her that you will trust her again when she has had two months with no evidence of possible stealing or other deceptions. Then keep your word.

Apply Your Knowledge

- If you have a child who steals, which of the reasons discussed above may be the cause of it?

- What plan do you have to help your child give up stealing?

- How can you prevent your children from stealing?

This chapter is short but important. It is not enough for our children to become obedient and well-behaved.

To be mature, responsible adults, they need to have internal values based on treating other people the way they want to be treated.

We need to encourage moral development so that our children will become caring adults with integrity rather than self-centered 'takers' or obedient rule-keepers.

Further Reading

Dosick, Wayne D. *Golden Rules: The Ten Ethical Values Parents Need to Teach Their Children.*
New York: Harper-Collins, 1995. Seems to be out of print.
Google search on Alibris for used copies.

Kohn, Alfie. *The Brighter Side of Human Nature: Altruism and Empathy in Everyday Life.*
New York: Basic Books, 1990

Unell, Barbara & Wyckoff, Jerry. *20 Teachable Virtues: Practical Ways to Pass on Lessons of Virtue and Character to Your Children.*
New York: Berkley, 1995

7

Love, Limits and Consequences:

How to Set Limits and Use Consequences

Chapter 7 covers most of what many parents think of as 'discipline'. That's why we've kept it for last – because the use of consequences should be a last resort. Our job as parents is to love and guide our children, not to control them with reward and punishment. The essence of limit-setting with our children is to have them respect us and other people, not to exert power as big people over small people.

Changing our own behavior and attitude is where our power lies. As we demonstrate not control over the child but rather control over ourselves, our children will also develop self-control – children do what they see done.

Still, we do need to set limits to point out personal boundaries. There are some situations in which logical consequences (such as removal of privileges) need to be used: if natural consequences are devastating, if safety is involved, if other people are getting hurt, if misbehavior is getting rewarded, or if natural consequences are too far away to have impact. This chapter talks about how to set limits and when it is necessary to impose consequences for our children. We discuss alternatives to consequences such as making I-statements and ignoring behavior which doesn't affect other people. We look at the dangers of punishing in anger and of making idle threats.

It's easy to use the same consequences over and over, especially Time Out, grounding, and removal of privileges. We discuss the pros and cons of these commonly used consequences, and the most effective ways to use them. We look at the differences between consequences and punishment, at the need to distinguish between rights and privileges before removing privileges, and at making a consequence relevant to the behavior for which it is used. We also look at how to and how not to use praise with our children.

1 - Limits, Boundaries and Power in the Family

Limits are essentially boundaries. Parents need to set limits on a child's behavior only with regard to family issues, issues to do with health, safety, and how family members treat one another. Once limits are set, consequences must sometimes be imposed.

The problem with using consequences is that all consequences involve a parent using power over a child. In 1970 Dr. Thomas Gordon, the founder of *Parent Effectiveness Training*, argued that the use of power and authority is unethical, and although it works in the short run, in the long run it produces rebellion and reactive behavior. We agree. He argued:

> *"Children want and need information from their parents that will tell them the parents' feelings about their behavior, so that they themselves can modify behavior that might be unacceptable to the parents. However, children do not want the parent to try to limit or modify their behavior by using or threatening to use their authority. In short, children want to limit their behavior themselves if it becomes apparent to them that their behavior must be limited or modified. Children, like adults, prefer to be their own authority over their behavior."* (*Parent Effectiveness Training*, p.189).

The Boundary Bubble

In what situations should parents set limits on their children's behavior? Very simply, when the behavior involves family issues rather than kid issues (see Chapter 5).

Kid issues are things which should be left for kids to handle; family issues require limits to be set on family members' behavior. Much misunderstanding and squabbling will be avoided if parents keep this distinction in mind.

Imagine a stretchy cellophane bubble containing the child's issues and experience. The bubble represents the limits we set. As they grow, children will push out from the inside, always testing the strength of the bubble. They need to know that the bubble exists but they also need to know that it will expand as they grow. Gradually, our role in maintaining the bubble will end and one day our children will be responsible for their own boundary bubble.

The Boundary Bubble

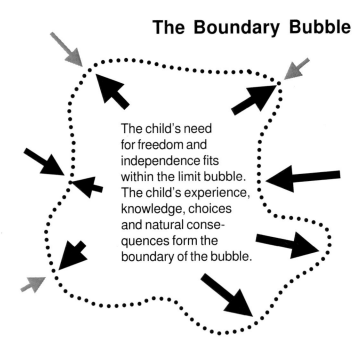

The child's need for freedom and independence fits within the limit bubble. The child's experience, knowledge, choices and natural consequences form the boundary of the bubble.

Parents implement family values as limits which form the outside of the bubble. Logical consequences stay outside the bubble. Limits change to reflect the child's level of responsibility.

As the child matures and takes on responsibility for herself, she develops her own limits according to her boundaries.

The limits represented by the boundary bubble concern safety, responsibility, values or respect. As the child matures, the area inside the bubble – the things that are the child's own responsibility – expands. These limits apply to the parents' behavior as well as the child's. When a parent pushes her way through her child's boundaries she steps into an area which really belongs to the child. Inside the bubble is everything we discussed earlier (Chapter 5).

Kid Issues are everything that a child is ready to take responsibility for on his own. Children should be given choices, trusted in their ability to make choices and allowed to experience the natural consequences of their decisions.

Parents should avoid crossing the child's boundaries by taking too much control of issues which rightly belong to the child. If the parent violates the child's boundaries, or the child violates the parents', conflict resolution should be used to reach decisions regarding limits and consequences. (See the chapter on Conflict Resolution in *The Parent-Child Connection.*)

Logical consequences apply to behaviors on the outside of this bubble. In some such situations, such as when the child rides a bike without a helmet, we need to impose a logical consequence. The limit is clearly defined and the consequence is carried through without judging, shaming, or debating. Use conflict resolution skills to discuss what the bubble should look like. In discussing the boundary with your child you create a win-win situation.

When the bubble is too small, we aren't giving children enough freedom and responsibility. They will either push on the limit or fail to grow towards independence. If the bubble is too big, we are not keeping them safe – the child can't feel the boundaries he needs. Giving too much responsibility to a child is neglectful. We must be open to the expansion and contraction of this framework as the child takes two steps forward and one step back in the process of maturing.

Below is an example of how a limit bubble grows. As the child demands more freedom, the parent can expand the bubble whenever the child's level of responsibility justifies more freedom.

Expansion of the Boundary Bubble

Example: Girl, age 11

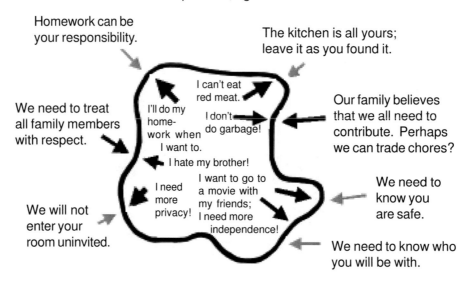

Homework can be your responsibility.

The kitchen is all yours; leave it as you found it.

We need to treat all family members with respect.

Our family believes that we all need to contribute. Perhaps we can trade chores?

We will not enter your room uninvited.

We need to know you are safe.

We need to know who you will be with.

I can't eat red meat.

I'll do my home-work when I want to.

I don't do garbage!

I hate my brother!

I need more privacy!

I want to go to a movie with my friends; I need more independence!

Small, Unimportant Rules

Stick to the basics with your framework of rules: limits involve respect for others, carrying through with responsibilities, values, and safety. If you have a bunch of small, unimportant rules you won't feel like following through with the million consequences which they will entail. It does not feel good to be a Consequence Cop and it is a role which is unnecessarily controlling. Such behavior only creates power struggles. When you don't have a bunch of silly rules, the rules you do have will be much more respected and less likely to be challenged. Children won't feel resentful at being over-controlled and they will have a more honest, open relationship with you. Where there is too much control, children withhold truth and are much slower at developing their own moral code. Trust your kids as much as you can and hand responsibility over to them.

2 - Before Using Consequences

Many parents think that good parenting means imposing consequences for every misbehavior. This is not so. Logical consequences should be used only as a last resort, when natural consequences are not effective or safe, and children do not seem to be learning. Before you rush into imposing a consequence, consider giving an I-message about how the behavior affects you or others. Also consider ignoring minor problem behaviors.

1. Give an "I-Message"

Stating limits without judging or attacking the child is the key to teaching respect and preserving self-esteem. (See chapter on Speaking Without Regrets in *The Parent-Child Connection*.) Give an I-message to express your feelings in a non-judgmental way. I-messages help children understand others' feelings and needs. They help children reach a higher level of moral development.

What to Say. State what you see or hear, state your feelings and your needs, and make a positive request.
● Example: "When I hear you call your brother a name I feel concerned. It is important to me that you are both treated with respect. Can you express your feelings instead?"

What Not to Say. Don't attack the child with a judgment about her character and don't bark out a command.
● Example: "How could you be so mean?"

Teaching Boundaries. Use I-Messages to define your personal boundaries and teach your child how you want him to treat you and others. This applies to interrupting, speaking rudely, and other annoying behavior.
● Example: "When I hear you talk about slugs (or even worse things!) at the table, it puts me off my food and I feel annoyed."

Apply Your Knowledge

● Think of an example where it would be appropriate to discuss the behavior of your child and how it makes you feel.

---

2. Decide What You Can Ignore

Even though a child may not be mature enough to understand the feelings and needs of others, he needs to have limits set for him; these limits give him a start on the road towards learning empathy. Essentially limit-setting means requiring our children to respect us and other people, and do no harm to others. For a child who does not yet understand others' needs and feelings, this limit teaches the fundamental truth that all human beings are equal. However, stating your boundaries does not mean you have to use your power to enforce them.

Ask yourself where the "tip of your (psychological or emotional) nose" is and ignore that space in front of it (your child's behavior which comes close to invading but does not quite invade your personal boundaries). This means, for example, ignoring toilet talk from your four-year-old, eye-rolling from your 12-year-old, and cursing under the breath from your teenager.

It pays to ignore what looks like 'attitude' rather than challenging it every time you think you see it. There is power in ignoring many behaviors – you know they will pass and you can't change them anyway. Often these things are done just to 'bug' you, so you take power if you ignore them and don't appear to be 'bugged'. It's hard to ignore behaviors which are deliberately designed to 'get your goat' but if you can do it, the behaviors will disappear simply because they don't get the reward of your attention. Children can find power in making their parents angry; don't give them this power.

Remember that doing nothing is doing something. Ignoring behavior is a very powerful act of self-discipline which teaches children that aggressive or inappropriate behavior doesn't win. How many times have you ignored a behavior only to find that in a short time the behavior passes? How many times have you tried to correct your child's behavior with a long-winded lecture or a consequence, only to have things get worse and your child resent you?

Apply Your Knowledge

- Think of an annoying behavior of your child for which ignoring would be the best discipline technique. Can you discipline yourself to ignore it?

---

3 - Logical Consequences

The term 'Logical Consequences' means consequences which are put in place by the parent or caregiver; these are not the result of a child's own act. We know that natural consequences provide real life learning experiences, but in some cases (see Chapter 5), we can't let these experiences happen, so we intervene by imposing consequences to teach our children limits.

A consequence is needed only when the child is not learning without one. Many times, however, a child will learn without our having to impose a consequence – simply because we give an I-message and he realizes he is hurting someone else. We don't need to impose consequences unless it is clear that the child is not learning without them.

We feel torn when recommending logical consequences at all; there is a danger that parents will hang onto them because they are easy. However, using consequences doesn't get the best results over a long period of time. It is easy to impose consequences on children and you don't need to take a course to learn how to do it.

However, parenting by consequences keeps kids stuck at the earliest stage of moral development, i.e. Reward-and-Punishment morality, where they believe something is wrong only if they get in trouble for it, or they believe something is good if they get rewarded or praised for it. (See Chapter 6). And if you have a lot of rules, your children may advance to the Law-and-Order stage but they won't develop the abstract understanding or the awareness of others' needs and feelings which are the essence of Love-Your-Neighbor morality.

Dr. Thomas Gordon puts it well: "Parental power does not really 'influence' children; it *forces* them to behave in prescribed ways. (...) Non-power methods of influence make it much more likely that children might seriously consider their parents' ideas or their feelings and as a result modify their own behavior in the direction desired by the parent." (*Parent Effectiveness Training*, p.192).

The most common situations in which we need to step in with logical consequences are those which cause us or someone else significant distress as a result of our children's actions.

Children must learn to deal with the consequences of their acts if they are to mature into healthy human beings and live social lives. This is what Alfred Adler called "the logic of communal living".

4 - Anger, Punishment and Discipline

Effective discipline consists of teaching children how to take responsibility and become mature, caring individuals. It should never be confused with punishment.

In the Heat of the Moment

You go into the recreation room in the basement. Your child was supposed to be doing his homework, but instead he is playing video games. The room is a mess and you see red. In anger you blurt out: "How dare you play that stupid game when you are supposed to be doing your homework! Look at this room! What a mess! You've got chips all over the floor and you drank all that pop! What a lazy slob! Get this mess cleaned up now! Get those books open and be prepared to go without video games or any friends over to this house for a week! Do you hear me?"

The Parent's Emotions:

Let's take a closer look at the very common scene presented above. How do you, the parent, feel?:
♦   Anger is the feeling which is expressed.
♦   Underneath the anger is disappointment: *"I thought I could trust him."*
♦   There is also frustration: *"Look at this damn mess!"*
♦   And resentment: *"I wish I had never bought that stupid game."*
♦   And there is fear: *"My kid is going to fail school and grow up to be lazy and worthless."*

The Child's Emotions:

How does the child feel? The child may be hurt by the words (the intent of which was to shame and punish), as well as ashamed, sad, and rejected. All of these negative emotions prevent the child from learning anything. Neither behavioral change nor intellectual growth can occur when strong negative emotions get in the way. The child is thinking about how mean you are, not about what a mess he made. He wants to *get even*.

Jenny, you're so clumsy! You always spill! Go to your room. And from now on, you get sent to your room every time you spill ...

But, Mom . . . .

No arguments!

But I'll be in my room forever! I don't know how to pour without spilling.

222

The Parent-Child Relationship

If a parent continues to be punitive, eventually the parent-child relationship will be damaged. When the parent-child relationship is damaged, children lose their desire to cooperate. The child will feel rebellious and (worse than that) will probably start treating younger children the way he is treated.

Positive behavior that results from punishment is temporary, but the damage to the relationship is long term.

It is important to remember that positive behavior which results from punishment doesn't last long. Sure, you may get instant results when you lash out. The child may jump to attention, clean up and do his homework, but the change is short lived! It is only temporary and he will surely repeat the negative behavior.

When we use our power to force our kids to do things, the price tag is much too high. The child's self-esteem is slowly chipped away because he feels bad about who he must be. When he loses control over his life he will eventually find other ways to try to get some power. He might lie or cheat or break whatever rules he knows his parents can't control.

De-escalating Your Anger

Here are some ways to reduce your level of anger:

- Use time out for yourself when you start to get angry.
- Let your children talk to you about their fears and your behavior.
- Have a 'hands in pocket' rule when you get angry. Don't touch your child at all when you are stressed.
- Give other family members permission to leave the room if they feel they are being violated.
- Watch what you think, and challenge old belief systems.

This is discussed in detail in the chapters on The Intelligence of Emotions and Conflict Resolution and Anger Management in *The Parent-Child Connection*. We know that most parents don't want to get angry at their children, especially if they lose control while punishing. If you tend to lean toward a more punitive parenting style, or are very reactive, take a minute to plan how you will recognize when your boundary is being breached and plan to limit your own behavior. You can give yourself a warning, time yourself out, and use 'I-Messages'.

Avoid lecturing, address issues early, and be consistent. List the behaviors that you react most strongly to and think about when in your reaction you need to change gears. Have a plan ready.

Start with one or two simple things that are kid issues: getting dressed, getting home on time, getting up for school, remembering homework, etc. Here's an example:

Anger Cool-Down Exercise

Child's behavior that drives me to reaction:	I will take action (change gears):	I will do this (instead of reacting):
Siblings' constant bickering drives me bananas.	When I first recognize my intolerance, before I get angry.	I will use an I-statement to express my frustration and give them a one-word reminder to listen to each other. If it continues I will remind them of the consequence.

Idle and Scary Threats

Most parents don't want to be ogres, but when we get angry we sometimes resort to threatening things we won't be able to carry out. How many times have you reached the end of your rope and blurted out a threat that you had no intention of following through with? When we make threats in anger and frustration, the proposed consequences are usually too extreme. Some parents blurt out those threats and then follow through because they need to 'make it the truth' in order to maintain their authority with their children.

For the most part, these things are blurted out to scare kids and perhaps get some cooperation. But when we don't follow through, our kids cease to respect our threats. So we may feel we have to follow through with them even though we know we are hurting our children; we do it just to maintain our parental authority. This usually backfires because children become resentful and hate us when we punish them too severely. And when we calm down we may feel guilty and know we have to backtrack because the punishment we have threatened was too severe.

Canceling Christmas

While visiting a friend one year before Christmas, I sat and watched while he tested his indoor lights, plugging them in and replacing bulbs. His children got very excited, and started to scream and play around the lights. I could hear him repeatedly ask them to stop and they were just not listening.

Getting irritated, he finally yelled, "If you don't stop playing with these lights, there won't be a Christmas this year!" The kids went running into the kitchen to their mother, crying and yelping about not having a Christmas. She simply asked her husband whether they should discuss canceling Christmas with the rest of the family first.

This father was trying to keep his kids safe because he loved them. He was also protecting his own personal boundaries, as it was frustrating and hard to concentrate. The problem is that the threat didn't sound loving at all, and children wouldn't interpret it as a loving act.

Or how about this one: "If you don't clean up your toys I am sending all of them to the poor children who will really appreciate them!" It would be pretty devastating if a parent actually did this! -- *Allison Rees*

The Orphanage Threat

I remember my mother phoning the orphanage to see whether they would take me when I was about three. We lived next door to one and I had some fear around it already. I will never forget the feeling; I really believed her. -- *Allison Rees*

Idle threats have unavoidable effects on the parent-child relationship. In the short run the child may believe you and feel devastated. In the long run, she will stop believing you and challenge you more.

Idle threats are on-the-spot attempts to change a child's behavior and get some control. They often come up in the heat of the moment when we're feeling angry. They are usually something we have no intention of following through with: "If you don't get your shoes on now, I won't take you to the birthday party!" But once a threat has been made, we're stuck with having to either follow through or back down.

If we follow through with punitive consequences, such as canceling birthday
parties or grounding for long periods,
our kids may resent us and feel unloved.

If we back down, we teach our kids to
argue and debate with us. This is better
than having them hate us. In fact, assertive kids who question consequences that
are overly severe become adults who
know their own minds and can speak up
for themselves.

However, if we frequently have to back
down from threats, our children will learn
not to believe what we say. Unless we're
so frightening that our kids are totally
intimidated, children will protest against
consequences which are too severe, so
by threatening them we are both provoking
them to anger and teaching them to argue,
debate, and drown us out. Then we wonder why our kids don't listen to us.

If we threaten children it teaches them
how to threaten us back. "I am not coming
out of this swimming pool and you can't
make me. I'm going to stay in here all
day." This threat is very effective if the
parent is fully dressed!

Quit fighting or go to your rooms.

"Quit fighting", I said, or go to your rooms.

Next time I mean it. Quit fighting or go to your rooms.

Apply Your Knowledge

● Do you ever use idle threats with your children? What kind of reaction do
you get from the children?

● Do your children use threats on you too?

● How do children feel when we blurt out an unfair consequence in anger?
If you find yourself blurting out a consequence in anger should you back
down? If you stick with the consequence, what does the child experience?

5 - How To Use Consequences

State What You Will Do

So what do you do when children are misbehaving and don't stop when asked? Even worse – what if it's a situation where safety is involved? State what you will do if they don't stop. Say it once, give fair notice, and then follow through with a reasonable action to protect the child. This is not an idle threat, it's a thoughtful loving promise, even if the children don't like what you'll do.

For example, the father with the indoor Christmas lights could have said: "It is important not to touch the lights. I am worried you will get hurt and I can't concentrate. If you continue to play around me, I will put the lights away and put them up after you go to bed." When it comes to safety, being consistent and taking action is important. You are able to follow through because the consequence you promise isn't too severe. The children have the choice of doing what you ask or watching you do what you said you would do.

It helps if you acknowledge the children's feelings while promising to follow through with consequences if they don't stop. For example, Dad could have gotten the children involved by offering them some suggestions as to how they might help. He could even have acknowledged their excitement. Just naming the children's feelings would have made them feel acknowledged and would have had a very calming effect. It might sound like, "It's pretty exciting, seeing the Christmas lights, isn't it? Here is the deal…"

A Consequence or a Punishment?

Consequences and Punishments are Different

Consequences...	Punishments...
• deal with what will happen next	• deal with the past
• are reasonable and related to the behavior	• are rarely reasonable or related
• are discussed ahead of time so the child is clear about the result of his choice	• are impulsive, often given out in anger
• come from a position of social order	• come from a position of authority

Let's make it clear: we don't believe in using punishment with children. The most significant difference between a consequence and a punishment is the tone the parent sets. The chart (on the previous page) from Rudolph Dreikurs' *Children: The Challenge* shows us the importance of discussing limits ahead of time with our children, and approaching new issues with conflict resolution strategies in place.

There is often a lot of judgment in punishment because the parent attacks the character of the child rather than just the behavior. Sometimes it can be in the form of a lecture or shaming comments. Words and tone of voice can turn a time out from a logical consequence into a punishment. The authority who punishes uses his power to communicate anger or disgust. "I'm the parent here and you will do as I say." Even with criminals, punishment hasn't been shown to be that effective. It sets up an 'us versus them' mentality in those who are punished, and they work harder on ways to continue to commit crime and escape punishment.

Letting our anger interfere can quickly goad us into punishment. If you are angry it is much better to take time to think rather than shout out a consequence. The heat of the moment is no time to make decisions. When we make decisions about consequences in anger, we can be very unfair to our children. In our work, we hear about children being sent to bed in the middle of watching a video specially rented for their enjoyment, being sent to bed without dinner, or having their birthday parties cancelled.

You can't leave the table until you finish dinner.

Sometimes our expectations are unfair in the first place, and when we impose such consequences our children really resist them because they are unfair.

For example, expecting children to eat their dinner when they don't like the food or aren't hungry can create huge power struggles. This very persistent child in the cartoon is determined not to eat food he doesn't like.

Distinguish Between Rights and Privileges

Children have a right to:

♦ physical safety

♦ food and drink

♦ sleep

♦ love and esteem

Children must always feel that they belong and – that no matter what – they are valued and loved. If a child is loved, he always receives:

♦ hugs and affection

♦ a story at bedtime or other sharing time

♦ birthday parties to celebrate his entry into your life

Privileges include:

♦ computer or TV time

♦ outings such as movies, skating, or swimming

♦ inviting friends over and having sleep-overs

♦ toys and sports and activities

We may deny privileges but not rights.

> **Never deny a child's rights as a consequence of their behavior!**
>
>
>
> **Children must always feel that they belong and that no matter what, they are valued and loved.**

Apply Your Knowledge

● How do you distinguish what should be your child's right and what can be a privilege which could be taken away as a consequence of behavior?

● Are you using any consequences which violate your child's rights?

● Does your child feel entitled to some things which you might be able to use as consequences?

Behavior and Consequences are Linked

For consequences to be meaningful, they should be related to the behavior for which they are imposed. There is no relationship between biking without a helmet and losing TV privileges, or between cheating at school and having to clean the kitchen. Don't use unrelated consequences; the child will only feel punished and won't learn from them.

Here are some examples of consequences which are directly related, from a child's perspective, to the behavior for which they are imposed:

- Having to spend time alone is related to being aggressive with others.
- Losing your bike for a couple of days is related to riding without a helmet.
- Having to vacuum your room yourself is related to not tidying it so that mom can vacuum.
- Having to do your own laundry makes sense because what isn't in the hamper doesn't get washed.
- Stopping at the vending machine is a suitable positive consequence for getting out of the pool when asked.

You get the idea? One mom just hated nagging her girls (age 8 and 10) to clear their plates, so instead of nagging she just left the plates there. It isn't very nice to sit down to a dirty plate at the next meal and the plate is hard to clean when it has sat there for several hours. You can go on strike if your teenagers don't contribute to cooking. Use those restaurant coupons you have always wanted to try and take a friend. You can leave a loaf of bread and peanut butter for the kids.

Another mom decided to pull the van over when her teens were arguing and swearing in the back seat. They chanted that pulling over wouldn't do any good and it couldn't make them stop. She simply got out of the car and went across the street to her favorite coffee shop. She could see the van rocking back and forth as she sipped on her coffee. What was more interesting was how the kids reacted when they saw mom getting picked up by her friend and getting a ride home.

Misbehaving Mother

Don't be boring. Get creative. When I take my kids to the mall my consequence is to dance or sing if they start to squabble with each other. At other times I walk like the Hunchback of Notre Dame. My daughter just wants to die. She immediately stops and begs me to behave.

I think my tactic works. I want them to behave; they want me to behave.

Other parents may plan to impose a positive consequence. "If you cooperate in the store, we will stop at the park, get that gum, etc." But it's kind of fun to misbehave.

-- *Allison Rees*

A Bribe is a Bribe is a ...

It's important to understand the difference between positive consequences and bribery:

◆   **Bribery:** offering kids something to stop behavior.
      e.g. "If you stop fighting I will buy you some gum."

◆   **Reward:** giving kids something for not starting bad behavior.
      e.g. "We went shopping and you made an effort to get along,
      let's get some gum."

Kids will start problem behavior because they can anticipate the bribe you will give them to stop it!

Choose Consequences that Matter

And remember, if you eat up all your chocolate cake, then you can have your spinach. And if you be sure and watch "Teenage Mutant Ninja Turtles", then we may let you take out the garbage.

"Son, if you don't stop hitting your sister, you won't get broccoli for a month!" might not work. Consequences need to have a little umph behind them. It has to be something that your child will feel motivated to work for. There are individual differences in what is rewarding and punishing.

Remember that what is rewarding is unique for each individual. For one child being sent to his room is unpleasant; for another it is a reward.

Kids have different temperaments (see Chapter 1) and therefore different likes and dislikes. A quiet, thoughtful child might like a book while an energetic child might like a noisy video game.

Plan Ahead

You can plan ahead, for example before going to the store, and talk about the limits that are expected. Giving children a voice when setting limits pays big dividends in cooperation. Eventually children just start to think of limits without any prompting from the parent. They get used to thinking and taking responsibility for themselves. The more they do it, the better they get at it.

Kid-Designed Shopping Rules

When my kids were about three and five, we went to the grocery store just so they could have the fun of pushing the little buggies. On the way, I recognized the possibility of chaos so I decided to ask them if they could come up with some good rules.

It was great. They pretty well covered everything, such as 'no running' and some very creative limits I wouldn't have thought of like: "No poking your finger through the plastic in the meat section" and "No running into old people". My favorite suggestion was to go through the check-out before leaving the store.

We were all set with our code of conduct made clear. It paid off to plan ahead and the kids felt great about themselves for having all these ideas. Everything was great until we went by the candy department. But hey, we will throw that one in next time. *-- Allison Rees*

Apply Your Knowledge

- Think of a situation in which you can plan ahead to set limits and use consequences. What will you do?

Consistency Matters

Parental Persistence

I saw a great example of teaching respect for other people's space at the doctor's office. Mom was in seeing the doctor while Dad and his son, around four years old, were in the waiting room. The little boy was playing with all the toys and having a great time. Finally Mom came out and it was time to go. "Come on David, it is time to put the toys away." David was the king of whining. "Ooooh, I'm so tired. I can't put all these toys away."

Both Mom and Dad reinforced the limit. "When you play with toys you put them away. That is the rule." You could see that they had enforced this enough times because he didn't resist (well, not physically, anyway). He put the toys away and cried the whole time, complaining about being tired. The parents were calm and unruffled by the spectators. They stuck to the limit, stayed firm and calm, and patted David on the back when it was over. *-- Allison Rees*

Why Consistency is Important to Children

- It eliminates confusion.
- It teaches through repetition.
- It shows that you mean what you say.
- It means equal treatment for all kids.

When a particular limit becomes an issue more than two or three times it usually means we need to make the rule clearer or request that it be followed. This means we need to be firm and consistent until the limit is established and the boundaries are straightened out.

Once we establish a limit we need to stick to it. Parents often give in to kids when they themselves are tired, happy or feeling guilty (that pretty well covers our entire waking hours). So if you are experiencing any of these feelings when your child asks

The best time to ask for something is when she's watching TV and doesn't want to be disturbed. The next best time is when she has those two little lines between her eyebrows. Then she'll yell at you, but give in afterwards. But if she's wide awake and not crabby, you might as well not ask.

for candy at the store, you will probably give in. If, however, you are determined and conscious of the limit, you will take thoughtful action to see it through.

It saves the child a lot of confusion when you stick to what you have already said (regardless how you feel). Kids don't really feel that great about themselves when they can see that they have pushed you into giving in to them because you are tired or in a vulnerable state. They may gain a sense of power over you, but what they really need to see is you having power over yourself. They need to see that you mean what you say.

Consistency is also important because young children learn through repetition. Look at how many times they want you to read them the same story over and over again. Until children are old enough to think abstractly, repetition is their main method of learning. (Just watch a toddler repeat a forbidden act a hundred times!)

This is your last second chance!

So if you want a child to learn your limit and your consequence, repeat it until the child has really got it!

Older kids are more concerned about fairness. If you apply limits and consequences consistently to all family members, including the parents, they can't accuse you of being unfair. They especially like it when a parent gets a consequence, for example a fine for swearing. Most parents find themselves explaining to little Johnny why his older brother gets to stay up later than him, or to Mary why her little sister gets carried into the house but she doesn't.

"Let me in," said the wolf. "No," said the pig.

You changed the words. You forgot, "I'll huff and I'll puff and blow the house down." Not just "let me in".

Apply Your Knowledge

• Are you able to be consistent when you set limits? What gets in the way?

• Have you noticed your children's concern about fairness? If you have more than one child, do you treat each of them fairly?

Escalating Consequences

Recipe for Consequence Cake

I was in a food store the other day. The tills had broken down and there were long lineups. My daughter and I were entertained by a squabble between a mother and daughter behind us. I am not trying to be cruel here; it just helped us pass the time and it was very interesting to see how the squabble developed.

I didn't catch the first part of this scene but picked up where mother got very upset because her (approximately) 10-year-old daughter called her an 'idiot'. Clearly not an okay thing to do. Four-year-olds may do it out of ignorance, but this child was old enough to know better and it wasn't done in anger. Probably a word her friends use and it just slipped out.

[continued on the next page...]

[... continued from the previous page]

Mom was upset and proceeded to lay down a consequence. I could tell by her language that she had had a lot of parent education and I was pretty impressed until she started layering the consequences. Her daughter was using all kinds of tactics, ranging from intimidation right through to clinging to her mother and begging.

Mom, however, locked into the power struggle and told the girl that when they got home she would have no dinner and go right to her room. By the time we got to the till, the child was going to have her new running shoes taken back to the store, no phone for a week, no dinner, and would be confined to her room for the rest of the day. What a mess they were in! Chances are, they were both hungry and tired and after supper Mom would realize that some of these consequences were not reasonable.

Mom needed to state that the daughter would have a Time Out when they got home then she should have disengaged from the discussion. Stopping at this point would not have been backing down; it would have been a wise decision to ignore attention-seeking behavior.

-- Allison Rees

So don't layer on those consequences, and make sure that the child is only given a consequence once.

If a child gets into trouble at school, don't add a consequence at home too. It has been dealt with by the teacher so leave it at that. Likewise, if one parent disciplines a child, avoid doubling up and layering another consequence on top.

Apply Your Knowledge

- Why would overusing logical consequences have a negative effect?

Presenting Consequences Positively

Logical consequences can be presented either as earned privileges or as punishments and deprivation. If kids take privileges for granted, they feel deprived and punished if they don't receive these privileges. You need to decide which things and activities will be considered their rights.

Your child may, for example, have a right to watch her favorite TV show once a week, but not to watch TV whenever she feels like it. She may have a right to play on her sports team and attend practices, but it might be a privilege to hang out with her friends on a Saturday.

You can then present your consequences in a positive manner, using 'when-then'.

For example:
♦ "When your chores are done, then you can hang out with your friends."
♦ "When your homework is done, then you can watch TV for an hour."

This sounds much nicer than:
♦ "You can't go out until your chores are done."
♦ "You can't watch TV until you've finished your homework."

6 - Specific Consequences

Time Out to Cool Down

'Time Out' is a very popular consequence. It has replaced spanking as today's most over-used consequence. Time Out isn't the be-all-and-end-all of discipline techniques.

We believe that Time Out should be used only as a cooling-down period. When a child acts aggressively or continuously intrudes on somebody's boundaries, it seems logical that he should have to spend time alone and cool off. It's not only the child who needs a cooling off period; frustrated parents need one too.

We often use Time Out when we feel at the end of our rope with kids' noise, constant questions and interruptions, or limit-testing. We use it when we're angry at our kids. Unfortunately, they sense our anger and feel insecure; they need reassurance but instead they get isolation.

We need to recognize that in many cases it is us rather than the kids who need the Time Out. When my kids were young, I (Alison Miller) used to tell them "I need some silence!" when I felt like that. They could understand this simple statement without feeling they had to be punished for just being kids.

Time Yourself Out

Timing yourself out of a situation is a wise move. It shows your children that you are willing to take responsibility for your own behavior. Talk about this with your children when you are not upset with them, to prepare them for the times when you need to take time for yourself. Explain that when you take time for yourself, it helps you to

If you don't stop that, Mary, I'm going over to that chair in the corner and sit down until I think of a suitable consequence.

calm down and control your temper. If they are prepared, they are less likely to be frightened by your withdrawal.

If your child is really young, put her in her crib and go to another room and breathe deeply. If she is older, help her understand that she shouldn't follow you into your room, and promise to come out as soon as you have calmed down.

When to Use Time Outs

As much as possible we need to accept kids' normal behaviors and not impose consequences on them for just being kids. If we use consequences of any kind for normal child behaviors, we are teaching our kids that it isn't okay to be kids.

Some kids will rebel; others will lose self-esteem and try to be the way they think we want them to be. Kids are noisy, messy, inquisitive, and intrusive; they can't help it. If we let go of our perfect houses and organized schedules, our kids can be happy and will mature without feeling bad about their inability to be 'little adults'.

Often parents with low sensory thresholds can't tolerate much noise and send their children to their rooms to give themselves a break. Just think of an intense child with a low sensory threshold parent (see Chapter 1). Earplugs are a great investment if you have young kids.

When parents use Time Out to deal with normal behavior which they misperceive as misbehavior, the Time Out is doomed to fail. Time Out is frequently used for toddlers when they begin to throw things, kick, monopolize toys, scream, whine, etc. If you always use Time Out to curb these normal behaviors, don't expect to see your child much for a quite a while, and expect that he may feel rejected and abandoned.

The truth is that lots of these behaviors simply exist because your child is immature, can't express his feelings, and might be hungry or tired or uncomfortable without knowing what is the matter. It's much more effective to figure out why the child is behaving this way (see Chapter 4 about behavior triggers) than to simply resort to a consequence like Time Out.

If we think of Time Out as just one of many possible logical consequences, we can get a better picture of when it's appropriate to use. If a child is so wound up that he can't calm down, if he is continuously bugging or provoking someone else, or if he's being aggressive to other people or pets, he probably needs a Time Out.

Give a Warning

An important part of a logical consequence is that the child has a choice about whether or not to engage in the misbehavior. In choosing the misbehavior, he is also choosing the consequence. Counting to three without yelling, lecturing or bargaining can give your child enough time to make a choice to stop a behavior if he knows the deal in advance. If you get to three the child is sent to Time Out.

Rejection, Fear and Abandonment

The level of our anger or our behavior when we put a child in Time Out can make him feel rejected, afraid and abandoned. To some children, it really does seem like solitary confinement. Remember to stay cool, and if your child seems afraid, try a Time Out place that is closer to you. Let him know you love him; reassure him that a couple of minutes on your own will help you (the parent) behave more lovingly.

Children with separation anxiety may simply be afraid to be alone. Time Out is not for them.

Do you want to be thrown into -- I mean -- do you want to be timed out?

Where Should the Child Be During Time Outs?

Some parents worry that frequent Time Outs in the child's bedroom will contribute to his resisting going to bed in the evening. This makes sense if Time Out is being used as a punishment by an angry parent. We believe that if you keep cool (at least until you're alone) and your approach isn't harsh, bedroom Time Outs are fine.

Some people are also concerned when the child doesn't seem to be upset about the Time Out and just carries on playing in her room. Remember that the reason for giving a Time Out is for everyone to calm down, to prevent your child from harming anyone, and to remove attention from the child's misbehavior. It doesn't have to be a punishment! So it doesn't matter if your child is playing alone in her room, as long as the Time Out assists her in calming down.

Others are concerned that their child will trash the room. This is a tough one. We suggest that you just let it happen. The natural consequence of trashing one's room is that your room is a disaster. After a while, the child may learn he is the one having to face the consequence of his actions, not the parent, and his behavior may stop. The key is not to rescue the child from his decision to trash the room. Let him experience the messy room for a little while.

The other choice is to have a Time Out area other than the bedroom (one without a lot of stuff to trash). This may be a bit of a luxury for many people. With my (Alison Miller's) kids we used a corner in a hallway; they could stand on their heads up against the wall but that's about all they could do there.

What's going on? You've been standing there for half an hour. I thought time out was 3 minutes?

It is 3 minutes from the time he's quiet!

 # ! ! ! Aaargh!!

Some parents are able to manage a Time Out with the child on a chair in the corner not too far from them. This feels safer to very young children. However, it can be difficult to keep them there and keep your attention away from them during this time. The key here is to keep it short.

How Long Should Time Outs Last?

The standard is roughly one minute per year of age. Keep it short. Be flexible, especially if this technique is new, or has been unsuccessful in the past. If your child has calmed down after a couple of minutes, open the door and welcome him back to your side. Young kids can't grasp how long 'four minutes' is, and may worry that it could be a long time. A visible timer can be useful. The important point you need to stress to the child is that the Time Out starts when he has calmed down. However, if he fusses for 10 minutes without calming down, give up on Time Out and use a different discipline technique.

Have a Time Out Drill

We prepare ourselves for earthquakes and fires, although hopefully we will never have to deal with them. How about preparing ahead of time for emotional whirlwinds? With younger children we can talk about those times when we need some space to calm down. We can practice going into our room (either parent or child) for two minutes so the child gets a sense of how long that is. Then after two minutes come out and have a hug. This gets them past the fear and uncertainty of Time Out.

Kids Time Themselves Out

Eventually, you may see your children timing themselves out. That truly is progress, especially when they can follow up by expressing their feelings in a healthy way. Some children like to draw, play or write rather than talk. Don't follow a child into her room when she goes in there. Give her space. You can teach a child to time herself out when she feels too wound up or upset. This is especially useful for kids with Attention Deficit Disorder (ADD). Let them decide when to time themselves out and for how long.

Take Teen Tension Around the Block

If you're in an intense conflict with your teenager, there is nothing wrong with leaving the house to walk around the block. Otherwise you may not get that time you need to cool down, and you'll find yourself engaging in a hostile power struggle. Just tell your child you need some 'cool down time' and leave.

When the Time Out is Over

We often make the mistake of lecturing, reprimanding, or reminding a child of what got them into the Time Out. Sometimes the Time Out happens when emotions run so high that the ability to think clearly and remember is clouded. Explanations should be brief and simple – never let it turn into a lecture or an interrogation.

How About a Time In?

Sometimes when a child is really upset and we time her out, she may become really unhappy about her behavior. With my (Allison Rees's) daughter, I call a 'Time In'. This is where the two of us will go into her room together. She may cry while I hold her or perhaps I will rub her back. I am showing her that I care and that I understand that she is just not able to have the self-control she needs at the moment. It is appropriate when she is tired or frustrated with what is happening around her. A *Time In* can be very effective, but be careful that you don't use it to reward negative behavior designed strictly for your attention.

Apply Your Knowledge

- Is Time Out an effective consequence to use with your child? Why or why not?
- For what kinds of behaviors might Time Out be effective?
- Do you ever consider timing yourself out?
- If you don't use Time Out what method do you use to discipline your child when he is acting aggressively?

Grounding

Grounding is usually taken to mean making your children or teens stay at home, without social contact with their friends. In some cases, it also means cutting off their telephone and MSN privileges. Like Time Out, this consequence is over-used. Parents of teenagers use it for many things including not completing chores, rudeness, and poor school grades. It is understandably tempting for parents to use grounding; a teen's social life is very important to her, so grounding is a consequence which she will really feel. But it is a very strong consequence and, like any other consequence, it should be reserved for behaviors which deserve it. Kids who get grounded a lot can become depressed.

Can Robert come out to play with me?

No, he's grounded.

Why'd he have to punish me, too? I didn't do anything.

"You can go out when your chores are completed," makes sense if it is a general family rule and everyone knows what to expect. But this kind of rule should not be used to prevent children from taking part in their sports activities or planned events which they are looking forward to. The effect on the child's friends should also be considered. We have both had our children suffer frequently and unexpectedly from the grounding of their best friends, when they were really looking forward to playing with them.

Grounding also punishes the parents, who are forced to remain in the same house with a bored, grumpy child. Grounding is a 'big gun' and in our view should only be used for 'major crimes'.

So when do you ground your child from going out and being with friends, or from communicating with friends via telephone and Internet? The consequence fits the behavior if grounding is used for doing something inappropriate in the company of friends. Grounding makes sense if an entire group of kids has done something together like having a party in a house when the parents are not home; the parents can agree together to ground all the kids for a weekend.

Grounding should not be for a long period of time. Teenagers really need to socialize; they are developing the social skills they will use in adulthood. One weekend is plenty. Another meaning of the term 'grounded' is mindfulness, being connected to oneself and present reality. Sometimes a kid needs this kind of grounding, when she has become so carried away with peer group activities that she loses perspective.

It can be hard for a teen to pull away from her peer group, even for a short time, and she may need her parents to do it for her. It can be helpful to keep her home for a couple of days; this will give her time to collect her thoughts away from the influence of her peers. It can give the parents and the whole family a chance to recover, rest, relax, and gain perspective.

Removal of Privileges

Sleep-overs can be a lot of work for parents and lots of fun for kids. Children shouldn't take sleep-overs for granted. It is reasonable to expect a certain amount of responsibility from your child so that this wonderful privilege can be earned. Offering it as a positive consequence is much more appealing than taking away something that is already in place. "If we can buckle down this week and get things done around the house (or whatever your expectation is) then I think having a sleep-over would be a nice break for you."

A good week can be celebrated with a trip to the pool or some other enjoyable activity. Children can be encouraged to see these activities as events which the whole family works toward. This teaches them not to expect to have all the fun without contributing to what makes it all possible.

Remember to present the sleepover event as a positive consequence rather than something you can threaten to take away.

Television and Computer Time

Many parents use the privileges of television and computer time as consequences, reporting that these are the only things their kids really seem to care about. It certainly won't devastate a child to go without TV or computer time.

Depriving a child of any privilege (e.g. TV time) can backfire though and set up an obsessive desire to get in as much of this privilege as possible. It makes sense to tell the child that the privilege will be reinstated as soon as a certain task is done. "When you put the dishes away, then you can watch TV." We think it is respectful to kids if we let certain TV shows with ongoing stories be regarded as rights rather than privileges – because we want those rights ourselves.

Communicating with friends through MSN is an important social need for teens nowadays, and removing this opportunity is a form of grounding and should be used only when appropriate (e.g. when the child's social activities have prevented her from completing her homework).

Young teens will want to have access to their friends and that can be a great thing, especially for less socially savvy kids who want to be part of the loop and connect with other peers. By the time kids are in their mid to late teen years they can govern their own activities and budget their time. If you are concerned about the amount of time your teen seems to spend on the computer, make an observation and express your concern for balance and health.

I (Allison Rees) recently mentioned to my daughter (almost 15 as I write this) that she seemed to spend a lot of time on her computer. It wasn't a judgment, just an observation. Half an hour later she handed over her ethernet card so that she couldn't access the Internet. She seemed to agree and she wanted a break. Over the weeks that followed she connected more with all of us in the family. She also started doing more reading, homework and now wants to take guitar lessons. She needed the break from peers and constant connection. Now she has a genuine frame of reference to find her own balance. It didn't come from external control but from the internal desire to be balanced.

So see both the positive and the challenging side to computer use. Guide your children into their future and give them enough freedom to experiment while under your loving eye and care. Pretty soon, they will be helping you understand the latest in technology. You may come to truly appreciate their knowledge and skills!

Toys

When kids fight over toys or the toys aren't put away, toys can be timed out. Today kids have so many of them that they often don't notice what is missing.

Some kids have lost so many toys because of 'bad' behavior that they have nothing left in their rooms but resentment. If it gets to that point, the consequence isn't working. Again, look for antecedents or triggers (see Chapter 4); why is the child struggling and what is the behavior about?

7 - When Parents Disagree about Limits

A lot of people say they argue about discipline, yet when we talk with them about limits there is often a lot of agreement. When couples take the time to discuss limits they find that limits aren't usually the problem. It is usually the anger and tone of voice with which one parent enforces the limits, or one parent's overturning the other's decisions, which causes the disagreement.

A couple was frustrated when their two pre-teen kids wouldn't contribute to household chores. Dad felt that Mom took their side whenever he tried to enforce the rules and for him it was one big nightmare. Dad admitted that he resorted to calling them lazy slobs on several occasions, and lost his cool quite often.

We decided that he should assign a set of dinnerware to each kid and make them responsible for their own dishes. If their dishes didn't get washed, they were just put into a basin under the sink. Obviously, when the kids left their dishes to sit in a dry basin all night, they were hard to wash in the morning. It didn't take long to get the dishwashing happening again. Dad kept his cool and the kids took on a responsibility that was long overdue.

Mom's part in this was to avoid rescuing and nagging. She needed to support the limit-setting. Now Mom and Dad were on the same page. She didn't feel a need to rescue when Dad kept his cool, which he did when he saw that the limits were being enforced.

Apply Your Knowledge

- When you are enforcing limits how can you avoid getting into an argument with your child?
- Your tone of voice should be calm yet firm when deciding on a consequence. Are you able to delay stating a consequence until you have had adequate time to cool down?
- How does your child respond if you lose your cool?
- If you're upset with your spouse about limits and consequences, what is it that upsets you? How can you put this into words for your partner?
- Do you or your spouse interfere with each other's discipline? What effect does this have on your relationship? On your child?
- Do your children hear or see you disagree about discipline? What effect does this have on them?

---

8 - About Rewards

Rewards can be effective when handing over a new responsibility, particularly one that the child doesn't want to take on. *Use rewards with caution* – the long-term effect of rewards is that children lose sight of the responsibility goal and look only to *"What will I get?"*

How Rewards Can Backfire

One woman explained to me that she was rewarding her nine-year-old boy for doing his homework. She had set up a system with the school counselor: at the end of every week, after mother signed a daily sheet confirming Junior had done his homework, he would get a reward.

At first the reward was fairly inexpensive. But soon she found that the only way she could keep her son motivated was to up the ante. The next thing she knew, they were talking ice-cream cakes and pet lizards.

She admitted she was in a conundrum and didn't know how to back out of it. It was putting a lot of stress on her. The positive natural consequence just wasn't kicking in. They hadn't set a time limit on this system and it was now an expectation. The reward had become the main focus and motivation.
-- Allison Rees

Rewards: Pros and Cons

Rudolf Dreikurs puts it well in *Children, the Challenge* (p.74):

> *"A reward does not give a child a sense of belonging. It may be a sign of parental approval of the moment, but what about the next moment? Do Mother and Daddy still approve? Or is another reward needed? Considering the number of moments, one soon runs out of rewards! If we withhold a special reward, it is interpreted by the child as a waste of his efforts.*
>
> *Parents face a serious problem if the child refuses to cooperate because he fails to get an answer to his question, "What's in it for me?" Unless he considers the reward sufficient, what is the sense of cooperating? Why should he bother to do as expected if he does not gain anything special in return? And so the attitude of materialism grows monstrous; there is no chance to satisfy the appetite of acquisition. A completely false value has been established, since the child assumes that the world owes him everything."*

The problem with reward is that it doesn't produce a thinking child. It's better to have a child who goes to bed because he's tired (yes, even it takes weeks of feeling tired to figure it out). At some point children need to take on responsibility for their rest. The same principle applies in many other areas. Kids are responsible when they learn to make their own lunches, schedule their own homework, and ensure that their own clothes are washed.

School systems are often quick to dish out rewards. The achievers might enjoy a reward and have no problems receiving one. Being recognized for something is wonderful. But it can alienate a child from her peers if she always gets the best marks or the awards. And meanwhile the children who don't get rewarded for effort or marks sometimes feel like failures. What about children with learning disabilities? What about kids who do try hard but just fall short? What about a child who is going through a family crisis?

One school principal we know has done away with the reward system. She said she couldn't stand seeing one more child in tears because they didn't make the cut. This system wasn't motivating kids to learn at all. She said that after an award ceremony, a first grade student came up to her and said, "I guess this means you don't really like me after all." That was it!

Reward and punishment are two sides of the same coin. If a punishment is withheld, that is a reward; if a reward is withheld, that is a punishment. Kids may feel punished, and react with anger, when you withhold rewards!

It is okay to use rewards on occasion and for a limited time. If you are going to use a reward, set up the agreement for a short period of time and ensure that the child understands that it is temporary.

Behavior Change Goal Charts

We have found that a **behavior change goal chart** can be effective and fun for getting certain behaviors started: self-help routines, new responsibilities, or new challenges such as music lessons, where the positive natural consequence is a little way off.

A behavior change goal chart helps children focus on what they need to do. Behaviors are listed on the left, and time periods (days or hours) along the top. When the child performs a desired behavior in one of the time periods, he is given a check mark or a star or sticker. The chart provides a record of how often the child performs the desired behaviors. Points are exchanged at the end of the day or week for agreed-upon rewards.

Step 1: List Only One Kind of Behavior

If a chart has too many behaviors the child will become confused and discouraged. The rule is: one behavior for each year of the child's age. But this rule works only if the behaviors are similar or connected. If the behaviors are entirely different, there needs to be fewer of them because a child will find them hard to remember.

Draw attention to natural rewards and praise the child for his behaviors (praise is also a reward). "Wow, your room looks so well-organized. You must be able find things so easily now." "You're brushing your teeth so often that I bet the dentist won't find any cavities." "You have so much more energy now that you're getting yourself to bed on time."

Step 2: Set up for the right period of time

For an older child two weeks
provides enough time to learn the
new skill and let positive natural
consequences (like having a clean
room or getting to school on time)
kick in.

But a preschooler can't wait two
whole weeks for his rewards, and will
lose interest, so he needs a shorter
period – even a day.

Step 3: Don't nag or remind

Not getting involved means that **you do not nag** the child about the chart – the tasks
become the child's responsibility.

Step 4: Don't Punish

If the chart does not work, **do not punish** the child. Not getting the reward is the
punishment. No tongue-lashings or lectures are allowed.

Step 5: Set a goal of reasonable success, not perfection

You can give a point for every successful behavior on the chart. If the total possible
points for a one-week period is 30 points, offer a reward for 20 points, a greater
reward for 25 and an extra special reward for 30 points. This stops the child from
feeling discouraged and giving up if he doesn't get maximum points on any particular
day.

This kind of chart can work well with early morning responsibilities: brushing teeth,
washing face and hands, and putting on coat and shoes.

The chart is a reminder; it replaces parental nagging and gives the child a chance to establish some positive new habits. It should not last forever. It's kind of like praising or rewarding your child for toilet training – you don't want to be doing it when she's a teenager!

Apply Your Knowledge

- Have you considered offering positive consequences for desired behavior? What kinds of rewards might be effective?
- What is the negative side of using rewards?
- Behavior charts work best with children between about three and 10 years old. Do you think a chart would be effective with your child?

Parenting Pointers

Use and Misuse of Praise

Positive Use	Misuse
♦ Specific (descriptive)	♦ Unspecific (general)
♦ Sincere (honest)	♦ Insincere (false)
♦ Non-Evaluative	♦ Evaluative
♦ Encouraging	♦ Perfectionistic

Praise is a verbal reward. It is often a double-edged sword. While praise can be a very effective way to change a child's behavior, it can have unintended side effects. Sometimes our attempts to use praise to get our child to behave better and raise his self-esteem only make our child feel that our love and esteem for him are conditional on his being what we want him to be rather than being himself. This is not a good thing.

Be Specific and Descriptive

Children need **specific and descriptive feedback** on what they have done rather than general comments. Rather than saying, "What a nice picture you made," describe the picture instead.

I (Allison Rees) did this with a little girl of four at one of my workshops. After my class she met her mother and me, clutching a picture she had painted in the child care room. I bent down and started describing what I saw. "I see lots of blue paint and a letter 'A' in some lines. Oh look, there is another letter inside a circle." She chimed in and pointed out some other aspects to her drawing that I had missed.

A week later when I was talking to another participant in my workshop, the young girl came up and stood beside me patiently waiting for me to finish talking. She looked at me and said, "I know how much you loved my drawing last time so I thought you would like to see another one." Being specific with my feedback not only showed her that I appreciated her artwork, it also encouraged her to do more of this kind of work.

Be Sincere

Some parents praise constantly, for every little reason. No matter what the child does, he gets some form of praise. Everything is 'wonderful'. This 'gusher approach' devalues praise itself. The child will tune out and stop listening to what you say because he doesn't believe you.

Don't Evaluate

Much of the praise we parents give tends to be evaluative. Without even thinking about it, we tend to phrase our expressions of appreciation in ways which are judgmental. Negative evaluative comments can hurt and discourage a child, of course, but so can positive evaluations, because they focus the child on whether he measures up rather than on the joy of what he's doing.

Good Boy

Recently I had a conversation with a young boy, James, who was complaining about how much his father praised him. "He's always saying 'good boy' or 'well done' – I hate it." The child was unable to explain clearly what he hated about it, but as I explored the topic with him, the problem was that he constantly felt evaluated. Whenever he was with his dad, he felt that he had to measure up to dad's standards, and that pleasing dad was supposed to be his aim in life. Even though his dad was trying to be positive, James was able to detect the underlying judgment, and rebelled against it.

James really couldn't stand being called "good boy". He felt his whole self was being evaluated on the basis of such trivialities as whether he remembered to hang up a towel after taking a bath. But even James was susceptible to evaluative praise in one area. He constantly pointed out to others how he was the best in as many respects as possible. He was successful in the pecking order at school, doing well academically and athletically. No doubt dad, and others as well, had praised him for excelling in competition with his peers.

See the first chapter of *The Parent-Child Connection* for the effects of basing approval on performance. *-- Alison Miller*

A child put in this position may try very hard to please and to measure up, liking himself when he does and disliking himself when he doesn't. Or he may rebel against being someone else's creature, valuing his autonomy (sense of running his own life) above pleasing the parent, and reject those evaluations, as James did. Effective praise helps the child develop his own standards of behavior; it does not impose the child's parents' standards.

Parenting Pointers

Supportive Praise

Here are some statements which may help your child enjoy his accomplishments and be proud of them:

- ◆ "You must feel good working and sleeping in a room that is so well-organized."
- ◆ "It must be really satisfying to know you can run that fast."

Parenting Pointers

Evaluation vs. Encouragement

Non-Evaluative Praise
[makes for positive results]

♦ encourages child to be herself

♦ encourages child to develop her own standards

♦ separates behavior from character

♦ recognizes contribution to others

Evaluative Praise
[produces undesirable results]

♦ praises child for pleasing you and others

♦ encourages child to measure up to your standards

♦ evaluates the child as a whole

♦ praises child for doing better than others

Praise should be encouraging. This means that we don't keep expecting more and more; we encourage our children by commenting positively on what they've done even if it isn't perfect. It is best to refrain from constantly suggesting improvements.

Apply Your Knowledge

- How do you feel when you are on the receiving end of gushy praise?
- How do you feel when someone makes a general comment about how good or competent you are?
- Have you experienced evaluative praise? How does it make you feel?
- How do you feel if someone praises you then suggests an improvement?
- What kind of praise do you find helpful?
- How do you praise your children? Is it specific, sincere, non-evaluative, and encouraging?

A Final Word

Limits and boundaries represent safety, respect, moral values and responsibility. In all of these areas we protect our children, we teach them, we guide them and most of all we model for them. It is more important for our children to understand the reason for limits and boundaries than for them to learn to be 'good' for the sake of approval.

Further Reading

Bayard, Robert T. *How to Deal With Your Acting-up Teenager.*
New York: Evans, 1986.

Leman, Kevin. *Making Children Mind, Without Losing Yours.*
Grand Rapids: Revell, 2000.

Wyckoff, Jerry & Unell, Barbara. *Discipline without Shouting or Spanking.*
Meadowbrook, 1984.

Glossary

ADHD (Attention Deficit Hyperactivity Disorder). A condition in which a child cannot focus his attention as well as others of his age, and is active in situations where he is expected to keep still. More extreme than Distractibility.

Altruism. Taking actions to help others out of kindness.

Antecedents. Events which happen just before a behavior and may trigger that behavior to occur.

Behavior Chart. A chart designed by a parent or teacher which lists a child's desired behaviors and checks them off when performed, so that the child can earn rewards.

Distractibility. A trait of temperament which involves being easily distracted and unable to focus attention on one thing for long.

Egocentricity. Being able to see other people and situations only from one's own perspective, not from theirs. All young children are egocentric.

Empathy. The ability to put oneself "in someone else's shoes" and see what things are like for them.

Extinction. Gradual disappearance of a behavior if it is not rewarded by attention or getting a need met.

Family issues. Issues regarding a child's behavior which affect other family members rather than just the child (e.g. making noise when others are sleeping, stealing, coming home too late).

Golden Rule. "Treat other people the way you would like them to treat you." Found in all major religions and cultures.

Grounding. Two meanings: 1) Keeping a child at home apart from interacting with friends; 2) Connecting with present-day reality rather than living in the past, the future, or the clouds.

I-messages. Communications which state your own needs and feelings rather than talking about the other person or supposed objective reality.

Kid issues. Issues regarding a child's behavior which affect only the child himself, so should be left up to him (e.g. homework, dirty laundry, forgetting his lunch).

Law-and-order morality. Morality which defines right and wrong by laws and rules.

Learning disabilities. Learning difficulties in specific areas such as reading, auditory processing, or coordination, even though a child is otherwise intelligent.

Limits. Boundaries a parent sets regarding what a child may or may not do. Limits often involve other people's needs and rights.

Limit bubble. The imaginary line which defines limits.

Logical consequences. Consequences which a parent imposes artificially for a child's misbehavior.

Natural consequences. Consequences for behavior which follow naturally from that behavior without having to be imposed (e.g. getting cold if you go out without a coat, being hungry if you don't take your lunch to school).

Persistence. A temperament trait involving persisting for long periods of time when trying to reach a goal. Not giving up easily.

Reward-and-punishment morality. Morality which sees right as any behavior which is rewarded, and wrong as behavior which is punished.

Sibling rivalry. Conflict and competition between brothers and/or sisters.

Temperament. A person's basic inherited nature.

Time Out. Putting a child in a quiet place for a specified period of time as a consequence of misbehavior, or to "cool down."

Transition stages. Stages in which a child changes his self-perception to a new level of maturity, e.g. from toddler to preschooler, from preschooler to school age child, or from child to adult. Children usually resist adult direction more in transition stages.

Triggers (antecedents). Events which "set off" an emotional reaction or misbehavior.

Index

Index

Index

Index

Index

History of the Authors and of LIFE Seminars

*From **Alison Miller**:*

It all began in 1981, when I was working as a psychologist at a treatment center for children and their families. At that time my own daughter was nine, my older son was five, and my youngest son had just been born (they're now 34, 30 and 25). I worked with family after family who were coming to see a psychologist because of problems with their children.

Living In Families Effectively

The first thing I learned is that seeing a psychologist doesn't help a child if his parents (often with the best of intentions) are still handling his behavior in ways that make it worse. It's more effective to work with the parents, to help them help their children.

Our center had about 10 child psychologists who sat in our offices and tried to help parents, one family at a time, learn more effective strategies to deal with their children's problems or their family relationships. And I realized, as I said the same things over and over again to each parent, that I could make this knowledge accessible to all parents, so that many of the problems could be prevented before they start. Even when the problems were already there, it made more sense for parents to take courses to learn parenting skills, without having to spend a lot of time and money on a mental health professional. So I began to develop parenting courses, and eventually LIFE Seminars were born.

LIFE stands for "Living in Families Effectively." The original LIFE Seminars were two long courses which I developed as a therapeutic and preventive program to address the many family needs I encountered while working with children, parents and families. Looking at the existing "packaged" parent education programs, I found some good information, but they didn't go far enough. Parenting is very complicated, and one six-week course can't teach it all. I began by putting together components from the one or two parent education programs that existed at that time, as well as material from various academic books and articles, which I translated from psychological jargon into everyday language.

Gradually I made the information my own, discarding what didn't fit from all the different sources. I kept adding components as I saw the need. I began with just behaviour management, then added communication, then child development, then handling feelings, then family systems, and so on. I would be teaching one night, get inspired, and suddenly come out with 10 or 15 minutes of new ideas which had come together out of my own experience and that of my clients and course members.

The people who were coming to me were often stuck in their ineffective patterns, and they wanted real answers. So did I, as I struggled with raising my own three children. My own family kept me humble. When I began that job, I kept seeing parents who were having the same difficulties that I was having with my own children. I had to search for answers for myself so I could be authentic with my clients. I also learned from my clients' mistakes, and from their successes too: it was as if I'd tried many different parenting styles to see what worked and what didn't. All this learning went into LIFE Seminars.

One thing I learned from all these people's experience was that it wasn't your type of family that made the difference in the effectiveness of your parenting. This knowledge helped me when I became a single parent when my children were 14, 10 and five. Allison Rees, who joined me in LIFE Seminars, has continued to be married. So I bring the knowledge of how to juggle all the demands of single parenting, and how to co-parent with your ex, and she brings the knowledge of how to parent with your spouse. She also brings many practical examples, the shining light of honesty, and a wonderful sense of humor.

Incidentally, my kids are still keeping me humble: they helped edit the material for this book!

From **Allison Rees**:

By the time I heard about the LIFE Seminars they were very popular and well supported by the community of Victoria, BC. At the time I had a three-year-old son and a six-month-old daughter and I was eager to raise my children as effectively and lovingly as I could. Participating in the courses satisfied this desire and more. I felt as if I had found the truth about parenting!

I joined LIFE Seminars first as a group facilitator, then as an organizer and the producer of the LIFE videos, and finally as the primary presenter of LIFE courses here in Victoria. I started adding my own stories and ideas as I taught the courses, and I learned daily from the many parents who shared their experiences with me in class and in counselling. Of course my most significant insights came from being a mother. Eventually Alison and I put our heads together to create the LIFE materials as they are now.

We have now been teaching parents to live in families effectively for more than 20 years. It's exciting to present a book that represents a culmination of our work as family counsellors, parent educators, and of course as parents.

From Both of Us:

Just like you, we've gone through sleepless nights with our toddlers – and then with our teens. We've wondered whether our children were normal. We've been confused about how two children from the same family can be so different. We've agonized about how to help them become kind, responsible adults. And for our children's sake we've looked at our own behavior, how we handle our feelings, how we guide our children without forcing them into our own mold, and what kind of an example we're setting for them.

We hope you've enjoyed this book and learned from it. To learn what else is available under the umbrella of LIFE Seminars, go to our website, **www.lifeseminars.com**, where you can learn about our videos or DVDs, our other books, the Good Medicine Family Life program for aboriginal nations (which uses our material), and our facilitator packages for people or agencies who want to teach LIFE Seminars courses. Or contact us by phone at 250-595-2649.

Alison Miller, Ph.D. and *Allison Rees, Ph.D.*

Now That You've Read "Sidestepping the Power Struggle"

Sidestepping is the first of our original two **LIFE** (Living in Families Effectively) books. It's based on the course of the same name. **Sidestepping** contains everything you need to know about your children's individual temperaments, their stage of development, "normal" and abnormal child behavior at each age, and what events can trigger difficult child behaviors. This book teaches you how to help children take responsibility for their own lives as they mature, and how to help them mature into ethical and competent human beings. It discusses effective and ineffective discipline techniques. If you read and practice everything recommended in this book you will be a pretty effective parent. **Sidestepping the Power Struggle** includes:

- ◆ **Understanding Your Kids** - All About Temperament, Ages and Stages From Tots to Teens, The Push and Pull Toward Independence, What is Normal?
- ◆ **Effective Discipline** - Raising a Thinking Child, How to Make Limits Stick, Exiting the Guilt/Anger Cycle, Handing Over Responsibility.
- ◆ **Everyday Challenges** - Bedtime, Mealtime, Homework, Siblings, Aggression and more.

The Parent-Child Connection, our second book, complements the material in **Sidestepping the Power Struggle.** We believe both books are a must-read for you to master all the essential principles of parenting. **The Parent-Child Connection** discusses the parent-child relationship in depth, including bonding, communication, boundaries in the family, handling emotions, and developing self-esteem. These are just as important as understanding child development and knowing discipline techniques. Even good discipline techniques can be misused if you don't have the relationship skills discussed in **The Parent-Child Connection**. Here's what's in it:

- ◆ **Successful Communication** - The Power of Words and How to Use Them, The Spirit of Listening, Working Through Issues and Conflicts, Emotion Coaching.
- ◆ **Where are the Boundaries?** - Where the Parent Ends and the Child Begins, Assertive Parents - Assertive Kids, The Deeper Meaning of Discipline.
- ◆ **Relationship Building** - Developing Emotional Intelligence, When Getting Closer Means Letting Go, Self-Esteem in Parents, Self-Esteem in Children.

If you like **Sidestepping** be sure to get **The Parent-Child Connection**. Check our website, www.lifeseminars.com, to see when it is available. You can order it from our website or by calling us at 250-595-2649. You may also be interested in our parent education lectures on DVD, listed on the website.

Alison Miller, Ph.D. and *Allison Rees, Ph.D.*

About the Production House

The services of desktop layout and design, digital pre-press, text editing contributions, and editorial management of *Sidestepping the Power Struggle* were provided by Brookeline Publishing House Inc.

Mary P. Brooke, B.Sc., Cert. PR
Publishing Consultant

Brookeline Publishing House Inc.
PO Box 42041, 2200 Oak Bay Ave.
Victoria, BC, Canada V8R 6T4

Web: www.brookeline.com
Toll Free: 1-877-595-6925
Phone: 250-595-6965
Email: publishing@brookeline.com

Notes: